Backing The Draw For Profit

by Graham Wheldon

web-site: www.sprintline.co.uk

e-mail: winners@sprintline.co.uk

Published by *Raceform* Ltd, Compton, Newbury, Berkshire RG20 6NL
Tel: 01635-578080 Fax: 01635-578101
web-site: www.raceform.co.uk

Photographs by Martin Lynch and Steven Cargill

Printed by Nuffield Press Ltd, 21 Nuffield Way, Ashville Trading Estate,
Abingdon, Oxfordshire OX14 1RL

Thanks to…
Dave Bellingham for his all-weather input. Check out Dave's weekly column 'King of the Sand' in the *Racing & Football Outlook* outside the proper racing season. Also thanks to David Chapman, Ashley Rumney, Richard Lowther, Peter Howes and, in particular, John Santer, for all their hard work.

Front cover: Showboat winning the 1999 Royal Hunt Cup up what seemed the favoured far rail. However, later races showed the stands' rail to be riding as fast at the meeting, continuing Ascot's current trend for unpredictability as concerns any draw bias (photo by John Beasley).

CONTENTS

INTRODUCTION

"On many British racecourses, the draw has more influence on the outcome of the races than any other single factor. In fact, it is possible to make a healthy profit simply by backing well-drawn horses. This cannot be said for any other feature of horse races, including the suitability of the going, ability of the jockey or trainer, or any type of performance rating system. Although it may seem that I am overstating the importance of the draw, personally I do not believe this is possible, and race results year after year support this view."

That was the opening paragraph to *The Effects of the Draw*, my first book on this most crucial aspect of Flat racing, and those sentiments hold as true now as they did then. Released in April 1998, *The Effects of the Draw* had sold out its print run within about six months and was *Raceform*'s best-selling book of the year.

So why the need for a follow-up volume, rather than a straightforward reprint? Well, since 1998, several courses have carried out work that has affected the draw biases in a major way, be it drainage work or a new watering system. Five of the racecourses that I listed in my top ten draw-affected courses in the country in '97 have dropped out of the revised list shown on pages 97 and 98, and plenty of others have seen a shift in bias. The likes of Yarmouth and Goodwood, rated 3rd and 9th in the '97 list, no longer play much of a role in my punting calendar, while Hamilton and Folkestone have become of greater interest.

I bet only on races likely to be affected by the draw, completely leaving alone middle-distance and staying events, and hope to convince you that this is the best way to make a profit from horseracing. I NEVER bet over jumps, it's just impossible to specialise in so many areas.

Jump racing has never appealed to me in quite the same way that Flat racing does, as I have never been able to find a consistent edge. There are just too many unquantifiables;

such factors as eight or (many) more obstacles, loose horses darting in and out, and the greater risk of your pick breaking down, to name but three.

There's a simple choice as far as I'm concerned, you can either back a horse in a 20-runner five-furlong handicap at Beverley, or back a horse in a 20-runner two-mile handicap hurdle at Cheltenham. In one, you can all but rule out 15 of the runners as a result of poor draws, still back yours at a decent price, and be almost 100% certain of being on a finisher. In the other, well let's see, your good work could get wrapped up in the starting tape, fall, unseat, be brought down, get carried out, break down, slip up, run out or, if you're lucky, he might even get over the first! But that's enough anti-National Hunt sentiment, for the time being at least.

As with any systematic approach, the important thing is to concentrate exclusively on races likely to be affected by a draw bias, which normally means any race run on a straight course. These will occasionally stretch up to a mile at the likes of Doncaster and Newbury, but will mostly be five or six furlongs. You will find that by following the system laid out in this book you will become au fait with most of the handicap sprinters, while your interest in other thoroughbreds may slip a bit, as it becomes clearer that this is the best area in which to make money. And ultimately, let's be honest, that's a big part of why most of us became interested in the sport in the first place.

Significant draw advantages are prevalent at about half of Britain's racecourses, and races that are affected by a bias clearly have to be treated differently afterwards to races run on a level playing field. In draw-bias races, some horses will have been flattered by racing on the best ground, while others will have seemed to have run way below form because they were racing on the worst ground. This will obviously affect where each horse finishes within the race and how far it is beaten, which in turn has major handicapping implications. Horses that run in bias races can be split into three distinct categories, those favoured by the draw, those hindered by it and those unaffected by it, and it is this evaluation that pinpoints future punts.

'He is a winner without a penalty' is a comment frequently attached to horses beaten a short-head in a handicap, but that is not strictly true as he is likely to be put up a few pounds in the weights. However, a horse finishing in front on his side when the field splits into two groups, but only fifth overall, is unlikely to go up in the weights, and may even come down a pound or two. Now that IS a winner without a penalty. This is looked at in more detail in Chapter 3.

I would say that the draw accounts for at least 90% of the thinking behind my selections, although other factors such as handicap mark, trainer form, jockey and ground do have to be taken into consideration before contemplating a bet. But it is the draw alone that provides the edge over the bookmaker, and it will continue to do so until the layers start accounting for it within the prices. Until then, we will continue to reap the benefits.

CHAPTER 1

DRAW BIASES COURSE-BY-COURSE

Rules of Racing No.28(v): The Starter shall call the names of the runners and, for Flat races, assign the horses to the places drawn by lot, all horses taking their place at the start in the order drawn for them. The rider who has drawn No.1 must always be placed on the left (as from behind the stalls) and the other riders must take their places in consecutive numbers from the left.

Presuming the Stands are on the outside of the course, on right-handed courses, low numbers will be towards the stands' rail at the start of the race. On left-handed courses, high numbers will be towards the stands' rail.

This Chapter deals with the effect of the draw at each course, and how it varies on different surfaces. The official going reports in this country still have to be taken with a pinch of salt, so I tend to use the *Raceform going allowance** in preference to the course's verdict (*The Racing Post* also produce their own set of going allowances).

* *The Raceform Going Allowance is a figure based on the race times at the course that day, and is published in Raceform, the Official Form Book, and in the results section of Raceform Update. The figure, expressed as seconds per furlong, is the time each furlong took under/over what it would have on good ground, according to Raceform standard times. A plus figure means that the ground was on the soft side of good, while a minus figure would mean it was faster than good.*

Many courses change the position of the stalls from meeting to meeting, so it is vital to check the racing press to see where they are placed, although yet again in 1999 there were at least two cases of stalls being placed on the opposite side to that which had been advertised.

Most embarrassingly from a personal viewpoint was the time Sandown positioned the stalls on the far rail having advertised them on the stands' rail. That day my tipping of Magic Rainbow, on the front page of *Raceform On Saturday*, had been almost entirely based on him having a high draw.

While a high draw wasn't a hindrance with the stalls far side, in a field of 12 it could have been a major help had the stalls been stands' side and had Bell instructed his jockey to go to the far side. So it is crucial to check out as near to the start of racing as possible where the stalls are to be positioned. On particularly bad ground, stalls can sometimes be dispensed with and flip starts used to start races.

ASCOT (R-H) - When the ground rides soft, runners invariably tack over towards the outside rail down the side of the course in round-course races of a mile and beyond. This part of the course is partially covered by overhanging trees and the ground is definitely at its quickest there, presumably as it is sheltered, but this seems common knowledge among the jockeys (Willie Carson brought Bahri wide all the way in the 1995 Queen Elizabeth II Stakes). The draw does not seem to make much difference though, with jockeyship playing a more important role in securing the best position. It is essential to check the racing press to make sure the far rail has not been moved on the straight course. This happened prior to the first August meeting in 1999, and led to the runners that raced hard up against it, including major punt Russian Revival (9/1 from 16/1) enjoying a major advantage over the stands'-side bunch.

It is a widely held opinion these days that low numbers are favoured in big-field races at up to a mile on the straight course, but recent statistics do not back up this theory, particularly over five furlongs:

5f races with 16+ runners at Ascot (1998-9)

Year	Race No	Going	Winner	Draw		Runners
1998	2054	G-S	Bint Allayl (2/1)	5	of	17
1998	2108	G-S	Bolshoi (10/1)	20	of	19
1998	2136	Good	Night Shot (7/1)	15	of	16
1998	3425	G-F	Double Oscar (8/1)	22	of	22
1998	4741	Soft	First Maite (12/1)	16	of	18
1999	2106	G-F	Mitcham (20/1)	3	of	17
1999	2107	G-F	Kalindi (12/1)	12	of	16
1999	4795	G-S	Superior Premium (20/1)	2	of	21

Essentially, Ascot should be treated in a similar way to Newmarket's July Course these days, in that, unless a strong bias appears at any given meeting, the draw should not be taken too much into account. The classic example as to the present uncertainty was the '99 Royal Meeting, where Showboat made it look as though it was crucial to be on the far rail, only for Deep Space and Halmahera to dominate the Wokingham, and Mitcham to win the King's Stand, up the stands' rail.

AYR (L-H) - Between 1995 and 1997, and in particular for the last two of those years, a high draw proved crucial in both the Gold and Silver Cups, with runners drawn low rarely getting a look in, but since then the bias has become less accentuated. Prior to '95, runners drawn between 5 and 15 used to be thought of as having the best of it when the ground rode softer than good, but in '99, if anything, a middle to high draw looked best when fields were at their largest for the Western Meeting. On the round course, low numbers enjoy a decent advantage when the fields are large, and runners who normally race prominently are likely to find a high draw a difficult hurdle to overcome.

> The next time the ground comes up genuinely soft for the Western Meeting, expect low numbers to have a definite advantage in the Ayr Silver and Gold Cups.

BATH (L-H) - Low numbers are favoured in races of a mile as the start is on a chute and the course turns left most of the way, but the advantage is minimal. The draw rarely has an effect in sprints, although those drawn very high in big fields can find trouble.

BEVERLEY (R-H) - High numbers are massively favoured in races over the straight five furlongs and also on the round course in races at up to 1m 100y on good to soft or faster ground. In sprints, the runners have to negotiate a right-handed jink not long after the start and it seems harder here than at any other course for runners drawn low to get over to the favoured rail, so Beverley has to be of interest to followers of the draw. Runners drawn high on the round course, especially in races over 7f 100y, are favoured as the course turns right soon after the start. When conditions are testing (soft or heavy), there is a strip of ground by the stands' rail that is significantly quicker than the middle of the course. Under such conditions, runners drawn very low hold a decisive advantage.

The stalls are invariably placed on the inside (far) rail, meaning that on soft ground, runners drawn low need to tack over to the stands' side in order to find the faster strip of ground, while those drawn high tend to stay central. It is well worth checking whether the stalls are being used here when the ground is heavy, since flip starts (which are used to start some long distance races on the Flat) are not uncommon. In such circumstances, runners do not always line up strictly in stall order, with shrewder jockeys often able to improve their position.

Subsequent Record of runners winning their side* in Beverley 5f races (1998-9) **

Year	Race No	Outlier	Draw 1st 4 (Ran)	Going	Next Time
1998	1137	**Dil**	12-19-18-5 (16)	G-F	**WON 2/1**
1998	1864	**Gold Edge**	15-11-17-**4** (18)	Good	4th 5/1
1998	2775	**Heathyards Jake**	12-10-**2**-14 (14)	G-F	3rd 13/2
1998	4405	**Red Amazon**	9-**5**-13-14 (14)	G-F	**WON 11/2**

1999	1102	**Rocco Tower**	12-9-14-**6** (16)	Good	**WON 14/1**
1999	2194	**American Cousin**	15-**5**-19-17 (19)	G-F	**WON 3/1**
1999	2515	**Kosevo**	11-8-13-12-**1** (13)	Soft?	**WON 16/1**
1999	2771	**American Cousin**	18-**10**-15-19 (20)	G-F	**WON 7/2**
1999	3952	**Mousehole**	10-**6**-12-13 (16)	Good	3rd 5/2

* 'winning their side' - In big-field races, the tendency is for runners to form two or three groups. The runner listed is the first one home on the unfavoured part of the course. These are known throughout as 'outliers'.

** On any surface bar soft or heavy, it is very unusual to see runners race up the stands' rail at Beverley, so runners shown above as winning their side are usually those that fared best towards the unfavoured centre of the course.

Beverley outliers have a record second to none of success on their next outing. In my estimation, the centre of the course here rides somewhere in the region of 5-6 lengths slower, on good to soft or faster ground, than the far rail. Consequently, any horse which finishes within that distance of the winner having raced there has to be considered to have run outstandingly well.

Followers of Beverley outliers enjoyed a very profitable time in 1999, when four of the five went on to win next time, including 14/1 and 16/1 victors. The ill-fated **Rocco Tower** was noted by *Raceform* Racereader Alan Amies as having raced wide (down the centre), so to finish less than 2l off the winner was a serious effort. He went on to win what looked at the time a hot maiden at Pontefract on his next run, a race in which John Dunlop's Mukayed, who held a Cork And Orrery entry at the time, was made favourite.

American Cousin was probably the most predictable sprinter of the season, twice running outstanding races at Beverley from impossible draws before following up at Doncaster within the space of a few days.

The day **Kosevo** came out comfortably on top of those to race up the stands' rail, the going had been given as soft, but the race times suggested it was good to soft at worst. It was clear from watching the amount of turf being kicked back by the runners on each flank that the far side was riding faster, so Kosevo became the outlier. He won next time at Haydock at 16/1.

Mousehole failed to complete the nap-hand for the year, despite being backed in from 5/1 to 5/2 favourite at Haydock next time after his eyecatching run.

<u>5f Races with 10+ runners at Beverley on good to soft or faster ground (1998-9)</u>

Year	Race No	Going	Winner	Stalls	Draw		Runners
1998	1119	Good	Mungo Park (7/1)	H	15	of	18
1998	1137	G-F	Talvera (14/1)	H	12	of	16
1998	1139	G-F	Flanders (11/8)	H	15	of	11

1998	1317	G-F	Poco (6/1)	H	9	of	10
1998	1864	Good	Royal Dream (9/1)	H	15	of	18
1998	1865	Good	Sweet As A Nut (9/1)	H	13	of	11
1998	2196	Good	Distant King (7/1)	H	10	of	13
1998	2490	Good	Alpha (16/1)	H	10	of	10
1998	2519	Good	Storyteller (7/2)	H	3	of	14
1998	2520	Good	Majalis (11/10)	H	4	of	11
1998	2775	G-F	Casimir (9/4)	H	12	of	14
1998	2776	G-F	Distant King (10/1)	H	4	of	19
1998	3159	Good	Dazzling Q'tet (11/1)	H	13	of	17
1998	3567	G-F	Goretski (15/8)	H	15	of	15
1998	3604	G-F	Bodfari Quarry (16/1)	H	7	of	13
1998	3831	G-F	Sound's Ace (10/1)	H	15	of	16
1998	3941	G-F	La Doyenne (25/1)	H	11	of	15
1998	3940	G-F	Most Respectfl (16/1)	H	5	of	12
1998	4303	G-F	Entwine (8/1)	H	1	of	20
1998	4304	G-F	Phantom Ring (14/1)	H	15	of	18
1998	4405	G-F	Open Secret (8/11)	H	9	of	14
1999	688	G-F	Sweet Haven (10/1)	H	10	of	12
1999	808	Good	Jaypeecee (7/1)	H	14	of	17
1999	1100	Good	Black Army (12/1)	H	20	of	19
1999	1102	Good	Francport (5/1)	H	12	of	16
1999	1448	Good	Princess Victoria (5/1)	H	12	of	10
1999	2194	G-F	Three Leaders (10/3)	H	15	of	19
1999	2771	G-F	Bollin Ann (11/2)	H	18	of	20
1999	2944	G-F	Agua Caballo (5/4)	H	10	of	14
1999	3163	G-F	Magic Of Love (5/1)	H	2	of	11
1999	3538	Good	Goretski (2/1)	H	14	of	16
1999	3949	Good	Bedevilled (11/4)	H	10	of	12
1999	3953	Good	Muja's Magic (33/1)	H	10	of	16
1999	3988	Good	Pertemps F-C (11/2)	H	10	of	13
1999	4325	Good*	Royal Romeo (10/1)	H	3	of	17
1999	4326	Good*	Palvic Lady (20/1)	H	1	of	12

* The going at this meeting was given as good, but the general consensus was that it had been over-watered and was, in fact, riding much slower than the official description.

Amazingly, backing the top six stalls in every race listed above would have returned a level-stakes profit, and that's with missing winners such as Muja's Magic (seven off the rail). It is not often wise to eliminate a runner drawn in the top stalls here solely because it is forecast to start at a big price, winners such as Black Army (12/1) and La Doyenne (25/1) being perfect examples.

5f Races with 10+ runners at Beverley on soft or heavy ground (1998-9)

Year	Race No	Going	Winner	Stalls	Draw		Runners
1999	1849	Soft	Step Ahead (6/1)	H	2	of	11
1999	1854	Soft	Pleasure (16/1)	H	1	of	16
1999	2515	Soft*	Cryhavoc (3/1)	H	11	of	13
1999	4443	Soft	Borders (7/1)	H	8	of	10

* The going at this meeting was given as soft, but race times suggested it was much nearer to good, hence the domination of those to race on the far side.

With such a small cross section of results to work with, it is hard to draw any cast-iron conclusions, but Step Ahead and Pleasure are examples of what should be expected the next time soft or heavy ground is prevalent at Beverley. Cryhavoc's win came on ground that was in reality good to soft, if not even good, while Borders had the pace and a sufficiently astute jockey to secure the stands' rail.

When there are 12 runners or more in a Beverley sprint and the ground is soft, runners drawn low can make use of a strip of decent ground under the stands' rail.

7f 100y & 1m 100y Races with 15+ runners at Beverley on G-S or faster (1998-9)

Year	Race No	Going	Winner	Stalls	Draw		Runners
1998	1116	Good	Bloom' Amazing (5/1)	H	15	of	15
1998	1117	Good	Night Of Glass (9/2)	H	12	of	18
1998	2485	Good	Fancy A Fortune (6/1)	H	15	of	15
1998	2516	Good	Ferny Factors (14/1)	H	1	of	17
1998	2771	G-F	Bay Of Delight (10/1)	H	11	of	15
1998	3562	G-F	Gymcrak Prem (9/4)	H	16	of	16
1998	3942	G-F	Kass Alhawa (10/1)	H	14	of	15
1998	4299	G-F	Samut (2/1)	H	10	of	15
1998	4300	G-F	Time To Wyn (14/1)	H	6	of	17
1998	4302	G-F	Master Caster (5/1)	H	14	of	18
1998	4406	G-F	Mr Speaker (10/1)	H	12	of	17
1998	4407	G-F	Margaret's D'r (14/1)	H	15	of	16
1999	684	G-F	Genuine John (11/2)	H	14	of	17
1999	685	G-F	Zulal (2/1)	H	15	of	16
1999	1097	Good	Komlucky (9/2)	H	15	of	16
1999	1661	Good	Tipperary Sun (15/2)	H	15	of	15
1999	2480	G-F	Bacchus (33/1)	H	2	of	15
1999	3952	Good	Bacchus (11/4)	H	15	of	15
1999	4320	Good	Dispol Magic (4/1)	H	9	of	15
1999	4321	Good	Elba Magic (7/1)	H	17	of	16

1999	4322	Good	Vintage Prem (10/11) H	8	of	15

Many are drawn into thinking that because Beverley's 7f 100y and 1m 100y courses are run on the round course that the draw doesn't have much of an effect, but the above results show it clearly does. Of the 21 15+-runner races to have been staged over the distances in the past two years, 18 were won by a runner drawn in the top half, while a staggering 15 went to a runner drawn in the top six stalls.

Best Examples		**5f**	**7f 100y-1m 100y**
	G-F	2194	
	Good	1100	3952
	Soft	1854	1851

* *The Best Example races are from 1999 unless specified*

BRIGHTON (L-H) - When the ground is soft or heavy, runners invariably tack over to the stands' rail in the straight. When this is the case, high numbers often hold the edge. Otherwise, low numbers have a minimal advantage in sprint races.

The perfect example of a jockey tacking over to the stands' rail and outfoxing his opponents was Richard Quinn on Double-O (Race 4713). On ground described as good to soft, all 16 runners bar Quinn's mount, from stall 10, stuck to the far rail. Two furlongs out, there looked to be little in it, but racing towards the stands' rail was a clear advantage, and Double-O had an eased-down 4 lengths to spare at the line.

Bizarrely, at the final meeting of '99, the complete opposite occurred when, in a field of 18 on ground again described as good to soft, only one runner chose to stay on the far side in the straight. That was Swynford Welcome, ridden by Gary Bardwell, and he too was successful, by an even easier 5 lengths.

All too often, this kind of occurrence, where the accepted draw bias gets turned on its head, is down to late-season ground. It is normally because the course has been raced on so much during the summer that it becomes more important to look for the strip of ground that is less chewed up. And it doesn't take too many races on rain-affected courses in the autumn for the turf to become churned up.

Best Examples		**5f 59y**
	G-S	4713

CARLISLE (R-H) - It has long been considered that high numbers do better in sprints, but there has been little evidence from race results to back this up in the past couple of seasons. The only time that a low draw can prove a hindrance on fast ground is if the horse in question needs to race prominently, otherwise Carlisle is a course where jockeyship plays as much of a role running into the bend as the starting position. Too many times during the '99 season, the winner seemed to come late, fast and widest out towards the centre of the track, to suggest that the far rail held any advantage. When the ground rides soft, low numbers seem to enjoy a distinct advantage, but genuinely soft ground is something of a rarity here, probably because they do not race after August.

CATTERICK (L-H) - When the ground is testing, the stands' rail is the place to be, which suits high numbers in five-furlong races. However, when the ground is good or firmer, horses drawn on the far side (low) hold the edge. Low numbers are marginally preferred in races run on the round course on all surfaces, particularly so over 5f 212y as runners have to take a left-handed bend into the straight. When the ground is soft, horses switched to race on the stands' rail are benefited.

Similarly to Brighton, there was one race where the supposed draw bias was turned on its head during '99, when Cartmel Park raced alone up the stands' side on good ground and won by 2½ lengths. Again this should be put down as a fluke on late-season (October 16) ground, although Ollie Pears deserves credit for the manoeuvre.

CHEPSTOW (L-H) - High numbers used to be favoured on the straight course, but these days the draw has no effect.

CHESTER (L-H) - Low numbers have an advantage, especially in races at up to 7f 122y, where a slow start from a high draw can be virtually impossible to overcome, given the constant turning nature of the course. Soft ground seems to accentuate the advantage enjoyed by runners drawn low, until it has been raced on a few times, when a higher draw becomes less of a disadvantage as the ground on the inside becomes chewed up.

DONCASTER (L-H) - The draw is only really an issue here during Lincoln weekend, when maximum fields are guaranteed in the Spring Mile and the Lincoln itself, but which side is likely to be favoured is almost impossible to predict from year to year. Neither side was conclusively favoured in 1995, low numbers were well on top in 1996, the centre strip of ground looked best in 1997 and again in 1999, after in '98 the draw had again had little bearing. As a rule of thumb, don't pay too much attention to the draw in the Lincoln unless the ground is soft, and look first and foremost to where the pace is. Low numbers do best in big fields on the round course.

> The next time the Spring Mile and Lincoln are run on soft ground at Doncaster, there is no reason why low numbers should not again dominate.

EPSOM (L-H) - When the ground is on the soft side, jockeys invariably tack over to the stands' side in races of six furlongs and beyond to look for the better ground. The ground is better here in such conditions as the course cambers away from the stands' rail towards the far side, keeping it drier. In five-furlong races, the stalls are always placed on the stands' side, so when the going is soft the majority of the runners are on the best ground from the outset. Horses drawn low in round-course races are able to take the shortest route around Tattenham Corner, and on faster ground have a decisive edge over six and seven furlongs and 1m 114y, particularly so front-runners and those that race prominently in their races. Over five furlongs, high numbers used to hold quite an advantage, but the bias is not so great these days.

Best Examples		**5f**
	Good	4013

FOLKESTONE (R-H) - Before 1998, Folkestone was never thought of as having that much of a draw bias, but nowadays it is common to see fields split into two groups in straight-course races, with runners rarely taken down the centre. The far rail rides faster than the stands' rail, favouring horses drawn high, apart from on heavy ground, something Miss Money Spider (Jimmy Fortune) took advantage of on two occasions in '99. Front-runners drawn high here are always worthy of close inspection.

Mammas F-C and Clonoe were two to win straight-course races during the '99 campaign racing up the stands' rail, both beating a bigger group on the opposite flank. However, rather than this being an indication of the ground on that side being not that much slower, I would be inclined to write off those two as races being won by horses who would have won easily from any draw. Mammas F-C had plenty in hand on official figures, and went on to prove herself in much hotter company, while Clonoe is almost certainly one of those horses who only performs to his capabilities when away from the main pack (see pages 95 and 96).

Straight race handicaps with 12+ runners at Folkestone (1998-9)

Year	Race No	Going	Winner	Stalls	Draw		Runners
1998	536	Good	Divine Miss-P (11/4)	L	6	of	12
1998	577	Soft	Clonoe (9/4)	L	16	of	14
1998	1689	Good	Resist The Force (7/2)	L	12	of	13
1998	2624	G-F	Frankie Fair (5/1)	L	14	of	16
1998	2625	G-F	Sihafi (10/11)	L	7	of	11
1998	3133	G-F	Suite Factors (5/1)	L	13	of	15
1998	3401	G-F	Suite Factors (11/4)	C	11	of	12
1998	3901	G-F	Alpen Wolf (3/1)	L	8	of	12
1998	4775	G-F	Mutabassir (9/4)	L	10	of	16
1998	4886	G-S	Compradore (8/1)	L	12	of	16
1999	532	Soft	Indian Blaze (14/1)	L	7	of	16
1999	655	Soft	Tinker Osmaston (7/1)	L	13	of	16
1999	764	Soft	Contrary Mary (8/1)	L	9	of	12
1999	1492	G-F	Forgotten Times (15/8)	L	2	of	12

1999	3142	G-F	Clonoe (20/1)	L	4	of	14

Clonoe was the one responsible for setting the trend of heading for the far rail in straight races, and since his success in the spring of '98 the majority of straight-course handicap winners have come out of the top half-dozen stalls.

Looking at the table, the 1999 results do not seem quite so clear-cut as those from '98, but in my opinion the bias was as strong as ever.

GOODWOOD (R-H) & (L-H) - High numbers are favoured on the round course, particularly over seven furlongs, except in very wet conditions when jockeys tend to tack over to the stands' side. The previously decisive advantage enjoyed by runners drawn by the far rail (high) in the Stewards' Cup disappeared in 1999, as a result of work to break up the surface by machine on that side, and in the end low numbers enjoyed a definite edge.

Subsequent Record of runners 'winning their side' in Stewards' Cup (1992-9)

1992	**Master Planner**	(6th)	next time	**WON 16/1**
1993	No Qualifiers			
1994	No Qualifiers			
1995	**Jayannpee**	(3rd)	next time	Unp 15/8
1996	**Wildwood Flower**	(5th)	next time	**WON 8/1**
1997	No Qualifiers			
1998	**Night Shot**	(6th)	next time	**WON 4/1**
1999	**Literary Society**	(3rd)	next time	Unp 14/1

HAMILTON (R-H) - It is absolutely imperative to be drawn high in sprints if the ground is good to soft or softer, and it is also an advantage when the ground rides good or faster. A high draw is also a clear advantage in races over 1m 65y as there is a tight right-handed loop into the home straight. It is not uncommon for the ground to become too bad for the use of stalls here.

Best Examples		**5f-6f 5y**	**1m 65y**
	Good	2238	
	Soft	4589	4591

5 & 6f Races with 12+ runners at Hamilton on good to soft or softer ground (1998-9)

Year	Race No	Going	Winner	Stalls	Draw		Runners
1998	560	Heavy	Arantxa (3/1)	L	9	of	12
1998	1075	Soft	Knotty Hill (5/2)	L	11	of	13
1998	2399	G-S	Superfrills (9/1)	L	11	of	12
1998	3576	Soft	Guest Envoy (6/1)	L	16	of	18

1998	4130	Soft	La Doyenne (7/1)	L	12	of	18
1998	4533	Soft	Red Amazon (11/2)	L	11	of	13
1999	500	Heavy	Sharp Edge Boy (25/1)	L	11	of	12
1999	637	Heavy	Unshaken (3/1)	L	17	of	17
1999	1206	Soft	Naissant (9/4)	L	11	of	12
1999	1425	Soft	Xcaret (5/1)	L	4	of	12
1999	1428	Soft	Denbrae (12/1)	L	6	of	16
1999	1855	G-S	Jacmar (14/1)	L	10	of	12
1999	4589	Soft	Golden Miracle (4/1)	L	16	of	16

Apart from the May meeting in '99 (perhaps best ignored as the ground was dead rather than genuinely soft), every winner came from well into the top half of the draw. Covering only the top three stalls in each race would have found nine of the 14 winners, for a very healthy £27.25 level-stakes profit (to £1 stakes).

HAYDOCK (L-H) - On soft ground, jockeys tend to bring their mounts over to the stands' side in races run on the round course as the ground usually rides better there. High numbers used to be favoured in sprint races when the ground was good or softer, but there now appears not much in it.

KEMPTON (R-H) - On the separate sprint track, when the stalls are on the stands' side and the ground is soft, a low draw is an advantage. When the stalls are placed on the far side, high numbers are clearly favoured, and when the runners stretch right across the track, high numbers comfortably hold the edge. The advantages become less defined on faster ground.

Best Examples		**5f-6f**
	Heavy	4431

LEICESTER (R-H) - It used to be considered that low numbers had an advantage on the straight course, particularly so on soft ground, but in recent years the bias has turned full circle and high numbers are now almost always favoured when jockeys choose to race down the centre of the course. On so many occasions in '99, the runners that raced nearest the stands' rail from low draws had little chance, despite looking to be in the battle two furlongs out. And the bias seemed to get forgotten by jockeys from meeting to meeting, with many electing to race up the stands' rail before again realising that was where the slower ground was. Towards the end of the season, however, the bias became less evident as low numbers just about held their own.

Best Examples		**5f-5f 218y**
	Good	3744
	Heavy	827

LINGFIELD turf (L-H) - The draw advantage is nothing like as defined as it was in years past, and now only the odd meeting seems to be affected. There were quite a few examples of high numbers dominating in sprints during '99, (mostly early season) but too many times horses racing down the centre prevailed to be bullish about any advantage. The one factor that can have a massive effect on the draw, though, is heavy rain falling onto firm ground. Presumably because of the undulating nature of the track and the fact that the far rail on the straight course is towards the bottom of a slope where it joins the round course, rainfall seems to make the middle and far side of the straight ride a lot slower. In these conditions, runners drawn right up against the stands' rail, often only the top three or four stalls, have a massive edge. The advantage does not seem to be anything like as great over sprint distances as it is over seven furlongs, and over 7f 140y, under any conditions.

To my knowledge, there have only been two 7f-7f 140y races to be run on recently rain-softened good or better ground at Lingfield in the past decade (to be fair they had to meet a very strict set of conditions). The result of the effect of the draw on both occasions, favouring runners drawn high, was very conclusive.

Best Examples		**5f-6f**
	Firm	1456

LINGFIELD all-weather (L-H) - The draw generally offers little advantage, although there are some striking exceptions. The statistics for races over six and seven furlongs are similar in that you do not want to be drawn very wide in a big field over either distance, so cross out any runner higher than stall 11 over six, and higher than stall 10 over seven. Interestingly, stall 1 has a particularly moderate record over seven. The statistics for races over 1m 2f during the 1998 and 1999 seasons make very interesting reading. Starting from any stall higher than 8 is a big disadvantage. The 1m 2f start is virtually on the winning post and, with a long, sweeping turn coming up after only half a furlong, any horse caught out wide is going to travel a good deal further than the rest. Tucking in behind the field has its problems too, as you then get the worst of the kickback. Although the number of races that are run over five furlongs is quite small compared to other distances, and the safety limit for the number of runners is only 10, stall 10 itself has a quite miserable record. No horse managed to win from that stall in either 1998 or 1999 and any runner starting from there can be eliminated on that basis alone.

Unlike on turf, all-weather racing does not suffer the frustration of repositioning of the stalls, or movement of the rails. This at least makes comparison of data from meeting to meeting consistent, which results in more meaningful statistics. There is still a problem with the official going reports, for although the official going is reported as standard 99% of the time, the truth is that the going is truly standard for only about 50% of meetings, slow for about 25% and fast for the other 25%. Occasionally, but very rarely, the ground will ride to an extreme, either very fast or very slow, usually as a result of freak weather conditions or some 'imaginative' track maintenance. The problem facing the Clerks of the Courses at the three all-weather tracks is that they can hardly go around and prod the surface with a stick like they can turf, and it is only by reflecting on the race times after the meeting that a true picture of the state of the ground begins to emerge. Fortunately for draw followers, the going does not have a major influence on the bias at any of the all-weather tracks, though track maintenance does.

MUSSELBURGH (R-H) - High numbers are favoured over seven furlongs and a mile. Over five furlongs, low numbers have an advantage, particularly on soft ground, irrespective of the size of the field, although this was not as great in '99 as in previous years. On the rare occasions that the stalls stretch right across the track, low numbers still do best, although the far rail (high) seems to ride quicker than the centre.

NEWBURY (L-H) - When the ground is genuinely soft, it is not uncommon to see runners race wide down the back straight and the side of the course in events of between 1m 3f 56y and 2m. It is particularly the case in races of 1m 5f 61y, which start on a chute at the far end of the back straight. In such circumstances, a high draw becomes a huge advantage. Many consider a low draw to be an advantage in big-field races over the round 7f 64y and 1m 7y courses, since there is a sharpish left-hand bend into the home straight not long after the starts. While this is pretty much the case when the ground is good or firmer, it is definitely not true when the ground becomes soft. After a few races, the ground on the rail becomes chewed up and horses that are drawn high are able to race on the better ground (often only four or five horse widths off the rail) and swing onto the better ground in the straight, so while they are travelling that bit further, the surface is that much better. In races run on the straight course, a high draw is an advantage on soft ground.

Best Examples		**5f 34y-6f**
	Soft	5032

NEWCASTLE (L-H) - On the straight course, it used to be a case of high numbers being favoured when the ground was good or firmer, and low numbers when the ground rode good to soft or softer. However, results from '99 suggested that the far rail was the place to be unless the ground was riding really fast, low numbers enjoying the edge on any ground good to firm or slower.

Best Examples		**5f-6f**
	Firm	2334
	Good	4984
	Soft	4636

NEWMARKET July Course (R-H) - Low numbers were favoured at the '99 Craven Meeting, while high numbers did best at the July Meeting. As often as not, the best guide is to look for any bias at the previous, or preferably current, meeting.

NEWMARKET Rowley Mile (R-H) - It is not uncommon to see fields of 30+ here, and when this is the case, runners up against either rail can have the advantage. When the going is soft, runners hard up against the far rail hold sway if the entire field stay on that side, but runners that tack over to the stands' rail are favoured over those staying far side. In late season, it has been known for the stands' rail to be moved to unveil virgin ground up against the stands' side. In these circumstances, runners drawn low can have a big advantage. As on the July Course, the odd meeting seems to pop up where one rail is favoured. In fields of around 15, stalls in the middle (between about 8 and 10) seem to do well, presumably because they can get covered up on such an open course. Over longer trips, when the fields are large, high numbers enjoy a slight advantage.

The course was not used for racing in 1999, and it remains to be seen if a year of inactivity and redevelopment has had any impact on the draw biases.

> The stands' rail is usually moved during the Champions' Meeting in October in order to accommodate larger fields, and horses racing on the fresh ground seem to enjoy a decisive advantage. When the rail is moved, runners drawn above 20 are faced with a major struggle.

NOTTINGHAM (L-H) - On the straight course, it used to be a case of low numbers being favoured when the stalls were on the far rail and high numbers when they were on the stands' rail, but these days the advantage does not seem that great. The occasional race will pop up where one side or the other has the edge, but this is normally more down to where the pace is than any bias.

PONTEFRACT (L-H) - Low numbers are considered best here for the same reason as at Chester, in that the course has several distinct left-hand turns with a short home straight, but the advantage is not that great. A high draw can be a big setback on fast ground, since it forces runners to either race wide or drop in behind and onto the rail, but on soft ground a high draw becomes a distinct advantage. When the ground becomes really wet, jockeys tend to head for the outside rail and runners drawn low can have little chance if the stalls are placed on the inside. However, the ground can become so bad that the stalls get moved to the outside of the course, negating any advantage in being drawn high in the first instance.

Best Examples		**5f-6f**
	Soft	4716

REDCAR (L-H) - It is not unusual to see fields verging on 30 in straight-course races several times throughout a season, and high numbers (stands' side) are often favoured. However, a majority of the runners seem to race towards that side of centre in these events and, considering relatively few go for the far rail, low numbers have held their own.

RIPON (R-H) - High numbers are slightly favoured on the round course. However, the draw has a massive effect in sprint races and any runner drawn in the centre stalls can usually be ignored. The optimum conditions for low numbers (although stands'-rail runners aren't as favoured over those down the centre as once was the case) seems to be when the ground is good or faster and there are 12 runners or fewer. I used to set the figure at 16 or below, but now there seems a greater inclination for jockeys drawn high in races of 13-16 runners to go far side. When the stalls stretch far enough across the course, there is a strip of fast ground towards the far rail which horses drawn high can utilise, and runners that go here enjoy a definite edge over those stands' side.

Best Examples		**5f-6f**
	Firm	1507
	Good	3663
	Soft	711

Sprint Handicaps with 14+ runners at Ripon (stalls low) (1999)

Year	Race No	Going	Winner	Draw		Runners	Raced
1999	614	G-F	Levelled (12/1)	5	of	19	Stands
1999	711	G-S	Whizz Kid (33/1)	13	of	16	Far side
1999	1507	G-F	Ballina Lad (14/1)	22	of	22	Far side
1999	2928	G-F	Bank House (14/1)	8	of	17	Stands
1999	3295	G-F	Kalar (8/1)	21	of	23	Far side
1999	3663	Good	Pipalong (16/1)	17	of	23	Far side
1999	3821	Good	Get Stuck In (20/1)	12	of	21	Far side
1999	4027	Good	Mammas F-C (11/1)	11	of	15	Far side

Levelled's race should be put down as a one-off where the stands' rail looked faster than the far side, as for the remaining races in '99 the far rail rode a lot faster. Bank House was brought to the stands' rail, as were all but one of the runners, in a race where every jockey bar Carl Lowther showed a lack of tactical knowledge. Interestingly, Lowther was also on board Get Stuck In when that one won from a central draw, making a bee-line straight for the far rail. He is clearly a jockey to watch here when there's a chance he can go far side.

SALISBURY (R-H) - Low numbers normally have the advantage on the straight course when the ground is soft, but as the '99 season wore on, runners that ventured over to the far rail on soft ground often came out on top. Much depends on the state of the course.

At the meeting where Nitwitty won (July 2, Race 2496), the going was given as good to soft, soft patches, but the race times suggested it was much faster. Tony Newcombe, trainer of third-placed Baptismal Rock, said the stands' side would be the place to be given that the far side had had a lot of sand put down on it. That day, those on the far rail were nowhere to be seen, but the bias was too variable afterwards to be able to draw any firm conclusions. Although one explanation could have been that a false rail was put up in July down the far side, which would have meant the far-rail runners were in fact racing down what is normally the slower strip centre to far side.

SANDOWN (R-H) - There is little or no draw advantage on the round course, but there certainly is on the separate sprint track. When the going is on the soft side of good and the stalls are placed on the far side (high), high numbers have a clear advantage. When the stalls are placed on the stands' side, low numbers enjoy a slight advantage when all the runners stay towards the stands' rail, but when a few break off and go to the far side, high numbers comfortably hold the upper hand again. The far rail is without doubt much faster than the stands' rail, which in turn is much faster than the centre of the course over five furlongs. The softer the ground, the greater the advantage becomes.

> If the stalls are placed on the stands' side and there are 10 or more runners, it is worth looking among the jockeys drawn in the higher stalls to see if there is a likely candidate to switch over to the far rail. Michael Roberts is one to have adopted this move successfully in the past couple of years on board Sweet Magic.

Best Examples		**5f**
	Good	1923
	Soft	825, 826

SOUTHWELL all-weather (L-H) - When the track is riding uniformly, as is the case at the majority of meetings, there is a notable draw bias in races run over both six furlongs and 1m 3f. In fact, the statistics for each distance are strikingly similar. This is perhaps not surprising as a sharp left-handed bend comes up after about a furlong in each case, and the bias is therefore towards low numbers. Basically, being drawn any higher than stall 7 is a big handicap and the really wide draws have a terrible record. Of the 40 horses that started from either stall 15 or 16 over six furlongs in the 1998 and 1999 seasons, none managed to win, while only five of the 141 horses that started from between stalls 11 and 16 inclusive over 1m 3f in the same period were successful. Mile races throw up some interesting draw statistics. Stalls 4 to 8 appear to hold an advantage over the rest, with those on the flanks, ie, stalls 1, 2 and 16 having particularly poor records.

The Fibresand surfaces at Southwell and Wolverhampton are affected much more by the power-harrowing that takes place during spells of very cold or very wet weather than the Lingfield Equitrack. On several occasions in the last couple of years a bias has existed soon after this harrowing has taken place. The only problem is that it is virtually impossible to predict where the bias will be until a few races have been run on the surface, and it is wise to wait a bit and see if a bias can be detected. It may be that those runners who race next to the inside rail down the home straight have an advantage over those who make their challenges down the middle, or perhaps the strip of ground down the centre of the track will be faster than on either side. That was certainly the case at more than one meeting at Southwell in the early part of 2000.

THIRSK (L-H) - In sprints during '99, high numbers were definitely favoured when the stalls were placed on the stands' side (high) and the ground was genuinely firm. But unlike in previous years, on good to firm ground or softer, the bias did not seem as great as it used to be. However, it could disappear completely in 2000 with the new watering system. When the going is on the soft side, low numbers can have the advantage as the far rail often becomes the place to be, although again the bias is not as pronounced as in the past. In races run on the round course, low numbers are favoured over 6f 216y and a mile.

Best Examples		**5f-6f**
	Good	4148

WARWICK (L-H) - Low numbers are slightly favoured on good or faster ground, but only because the course turns left-handed at some point over all distances. However, when the ground is genuinely soft, high numbers have the edge over most distances as the stands' rail (outside rail) rides that bit faster.

WINDSOR (Fig. 8) - It is not uncommon to see large fields right through the summer at Windsor, particularly over sprint distances. Over 1m 67y, runners drawn high enjoy a slight edge since the start is set on a chute and the course follows a tight right-handed loop to the point where it joins the sprint track. In sprints, high numbers hold a definite advantage when the ground is good or faster, and a very low draw can become a difficult hurdle to overcome in big fields. Soft ground swings the bias to the exact opposite, when a high draw is a major drawback. For whatever reason, the biases seem at their greatest early season.

Best Examples		**5f-5f 217y**
	Good	1138
	Soft	5110

WOLVERHAMPTON all-weather (L-H) - Wolverhampton has the biggest bias of the three British all-weather tracks, at least when power-harrowing has not taken place during very cold, or very wet, weather. The way in which the bends are cambered means that the Fibresand rolls towards the inside rail, making the ground there deeper. This means that racing away from that rail, especially once into the home straight, is a big advantage. There has been work carried out on the surface recently to eliminate the bias, but it still appears to exist. Therefore, a middle draw is often best over most distances. If drawn low, you not only have to race in the deeper stuff but, unless a front-runner, you also get all the kickback and need luck in running. If drawn too high, you can be forced so wide that you lose too much ground. When power-harrowing has taken place, the bias switches towards the inside rail and a low draw is a big help, due to the fact this is the quickest way home. Front runners with low draws are especially favoured under these conditions. To be fair, Wolverhampton are very good at advising the public over the PA that power-harrowing will take, or has taken, place. The only distance where the draw does not seem to make much difference is over 7f. This is because the start is on a left-hand bend and those horses with low draws and early speed can more or less choose where they want to race. Any draw between 1 and 6 is an advantage, with stalls 1 and 2 boasting particularly impressive records in the 1998 and 1999 seasons.

YARMOUTH (L-H) - High numbers have an advantage when the ground is firm and the fields are large, but nothing like as much as they had in '96 and '97. The implementation of a new watering system seems to have had the desired levelling-out effect.

YORK (L-H) - The draw at York has been thoroughly unpredictable in the past few seasons and neither side of the track seems to have that much of an edge. Very high draws and very low draws continue to look worst off in big-field sprints, but the main requirement seems to be to race with the main bunch and thus closer to the pace. The last time that the draw played a major role was at the 1991 Ebor meeting, when the ground had been watered in the run-up, only for significant rainfall to follow. That week, low numbers were favoured on the round course as trainers and jockeys complained of false ground.

CHAPTER 2

RACECOURSE DETAILS AND MAPS

Distances open to change when 'dolling out' occurs are shown in **bold**. Dolling out (moving the inside rail), can cause the actual race distance to vary from the distance shown. Such races are advertised in the racing press prefixed by the word 'about'.

Excuse the drainage jargon, but I'm not sufficiently up to speed with these things to be able to explain them in detail. Essentially, though, Vertidraining is similar to sand-slitting, but the former goes to a depth of approximately 14", while the latter goes to only 6".

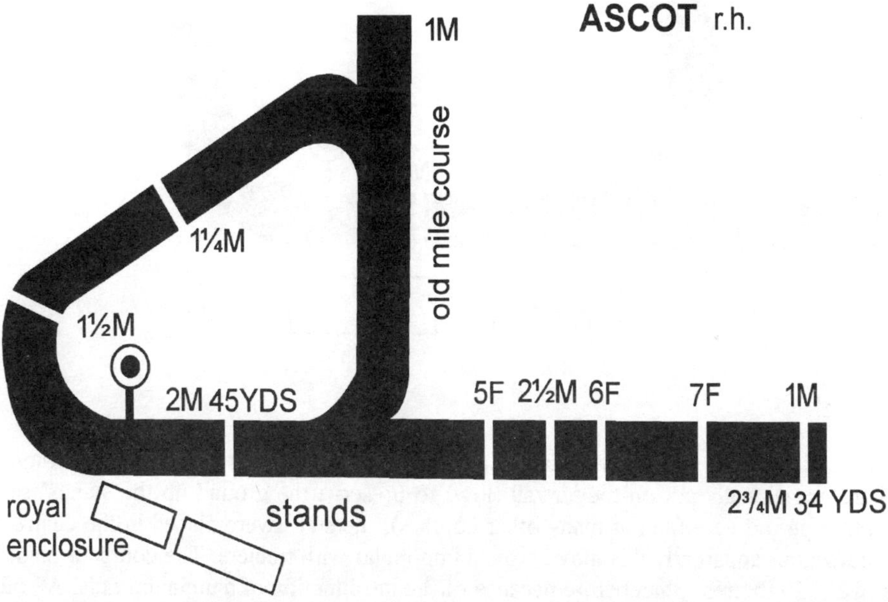

Ascot put the stalls on the stands' side (low) nine times out of ten in races run on the straight course, but they can occasionally go on the far side or down the centre. Both rails on the straight course, which is about 35 metres wide at the mile start and gradually diminishes, used to be permanent, but the far rail can now be moved. As there are more meetings this summer, more frequent adjustments may have to be made from now on. The straight course runs west and watering is achieved mainly by the Upton irrigator pop-up system or the Briggs (which is not affected by the wind). Clerk of the Course, Nick Cheyne, believes that the use of the Upton irrigator in the last three years has greatly reduced any draw bias. Compaction is reduced by Vertidraining and by slitting.

Maximum runners: 5f (28), 6f (30), 7f (30), 1m (st) (32), 1m (rnd) (30), **1m 2f** (18), 1m 4f (20), **2m 45y** (20), **2m 4f** (29), **2m 6f 34y** (32)

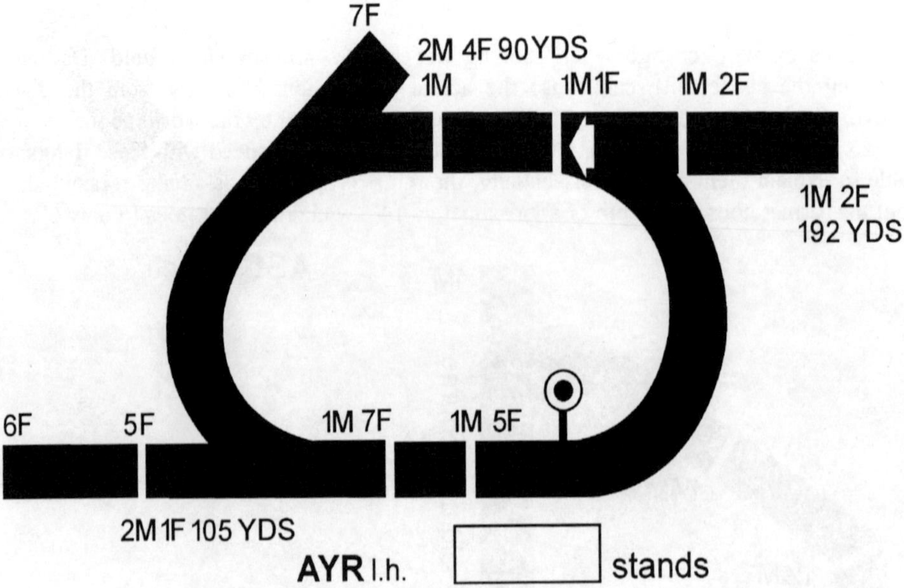

Ayr normally put the stalls on the stands' rail (high) in races at up to six furlongs, although they are occasionally put on the far rail (low) to preserve the ground up the stands' side. For a trial period here (and at many other courses), the stalls were placed in the centre of the course, but apparently this move proved unpopular with trainers. The course is slightly narrower - 29 metres - than before because of the introduction of aluminium rails. All rails can be moved, and are frequently (by up to 3 metres) dependent on ground conditions. The straight course runs west. A towline watering system was used in the past, but groundsman Jimmy Deans says: "We now have the latest model (the Briggs) which is slow-moving and covers the full width of the track, and with the new system, the wind, which blows off the sea, has no effect." No major drainage work has been done recently, only some insignificant bits and pieces, localised at the three-furlong point, and between the mile and 1m 1f points. Ayr suffers no compaction problems, and just undertake normal turf husbandry such as spiking.

Maximum runners: 5f (20, 27 at Western Meeting), 6f (20, 29 at Western Meeting), **7f** (18), **1m** (20), **1m 1f 20y** (20), **1m 2f** (20), **1m 2f 192y** (20), **1m 5f 13y** (20), **1m 7f** (20), **2m 1f 105y** (20)

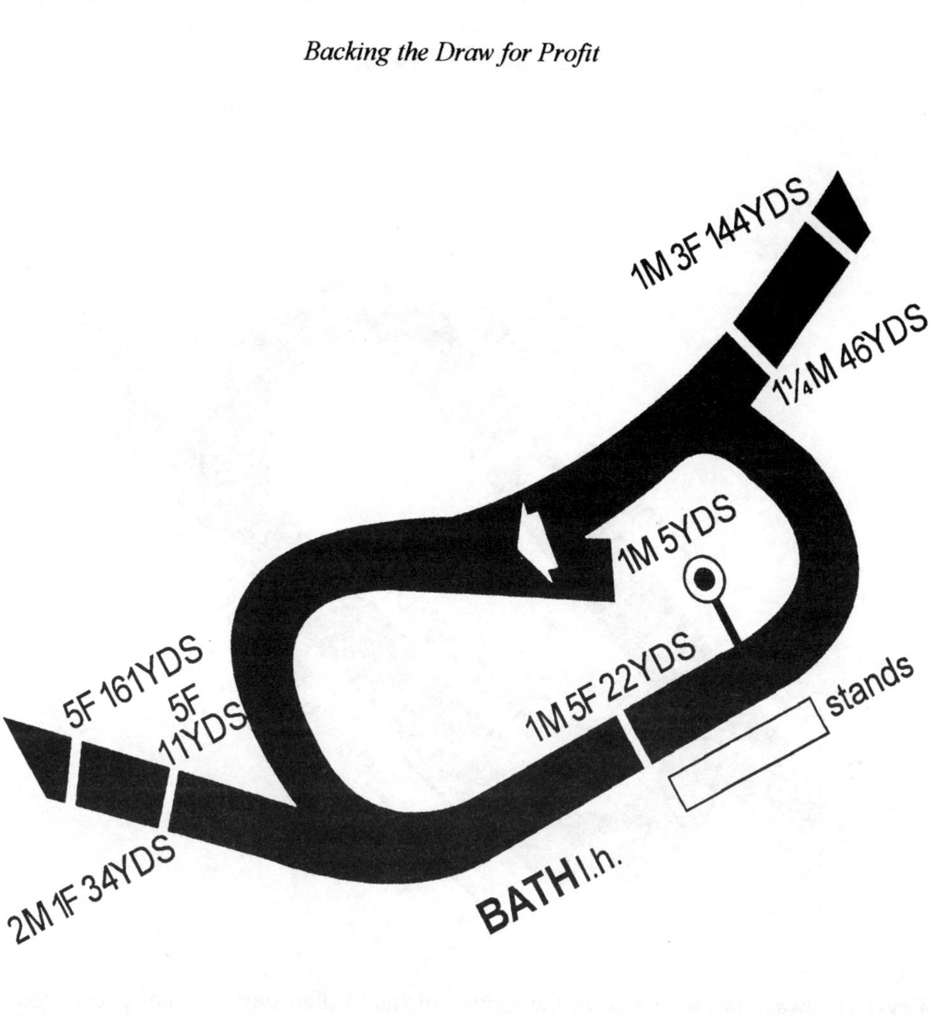

Bath place the stalls on the inside (low) over all distances. Realignment work was carried out on the home turn in 1994/5, and while both rails can now be moved, this is not the preferred method, and they tend to construct false rails by dolling out where necessary. The 5f 11y start is about 34 metres wide, considerably wider than the 5f 161y start, which is only 19 metres across. The home straight faces west/north west. Because of its height above sea level, Bath is unique among Flat courses in having no watering system, and in the words of Clerk of the Course, Rodger Farrant: "Bath is one of the best-draining courses in the country, so no work is necessary in that area." The only turf husbandry that takes place is basic spiking.

Maximum runners: **5f 11y** (20), **5f 161y** (19), **1m 5y** (16), **1m 2f 46y** (20),
1m 3f 144y (20), **1m 5f 22y** (15), **2m 1f 34y** (20)

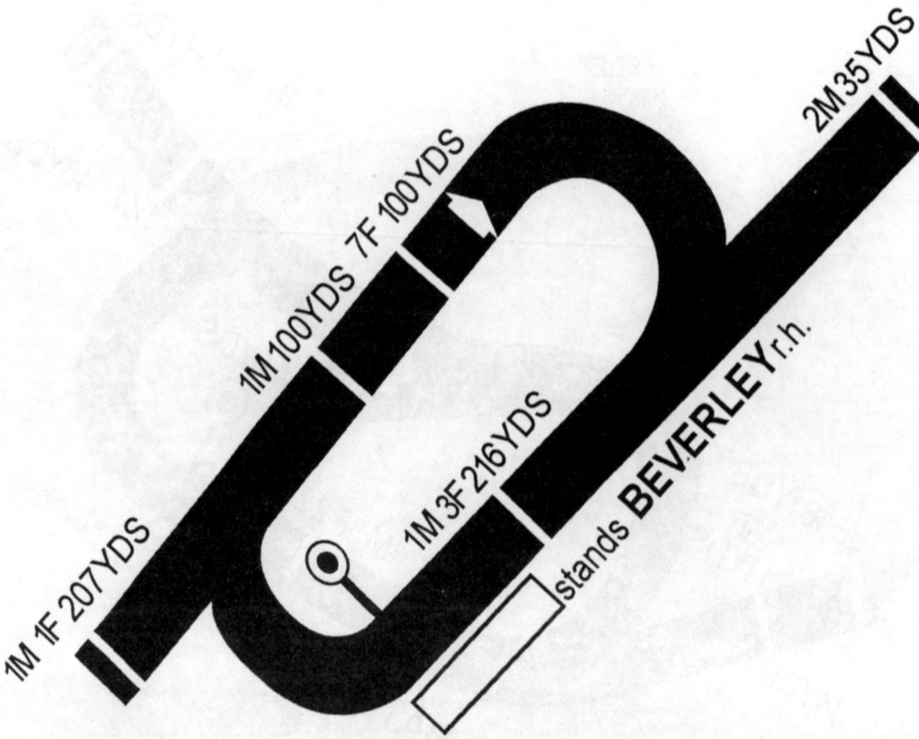

Beverley always put the stalls on the inside rail (high). Flip starts are not uncommon in five-furlong events, since it is difficult for the stalls to be moved across the centre of the course to the starting point when the ground is wet. The rails in the straight course, which is about 31 metres wide and faces west, cannot be moved. Drainage work was carried out in the autumn of 1997 at two points, just after the winning post and on the bend by the 1m 1f 207y start. The safety figures were reduced from 25 to 20 at the start of the 1996 season, to aid stalls' accessibility. A dragline is used for watering and can be adjusted to offset wind effects. Steve Jessop, the groundsman, said: "Sand-slots in the last furlong were made about five years ago and topped up this winter. The last furlong has been a tad slow in the past, but should now be faster." No breaking up of the ground has been necessary.

Maximum runners: **5f** (20), **7f 100y** (16), **1m 100y** (17), **1m 1f 207y** (19),
1m 3f 216y (15), **2m 35y** (20)

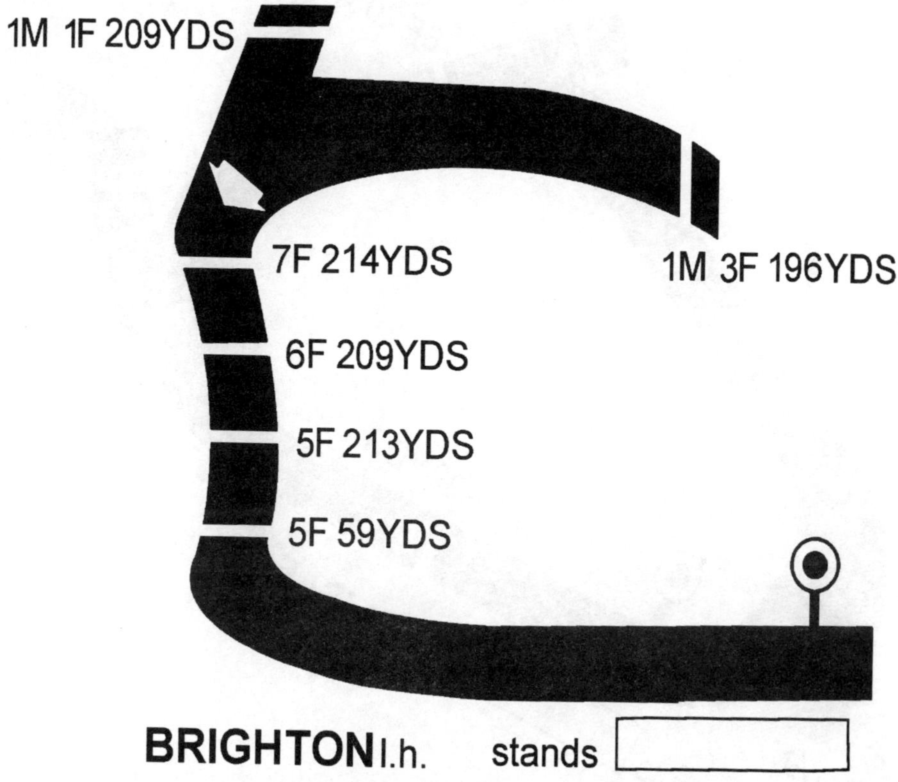

Brighton place the stalls on the inside (low) except for the 1m 2f and 1m 4f starts when they go on the outside. The width of the course at the 5f 59yds start is approximately 21 metres. The prevailing wind off the sea comes from the south, the same direction as the straight faces. A boom watering system is employed, which spreads water equally, and any wind effect is therefore slight. The course is based on chalk soil, so no drainage work has been required, and maintenance is minimal.

Maximum runners: **5f 59y** (16, **14**), **5f 213y** (18, **16**), **6f 209y** (18, **16**), **7f 214y** (15), **1m 1f 209y** (20), **1m 3f 196y** (18)

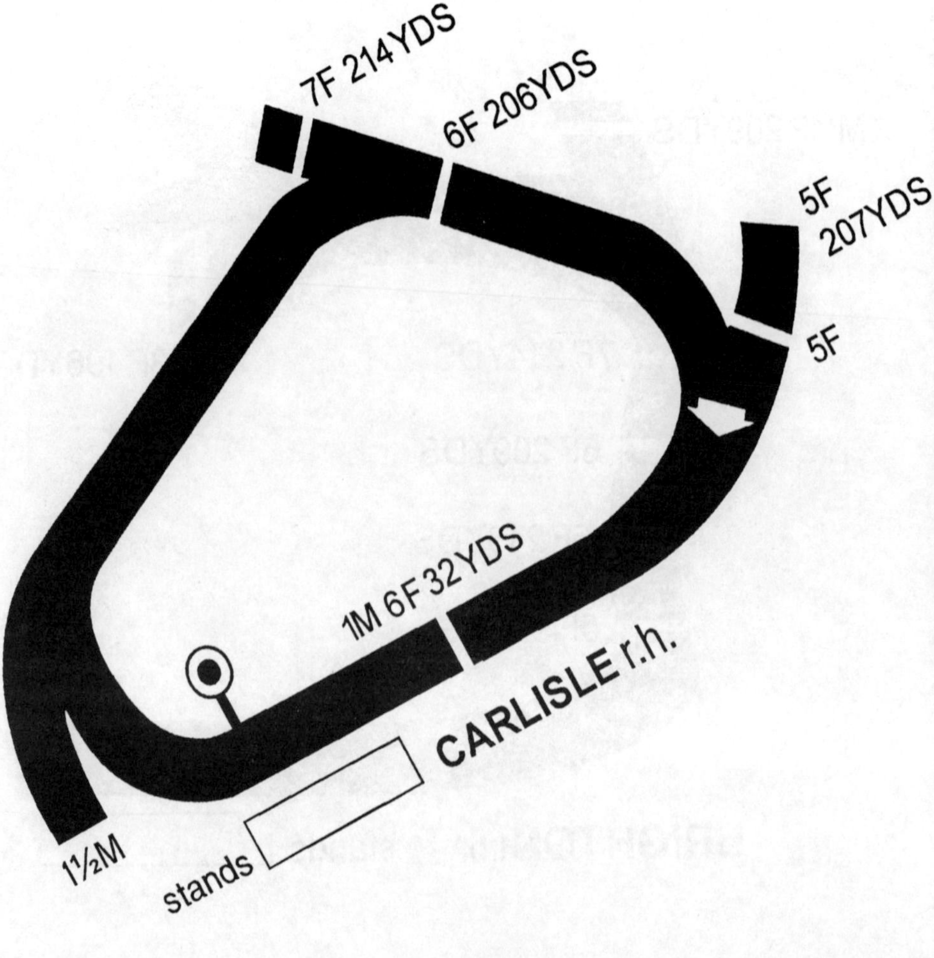

Carlisle normally put the stalls on the inside (high) at all distances, although they sometimes go down the centre in sprints, where the course is about 22 metres wide. The rails are moveable, but only by about a yard when the ground is really cut up. The home straight runs south, and the prevailing wind is normally a westerly. A gun watering system is in place, but clerk of the course Johnnie Fenwicke-Clennell said: "We've had no need to use it yet. As far as drainage work is concerned, we have put sand-slits in all over the place. We Vertidrain twice a year and use a spiker."

Maximum runners: **5f** (20), **5f 207y** (20), **6f 206y** (15), **7f 214y** (18), **1m 1f 61y** (16), **1m 4f** (20), **1m 6f 32y** (14), **2m 1f 52y** (18)

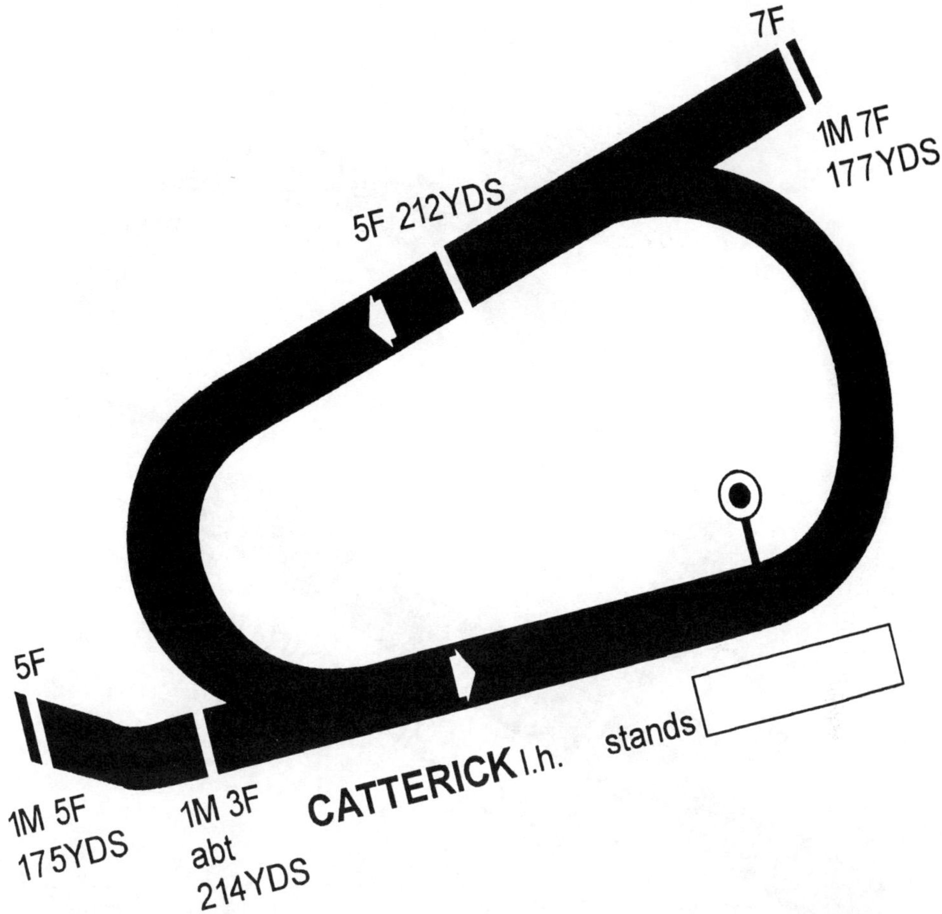

Catterick usually place the stalls on the far rail (low) over five furlongs and at every other distance apart from 5f 212y, where they are often placed on the outside (high). The inside rail can be moved by as much as 3 metres in the home straight (which is between 24 and 28 metres wide) and on the home bend by as much as 4-5 metres, but the stands' rail is permanent. The straight course runs north. A towline watering system is used, and it can be adjusted to offset the effects of the wind. No major drainage work has taken place, just spiking and general turf husbandry.

Maximum runners: **5f** (20), **5f 212y** (14), **7f** (18), **1m 3f 214y** (20), **1m 5f 175y** (20), **1m 7f 177y** (20)

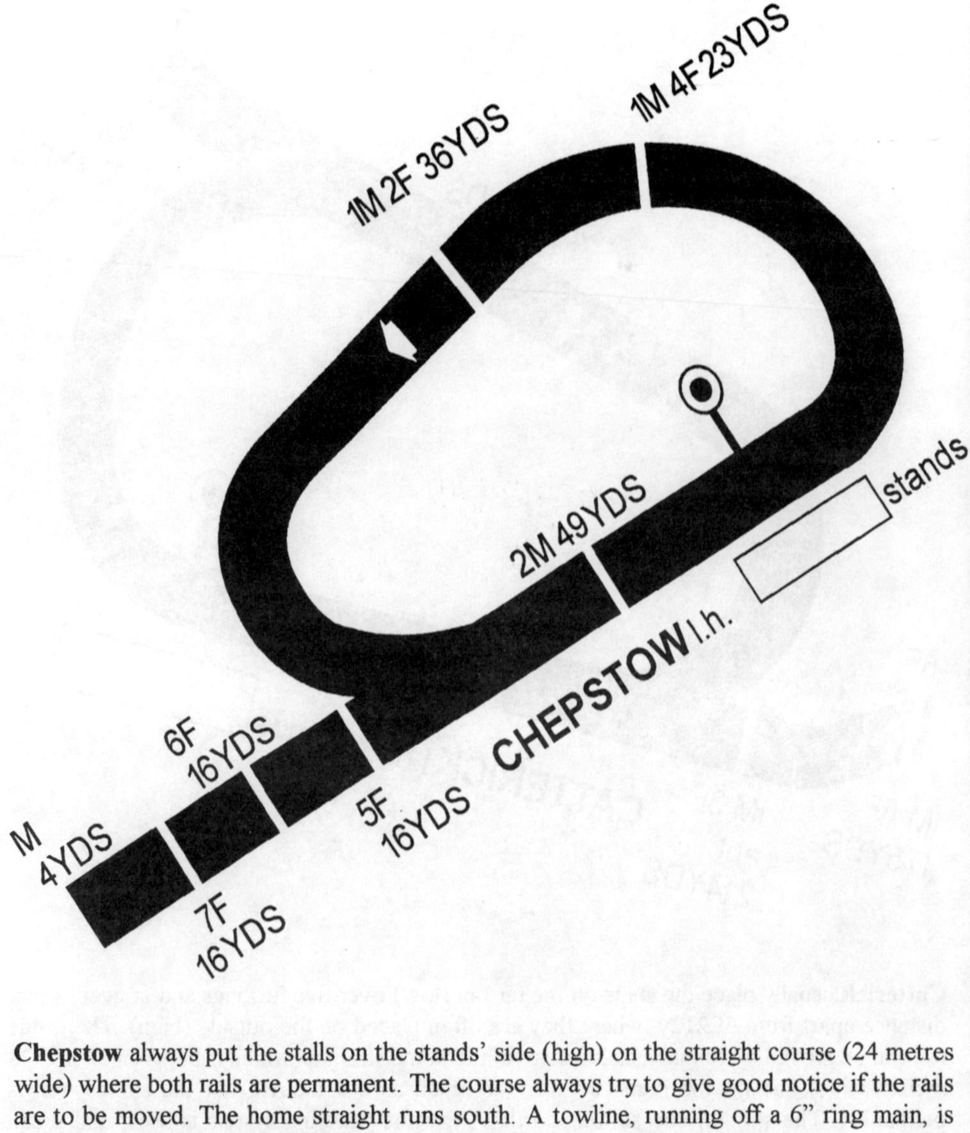

Chepstow always put the stalls on the stands' side (high) on the straight course (24 metres wide) where both rails are permanent. The course always try to give good notice if the rails are to be moved. The home straight runs south. A towline, running off a 6" ring main, is used and can be adjusted to offset any wind effects. No drainage work has been necessary, but regular Vertidraining takes place.

Maximum runners: 5f 16y (20), 6f 16y (20), 7f 16y (20), 1m 14y (20), **1m 2f 36y** (16), **1m 4f 23y** (19), **2m 49y** (flip start) (20), **2m 2f** (18)

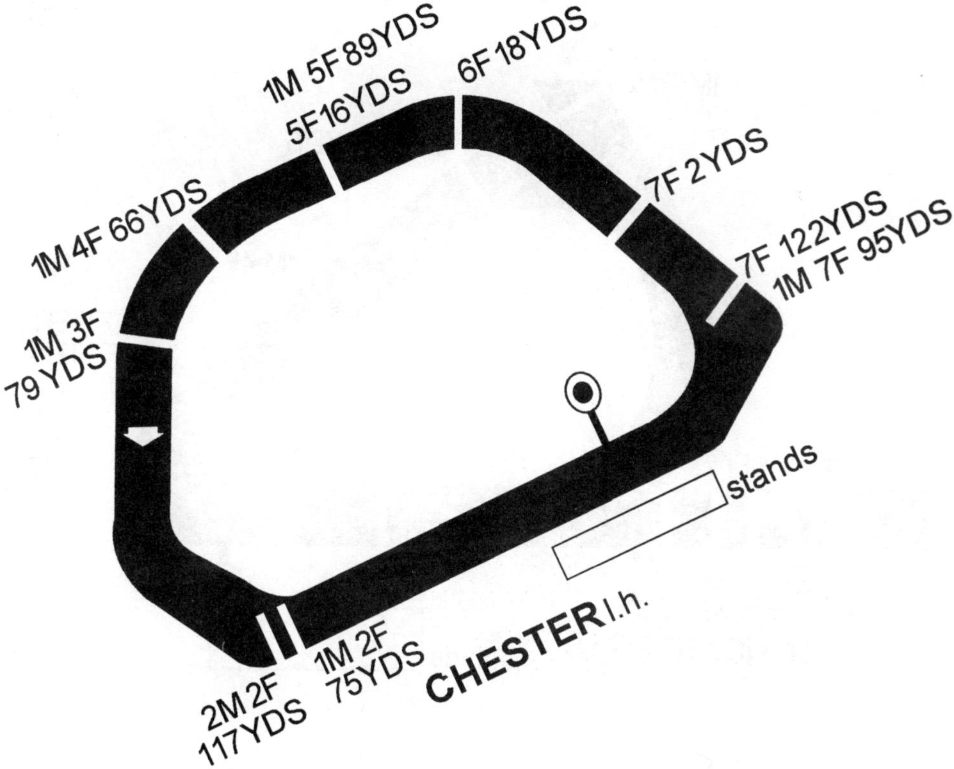

Chester put the stalls on the inside (low), except for races run over 1m 2f 75y and 2m 2f 117y (same starting points) where they are put on the outside (high). However, sometimes the stalls will be advertised as low in all races, but the starter (dependent upon who it is) may have them pushed nearer the centre in a bid to offset the strong low bias. The ground can become wet enough for flip starts to become necessary. The inside rail can be moved, from the 5½-furlong from home point to the furlong pole, going out by as much as 4 metres at the furthest point. It is usually moved on the Thursday of the May meeting, and often in August and September. A computer-operated pop-up system is used and the wind apparently has no effect. There has been no recent drainage work, just Vertidraining.

Maximum runners: **5f 16y** (16), **6f 18y** (16), **7f 2y** (16), **7f 122y** (18), **1m 2f 75y** (17), **1m 3f 79y** (16), **1m 4f 66y** (16), **1m 5f 89y** (16), **1m 7f 195y** (18), **2m 2f 147y** (18)

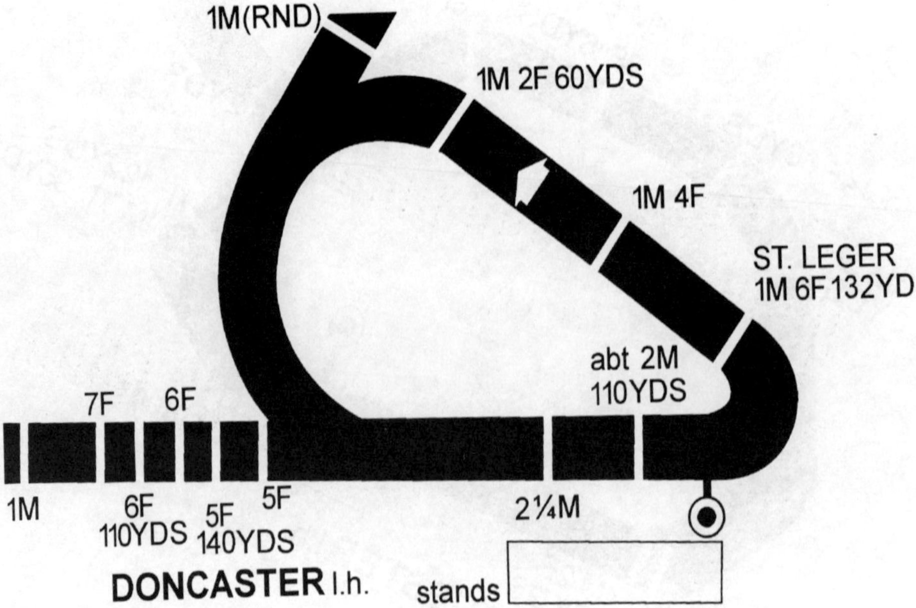

Doncaster normally put the stalls on the stands' rail (high) in the straight, and on the inside rail (low) at distances of 1m 2f 60y and beyond. Over the round mile, they are now placed on the outside, as during a trial period in 1996 when they were placed on the inside it was found that jockeys on runners drawn high were inclined to chop off those on the inner. The straight course, which faces west, is about 25 metres wide at the mile start, tapering down to 18 metres at the winning post. A towline is used and watering is done 1 metre off the rail to offset the wind effect. No recent major drainage work has been carried out, just Vertidraining when necessary in April. During the summer, spiking is done prior to watering.

Maximum runners: 5f (22), 5f 140y (22), 6f (22), **6f 110y** (22), 7f (22), 1m (straight) (24), **1m (round)** (25*), **1m 2f 60y** (20), **1m 4f** (24*), **1m 6f 132y** (24*), **2m 110y** (18), **2m 2f** (20)

* Safety figures only apply to Lincoln meeting, Leger meeting and November Handicap

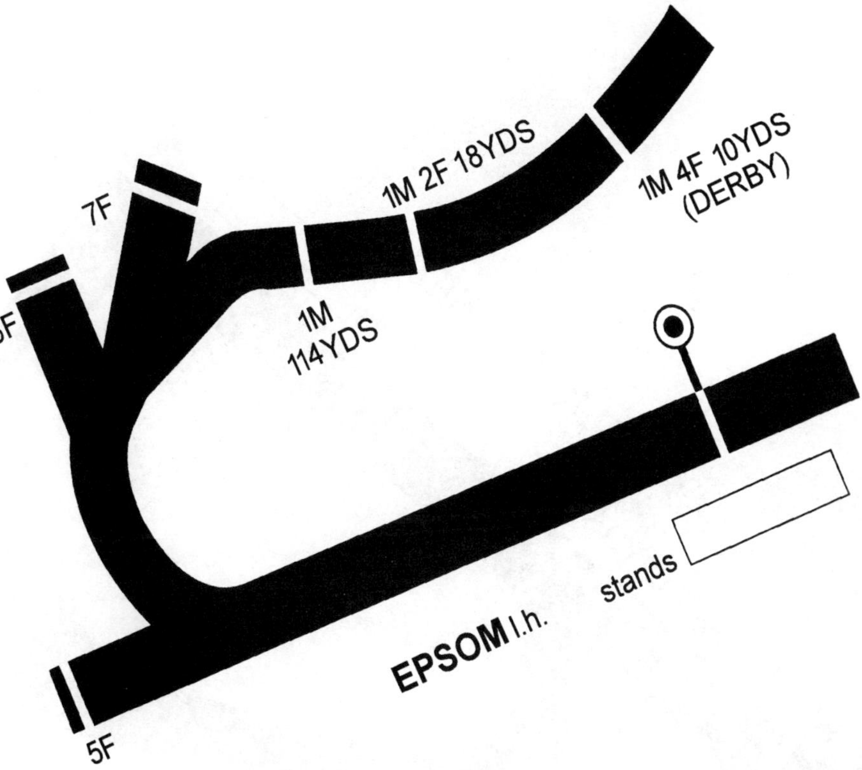

Epsom invariably put the stalls high (stands' side) over five furlongs and over six furlongs (which starts on a chute). The rails are moveable for the few races staged on the five-furlong course, which is 35 metres wide, and whether they are depends upon how much racing has been staged on the round course. The straight course runs in a south-westerly direction. Brian Clifford, assistant Clerk of the Course for United Racecourses, said: "It can get very breezy up here and the wind can come from all directions, but the groundsman is a master at adjusting the towline system to adjust to all conditions. Epsom is self-draining, and only requires Vertidraining, slitting and general turf maintenance."

Maximum runners: 5f (20), **6f** (17), **7f** (17), **1m 114y** (20), **1m 2f 18y** (30), **1m 4f 10y** (30)

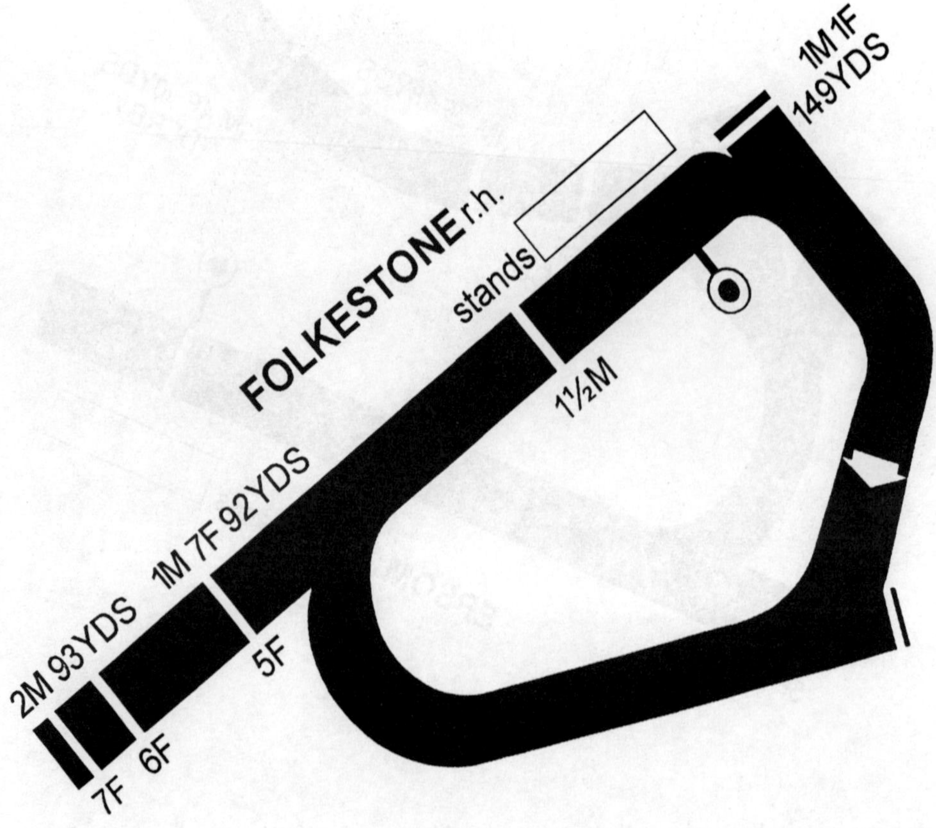

Folkestone usually put the stalls on the stands' rail (low) for straight races. The rails in the straight course, which is 23 metres wide and faces west, are never moved. Watering is achieved by draglines, which are repositioned when necessary. No recent major drainage work has been done, just routine turf maintenance.

Maximum runners: 5f (16), 6f (16), **6f 189y** (16), **7f** (16), **1m 1f 149y** (15), **1m 4f** (normally 18, temporarily 16), **1m 7f 92y** (16), **2m 93y** (16)

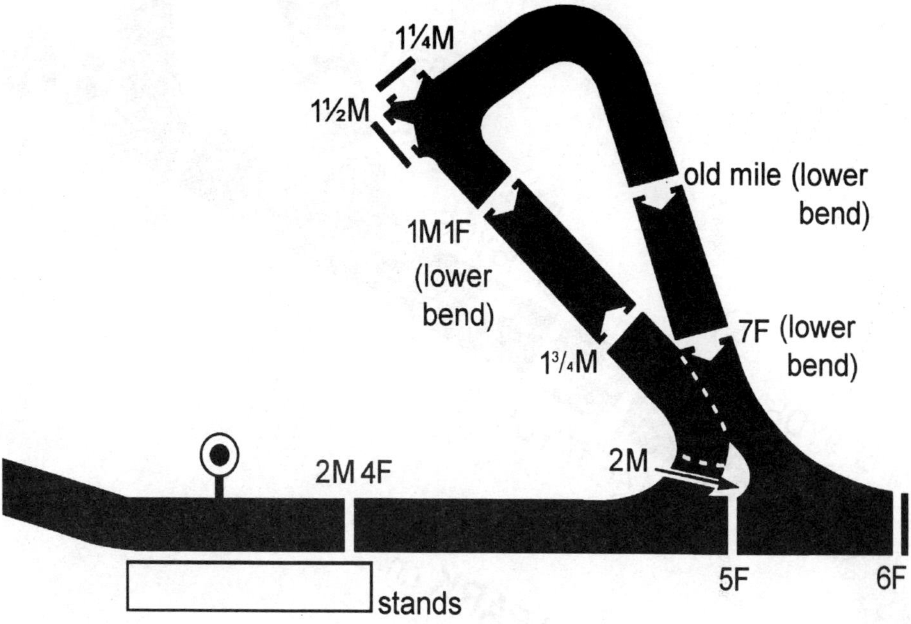

GOODWOOD r.h.

Goodwood try to put the stalls on the stands' side (low) wherever possible on the straight course and only switch them to the far rail in exceptional circumstances. The stands' rail is permanent but the far rail can be moved, right the way down to the winning post, by as much as 5 metres. The straight course is about 31 metres wide. An Upton irrigator is used, so the wind has no major effect. There has been some minor drainage work in the final furlong, and a compaction-breaker was used last year on all parts of the course.

Maximum runners: 5f (30), 6f (30), **7f** (20), **1m** (22), **1m 1f** (22), **1m 2f** (22), **1m 4f** (16), **1m 6f** (17), **2m** (16), **2m 4f** (22)

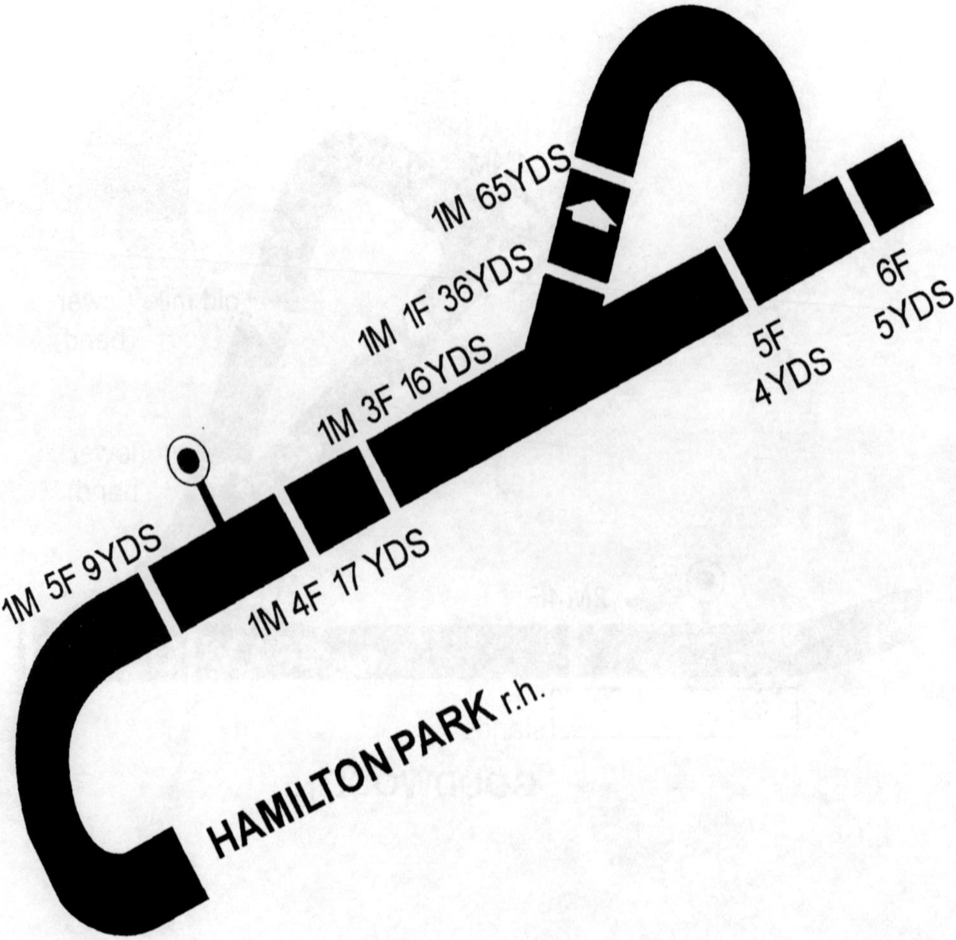

Hamilton normally put the stalls on the stands' side (low) on the straight course, which is about 22 metres wide. The inside rail on the 'loop' can be moved by up to 10 metres, but both rails in the straight are permanent. The straight course runs north. An Upton irrigation system is used, and there has been quite a bit of drainage work done recently; sand-slitting from half a furlong out to halfway round the pull-up, and in the dip at the top of the 'loop' - about 3f 110y out. Vertidraining is done every season.

Maximum runners: 5f 4y (18), 6f 5y (18), **1m 65y** (16), **1m 1f 36y** (18), **1m 3f 16y** (18), **1m 4f 17y** (18), **1m 5f 9y** (18)

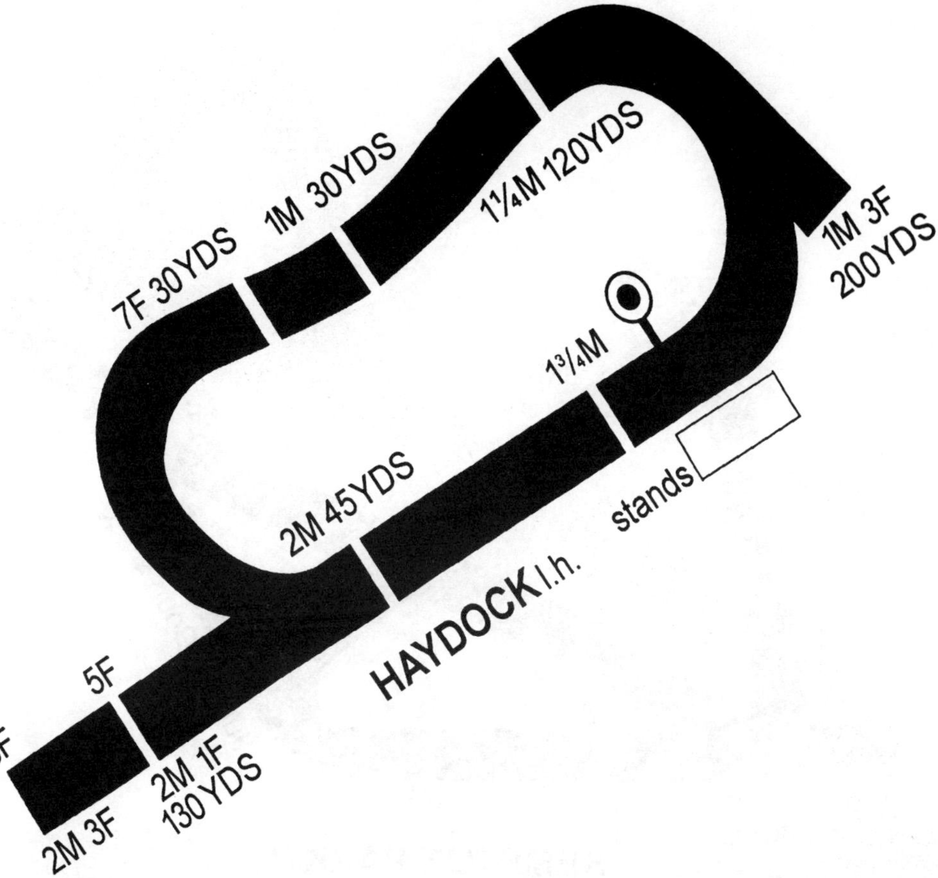

Haydock put the stalls stands' side (high) on the straight course, which is about 26 metres wide. The rails in the straight are very rarely moved, although they were for one meeting last October to avoid very wet patches, particularly at the 4f marker. The course runs west and is watered by an Upton irrigator, so the wind effect is minimal. Lisa Rowe said: "An enormous amount of drainage work has been done since we finished in October. At the six- and five-furlong areas, there are 6mm gravel drains, topped with rootzone, and we have injected slits to interlink with those drains. Vertidraining, which goes in 6-8", is carried out in certain areas up to four times a year, but no deeper upheaval work is to be done."

Maximum runners: 5f (24), 6f (24), **7f 30y** (16), **1m 30y** (18), **1m 2f 120y** (20), **1m 3f 200y** (20), **1m 6f** (20), **2m 45y** (20)

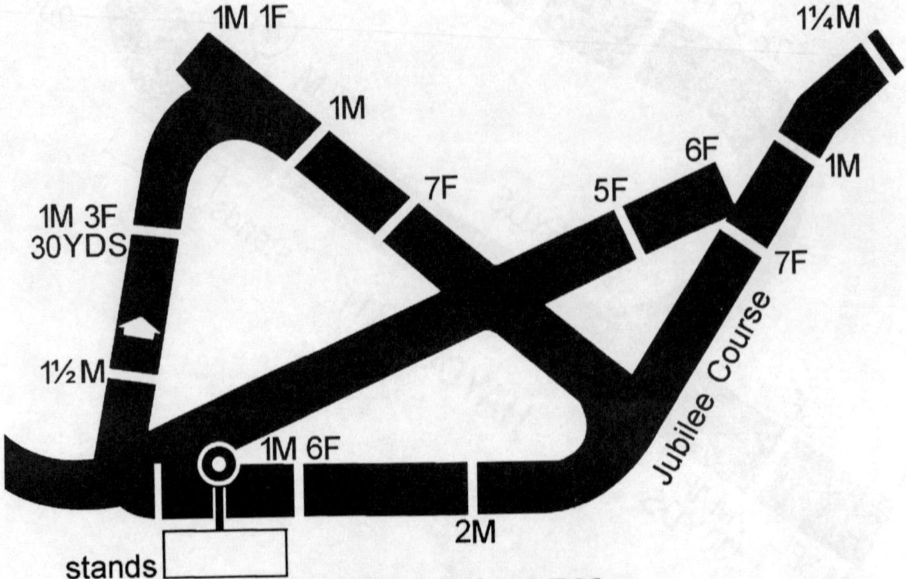

Kempton alternate the stalls between the far rail (high) and the stands' rail (low) on the sprint course, which is about 30 metres wide. Neither rail on the separate sprint chute, which faces south-west, is moveable. A pop-up watering system is used, and no drainage work has been necessary, just general turf husbandry.

Maximum runners: 5f (26), 6f (26), **7f** (Jubilee) (17), **7f** (round) (17), **1m** (Jubilee) (20), **1m** (round) (18), **1m 1f** (20), **1m 2f** (Jubilee) (20), **1m 3f 30y** (20), **1m 4f** (20), **1m 6f 92y** (14), **2m** (18)

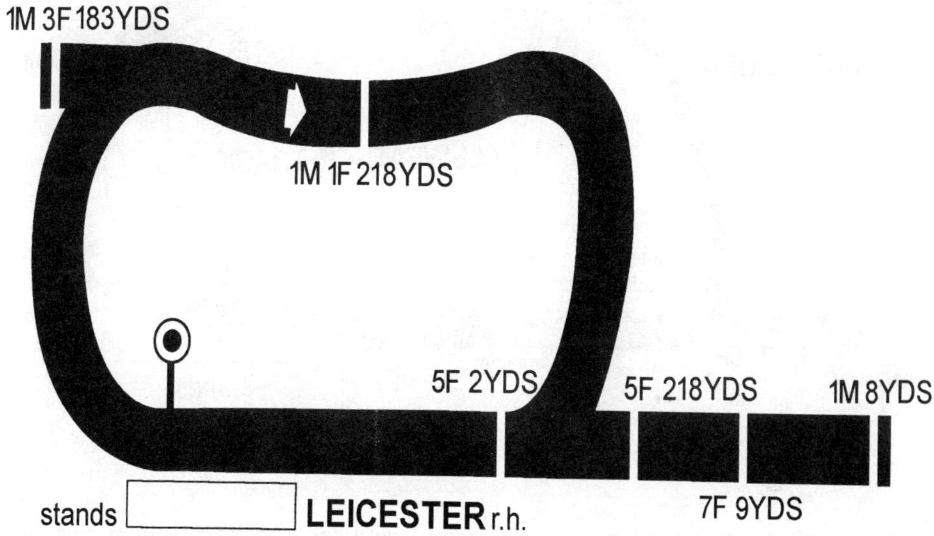

Leicester normally put the stalls on the stands' rail (low) on the straight course, which runs east. Both rails in the straight, which is about 25 metres wide, are permanent. Nick Lees, Clerk of the Course, said: "We use pop-up sprinklers, and were the first in England to use them in the mid-60s. In the summer, when watered, it can be faster up the centre if there is a wind blowing and causing a dry patch. In the long term we might get a boom system as an accessory, funds permitting. It's a clay course, so we have to mess about a bit with the drainage, but nothing major has been done. Vertidraining is done to aereate the ground."

Maximum runners: 5f 2y (25), 5f 218y (22), 7f 9y (20), 1m 8y (20), **1m 1f 218y** (19), **1m 3f 183y** (22)

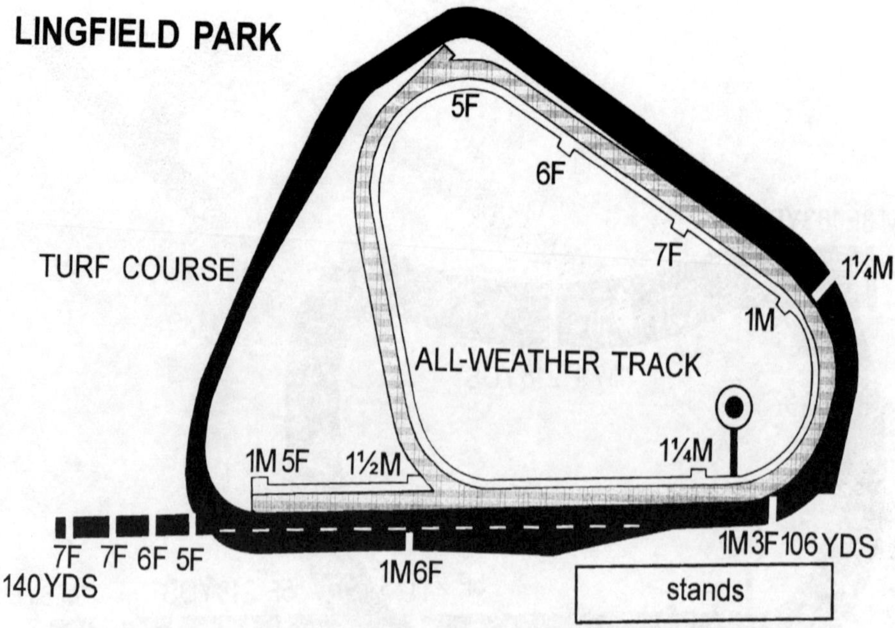

Lingfield turf usually put the stalls on the stands' rail (high) for races between five and seven furlongs, but down the centre for races over the straight 7f 140y. While it is rare for them to be placed on the far rail (low), that can occur in late season. During the summer, the option is there to put the stalls away from the stands' side, which reduces the safety factors, by moving the stands' rail by as much as 3 metres inwards. The straight course runs north. A Boom irrigation system is used, which means there is little wind effect, though sometimes it blows straight down the course. No recent drainage work has been carried out, just routine turf maintenance.

Lingfield all-weather put the stalls on the inside (low) for every distance bar five furlongs, when they are invariably on the stands' rail (high). The entire course is 20 metres wide.

Maximum runners: **turf** 5f (20), 6f (20), 7f (18), 7f 140y (18), **1m 1f** (14), **1m 2f** (16), **1m 3f 106y** (16), **1m 6f** (20), **2m** (20)
all-weather 5f (10), **6f** (14), **7f** (16), **1m** (12), **1m 2f** (14), **1m 4f** (18), **1m 5f** (18), **2m** (14)

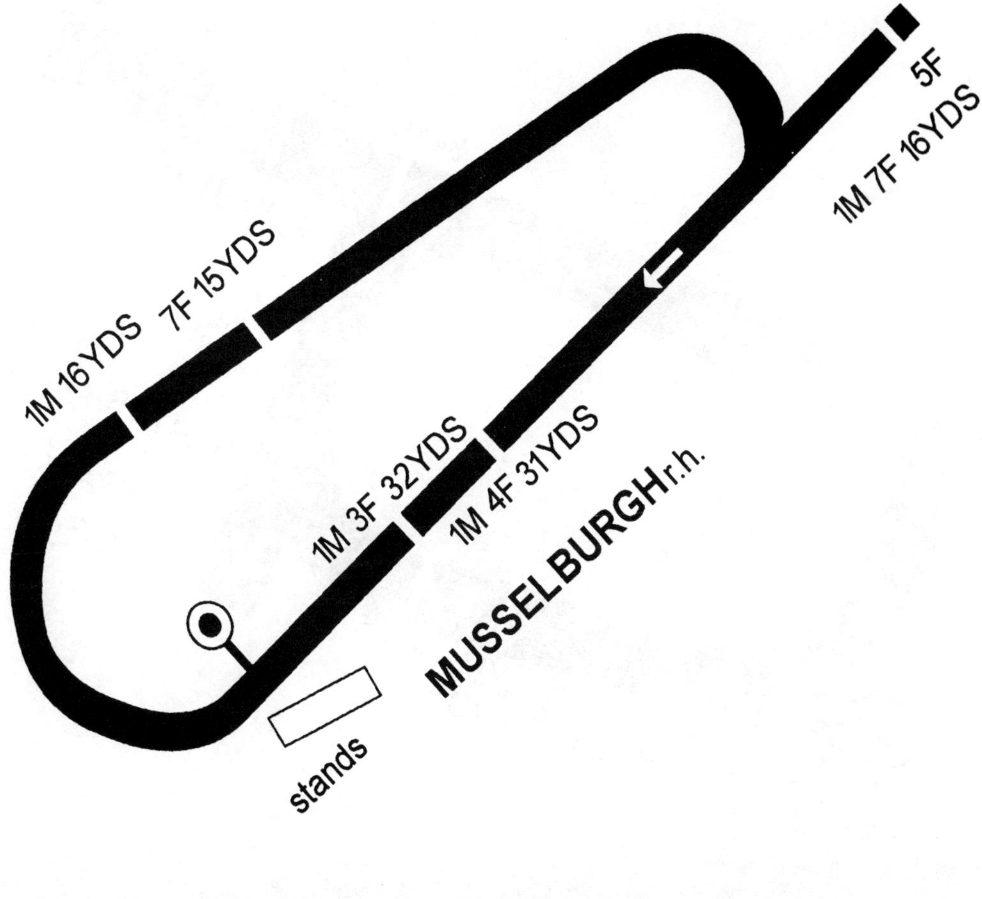

Musselburgh vary the stalls' position, last year putting them on the far side (high) for the first half of the season and on the stands' side for the second half. No policy has yet been decided for 2000. The groundsman feels that when they are on the far side, there is no draw advantage, but that there is a slight kink on the stands' side which can favour low numbers when the stalls are low. The straight course, which runs west, is about 19 metres wide. A towline is used for the back straight and bend, a Briggs boom for the straight, and the wind has little or no effect. No drainage work has been necessary, as the course is based on sandy soil.

Maximum runners: **5f** (17), **7f 30y** (14), **1m** (14), **1m 1f** (16), **1m 4f** (16), **1m 5f** (16), **1m 6f** (12), **1m 7f** (16), **2m** (17)

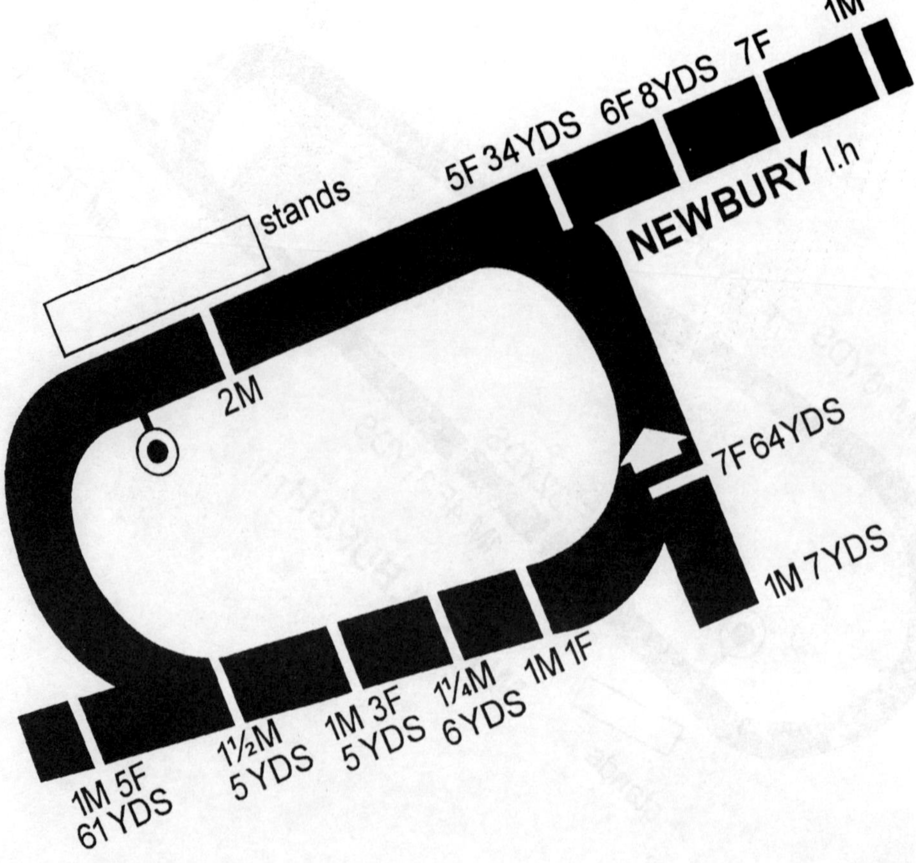

Newbury put the stalls down the centre for important races, but on the stands' side in big-field straight races in order to preserve the ground on the inside for round-course events. The straight course is 32 metres wide at the mile start, tapering down to 18 metres at the finish, and a moveable 'dummy' stands' rail can go out by up to 5 metres for safety reasons (wear and tear). The straight course runs west. The pop-up system used in the past was affected by the prevailing south-westerly wind, but there is no affect with the new Briggs system. No drainage work has been done recently.

Maximum runners: 5f 34y (27), 6f 8y (27), 7f (straight) (27), **7f 64y (round)** (18), 1m (straight) (27), **1m 7y (round)** (20), **1m 1f** (18), **1m 2f 6y** (22), **1m 3f 5y** (22), **1m 4f 5y** (22), **1m 5f 61y** (20), **2m** (19)

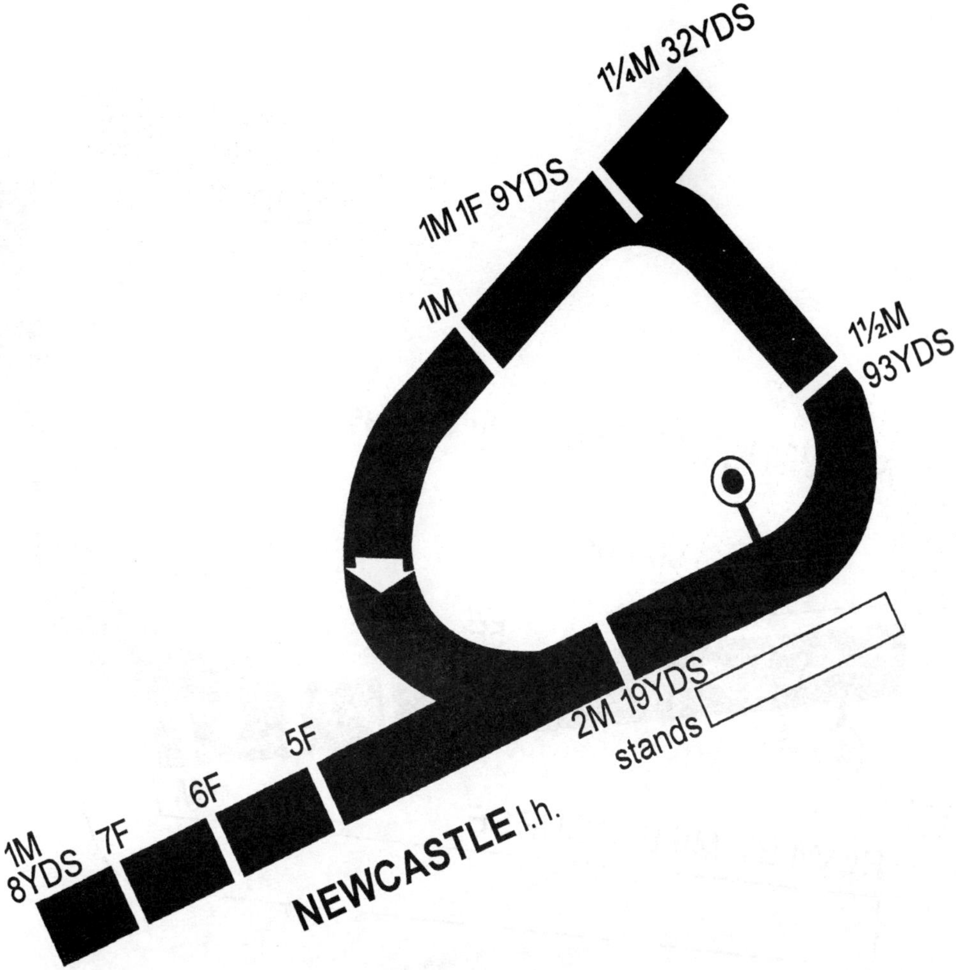

Newcastle normally place the stalls on the stands' side (high) on the straight course, and maybe twice a year on the far side, otherwise the ground between the 1m 3y start and the four-furlong point on that side is never used. The 21-metre wide straight course runs west and both rails are permanent, but plenty of 'dolling out' takes place during a season. An Upton irrigator is used for watering, so the wind has no effect, and no major drainage work has been done since '95, just regular Vertidraining.

Maximum runners: 5f (20), 6f (20), 7f (20), **1m (round)** (20), 1m 3y (straight) (20), **1m 1f 9y** (20), **1m 2f 32y** (20), **1m 4f 93y** (20), **2m 19y** (20)

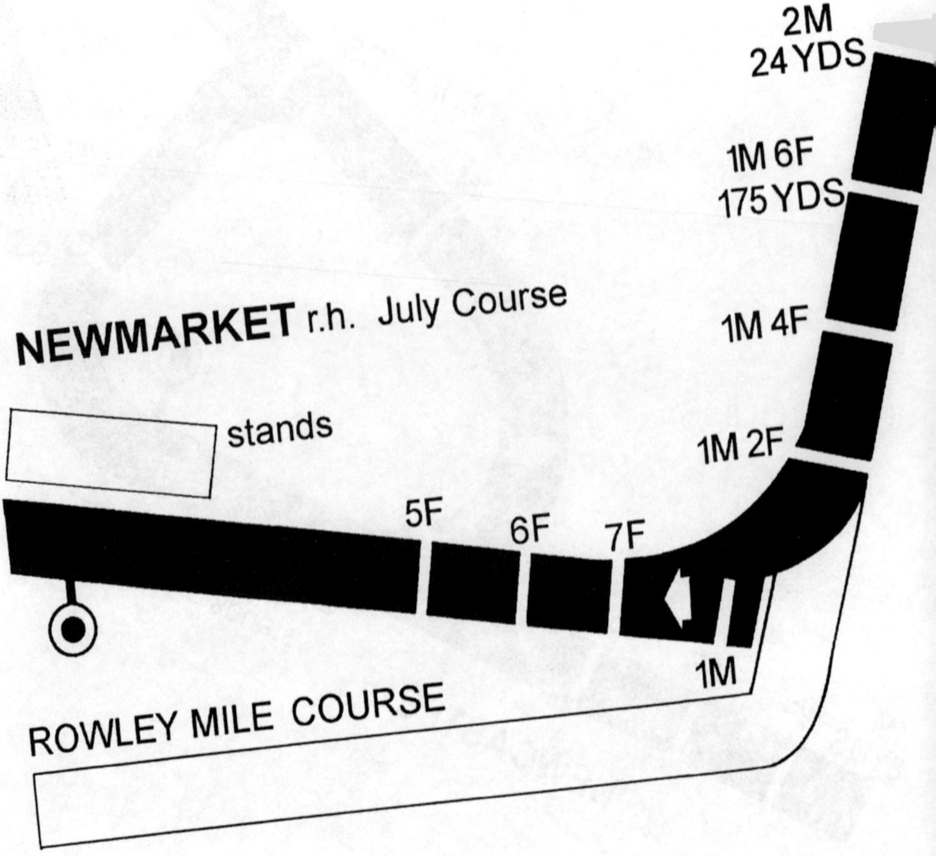

Newmarket July Course vary the stalls' position fairly equally between the stands' rail (high), the far rail (low) and the centre of the course. There is a permanent dividing rail down the centre of the course, which effectively creates two different tracks, and racing is divided up pretty much equally between the two. All the rails are permanent from the 7½-furlong point in the straight, which faces south-east. No drainage work has been required.

Maximum runners: 5f (20), 6f (20), 7f (20), 1m (20), 1m 110y (20), **1m 2f** (36), **1m 4f** (36), **1m 6f 175y** (36), **2m 24y** (36), **2m 1f 65y** (36)

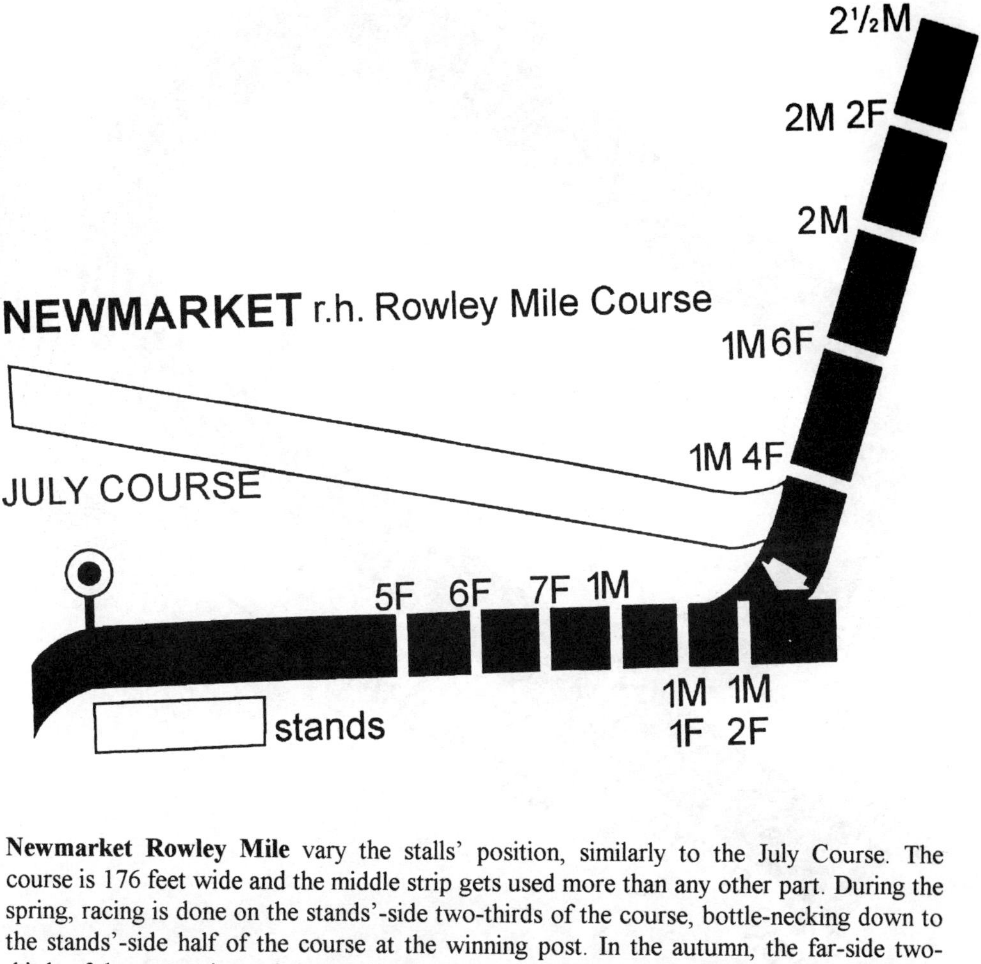

Newmarket Rowley Mile vary the stalls' position, similarly to the July Course. The course is 176 feet wide and the middle strip gets used more than any other part. During the spring, racing is done on the stands'-side two-thirds of the course, bottle-necking down to the stands'-side half of the course at the winning post. In the autumn, the far-side two-thirds of the course is used, narrowing down to the far-side half at the line. This means that there is a triangular shaped piece of ground down the centre which is in use all the time. Both rails are moveable. The straight course, which points south-east, narrows from being 53 metres wide at the mile start, down to 36 metres at the five-furlong start. Towlines are mainly used, half a furlong at a time in three parallel lines, because the course is so wide, and the course also has the Briggs boom, the choice assuring the wind doesn't affect distribution. No drainage work has been required.

Maximum runners: 5f (30), 6f (30), 7f (30), 1m (30), 1m 1f (30, Cambs 35), 1m 2f (30), **1m 4f** (36), **1m 6f** (36), **2m** (36), **2m 2f** (36)

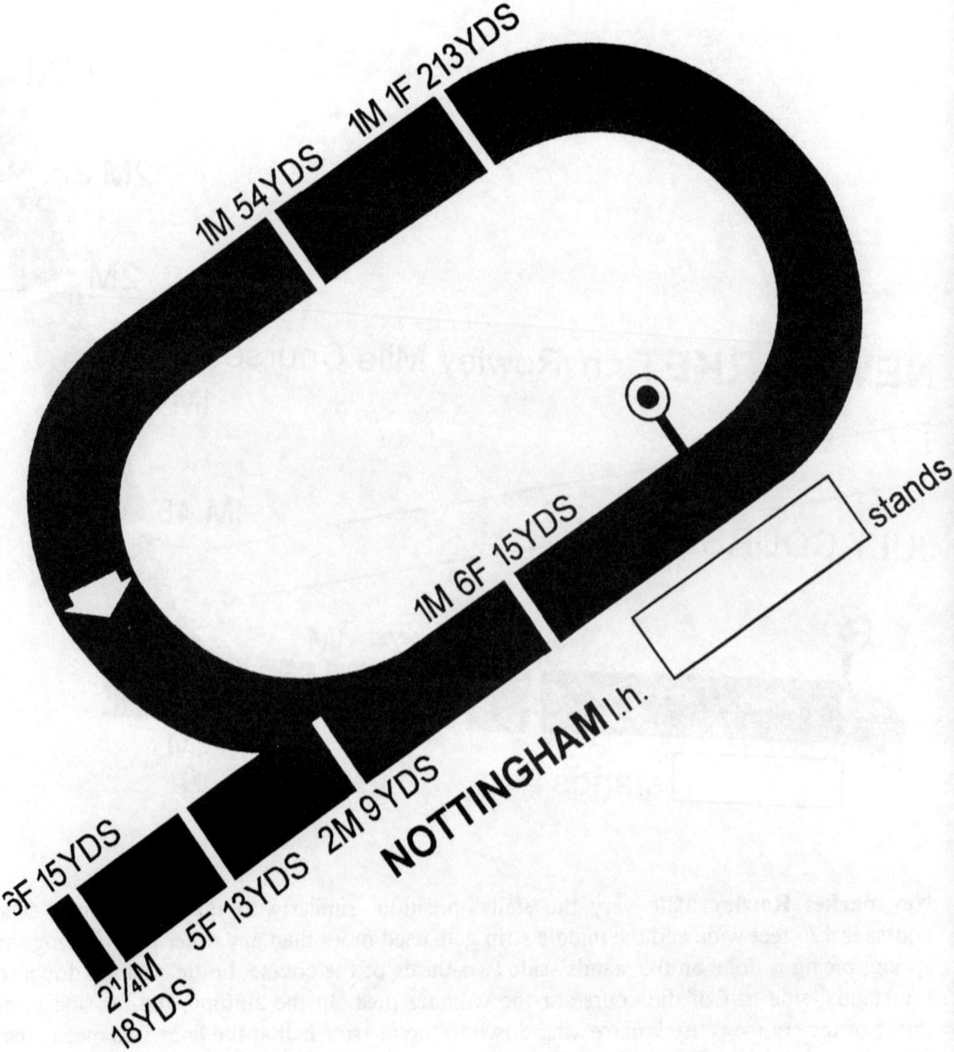

Nottingham prefer to keep the stalls on the stands' side (high) in straight races, but they can sometimes go on the far rail (low). The straight course, which faces west, is about 23 metres wide and both rails can be moved. An Upton irrigator is used for watering, and no major drainage work has taken place, just Vertidraining and air injection.

Maximum runners: 5f 13y (20), 6f 15y (20), **1m 54y** (18), **1m 1f 213y** (18), **1m 6f 15y** (16), **2m 9y** (18), **2m 2f 18y** (18)

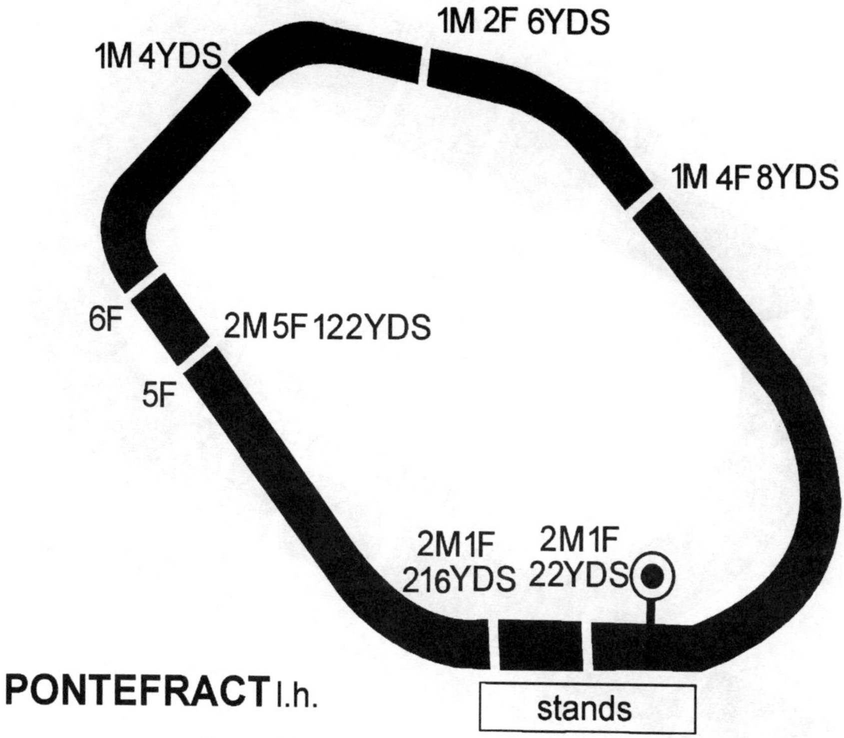

Pontefract put the stalls on the inside rail (low), unless the ground becomes soft, when they are sometimes moved to the outside. The five-furlong point is 18 metres wide, and the finishing straight 19.7 metres across. A temporary rail is erected from the six-furlong pole down to the winning post, 4 metres outside the permanent rail, before the fourth meeting of the season to make use of fresh ground and is taken down before the Friday meeting in mid-July. The short straight runs west. An Upton irrigator is normally used for watering, with a towline system in place as a back-up. The drainage work is ongoing (the course was built between 1916 and 1918 through a bank, which means there isn't much top soil on top of clay). This winter, sand-slitting took place on the bend into the straight, and also to a lesser extent in the dip four furlongs out. Vertidraining is done twice a year, once in October after the season ends, and once in mid-May before dolling occurs.

Maximum runners: **5f** (18), **6f** (18), **1m 4y** (20), **1m 2f 6y** (19), **1m 4f 8y** (18), **2m 1f 22y** (19), **2m 1f 216y** (19), **2m 5f 122y** (20)

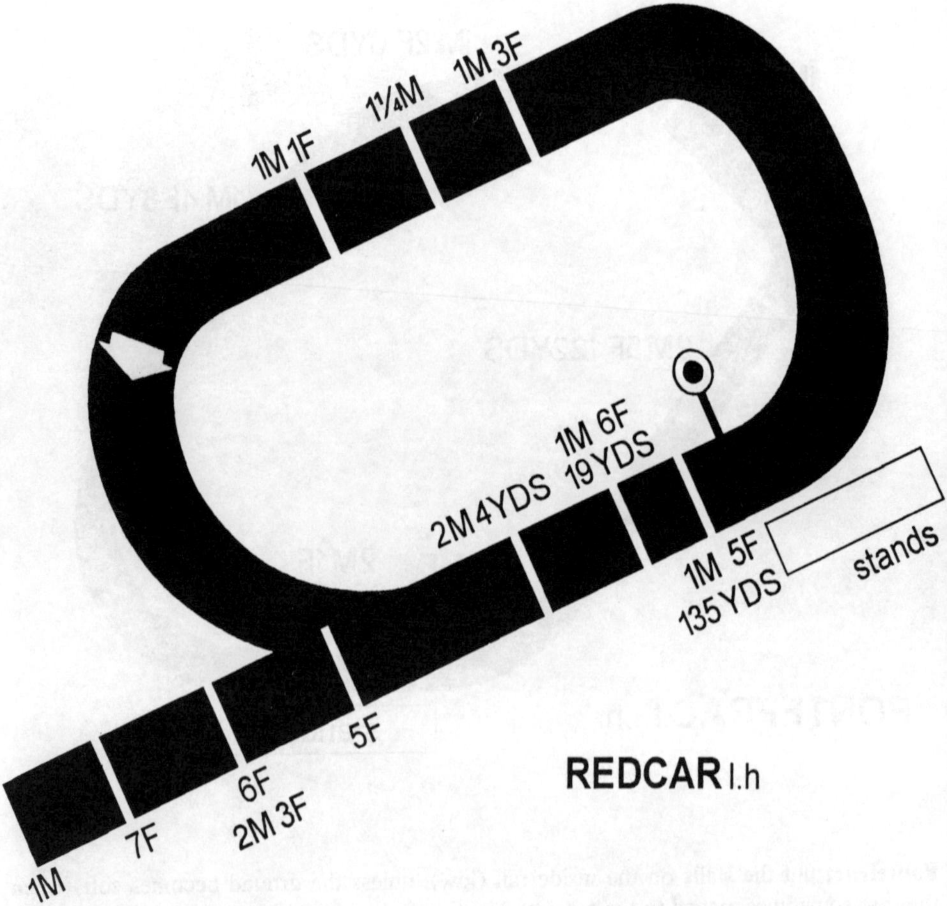

Redcar put the stalls close to the stands' rail (high) the majority of the time, but not right on it because of the shape of the course towards that side. Both rails in the straight course, which runs in a north-easterly direction, can be moved but never are. The straight course narrows from being 30 metres wide at the mile start down to 25 metres at the five-furlong point. A pop-up watering system is used, and water distribution can be affected by the wind coming from the west. No major drainage work has been carried out, just slitting in the back straight, Vertidraining and spiking.

Maximum runners: 5f (23), 6f (26), 7f (29), 1m (30), **1m 1f** (16), **1m 2f** (17), **1m 3f** (17), **1m 5f 135y** (15), **1m 6f 19y** (16), **2m 4y** (18), **2m 3f** (18)

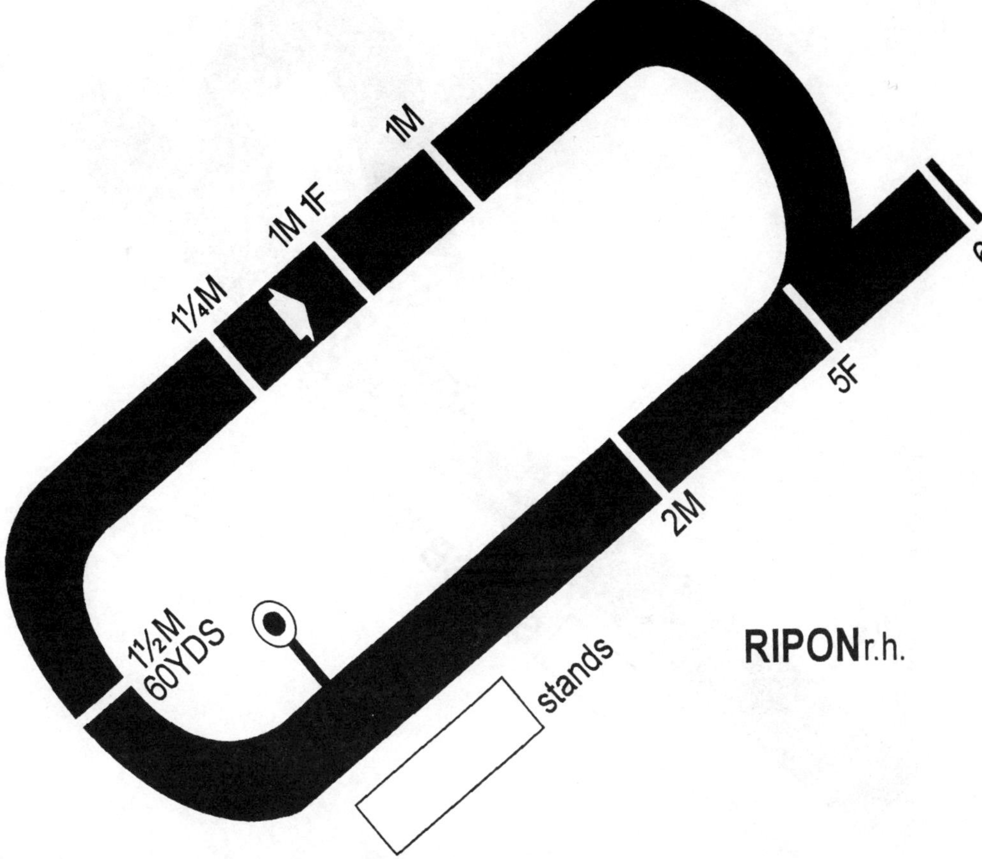

Ripon try to keep the stalls on the stands' rail (low) in sprint races wherever possible. A new pop-up sprinkler system was implemented in August 1997 to cover both rails in the straight, but the westerly wind, which tends to prevail, blows away from the stands' rail and can make even watering difficult. Consequently most watering is done during the night when conditions are calmer. The inside rail is moveable between the mile and five-furlong points, but both rails in the straight are permanent. The straight course, which points north-east, is about 24 metres wide. Vertidraining takes place currently only in the winter, but may occur more frequently in future.

Maximum runners: 5f (23), 6f (23), **1m** (20), **1m 1f** (25), **1m 2f** (25), **1m 4f 60y** (20), **2m** (20), **2m 1f 203y** (23)

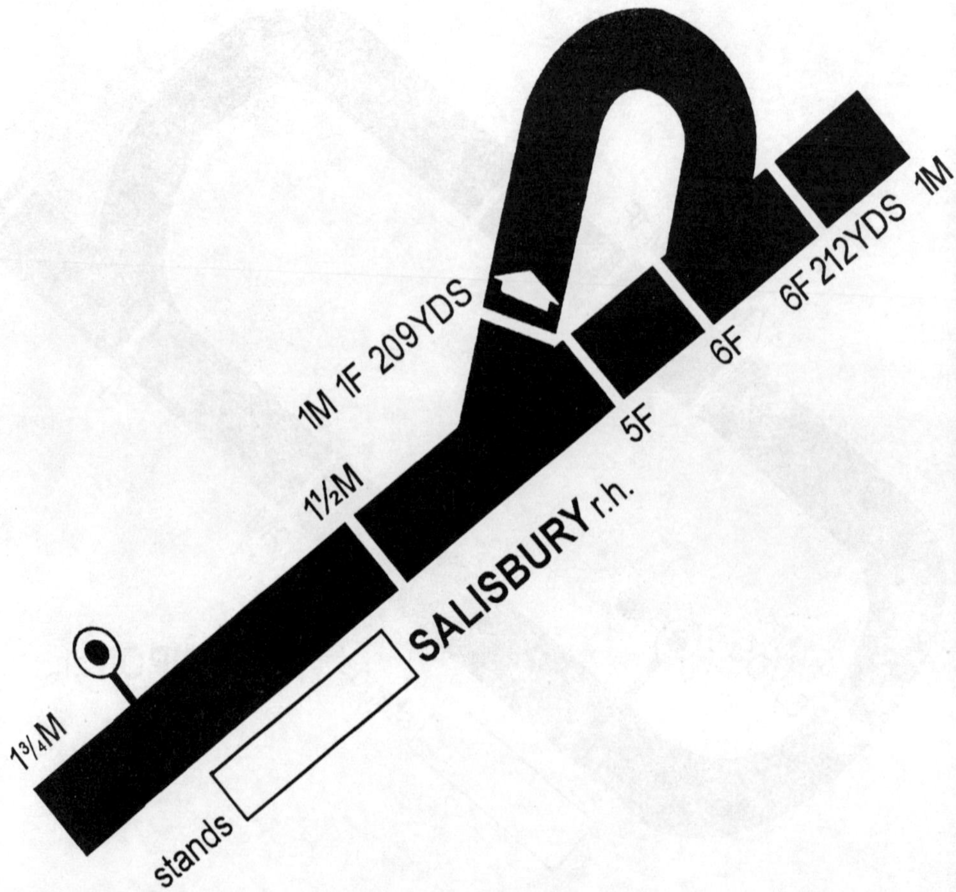

Salisbury normally place the stalls on the far rail (high), except in July and August, when a bit of false rail on the far side makes their position more central. However, on softer ground, they tend to go on the stands' side. The straight course widens from being about 19 metres wide at the mile start, up to about 29 metres at the five-furlong point. The rails are not moveable, except in mid-summer, when the far rail comes in by 4 metres. The straight course runs west. Towline and Upton irrigator systems are employed, with the latter used when it is windy to avoid any effect. Minor drainage work has been carried out at about the seven-furlong marker; and slitting, spiking and, occasionally, Vertidraining take place.

Maximum runners: 5f (20), **6f** (20), **6f 212y** (20), **1m** (18), **1m 1f 198y** (18), **1m 4f** (20), **1m 6f 15y** (flip start) (20)

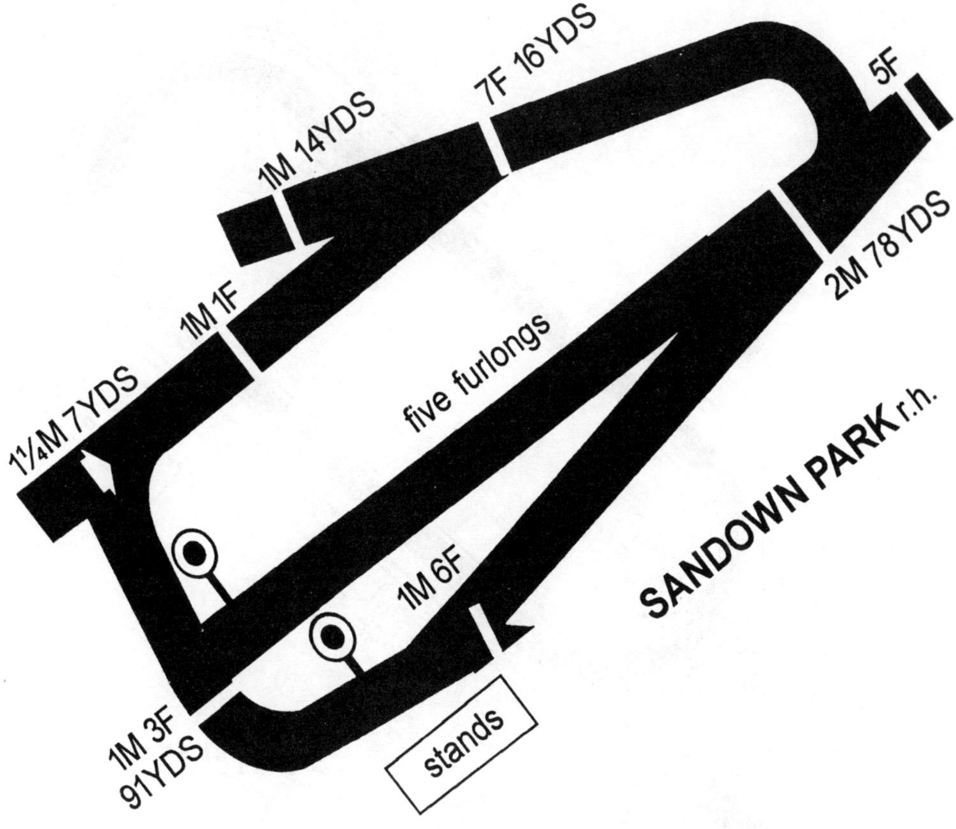

Sandown alternate the position of the stalls on the straight five-furlong course between either rail, although they tend to go on the stands' side in the early stages of a season. The whole inside rail on the round course can be moved, but both rails on the separate sprint course are permanent. The sprint course is about 34 metres wide, although there is the option to doll off to bring it down to about 25 metres, and points south-west. Briggs, pop-up and towline watering systems are used, although mostly towline because it is easier to bring into operation. The old drains have been renewed, and the course tends to require quite a bit of spiking, Vertidraining and general turf husbandry.

Maximum runners: 5f 6y (20), **7f 16y** (16), **1m 14y** (18), **1m 1f** (16), **1m 2f 7y** (20), **1m 3f 91y** (14), **1m 6f** (18), **2m 78y** (20)

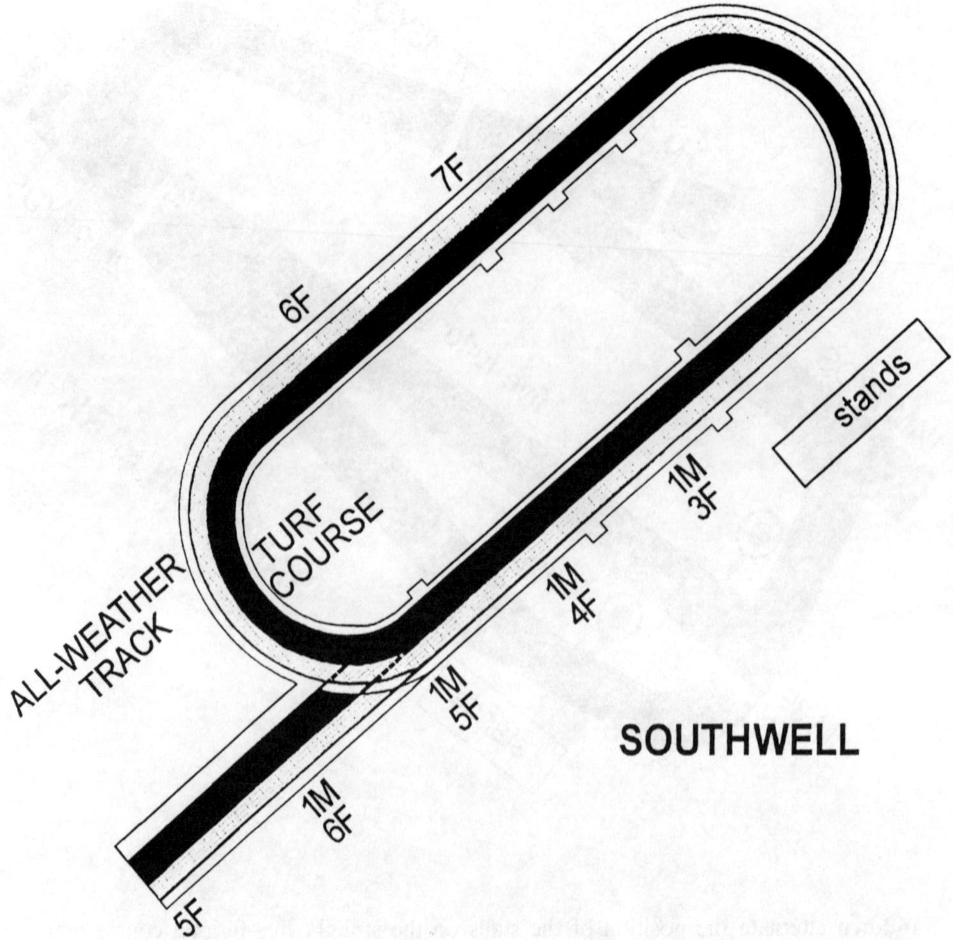

Southwell all-weather re-laid the entire track in October, 1997 and it now rides much quicker than before. Amateurs and apprentices do not race over six furlongs. The straight course is about 18 metres wide.

Maximum runners: **turf 6f** (14), **7f** (16), **1m 2f** (14), **1m 3f** (16), **1m 4f** (16), **2m** (16)
all-weather 5f (17), **6f** (16), **7f** (16), **1m** (16), **1m 3f** (16), **1m 4f** (17), **1m 5f** (17), **1m 6f** (17), **2m** (16), **2m 2f** (16)

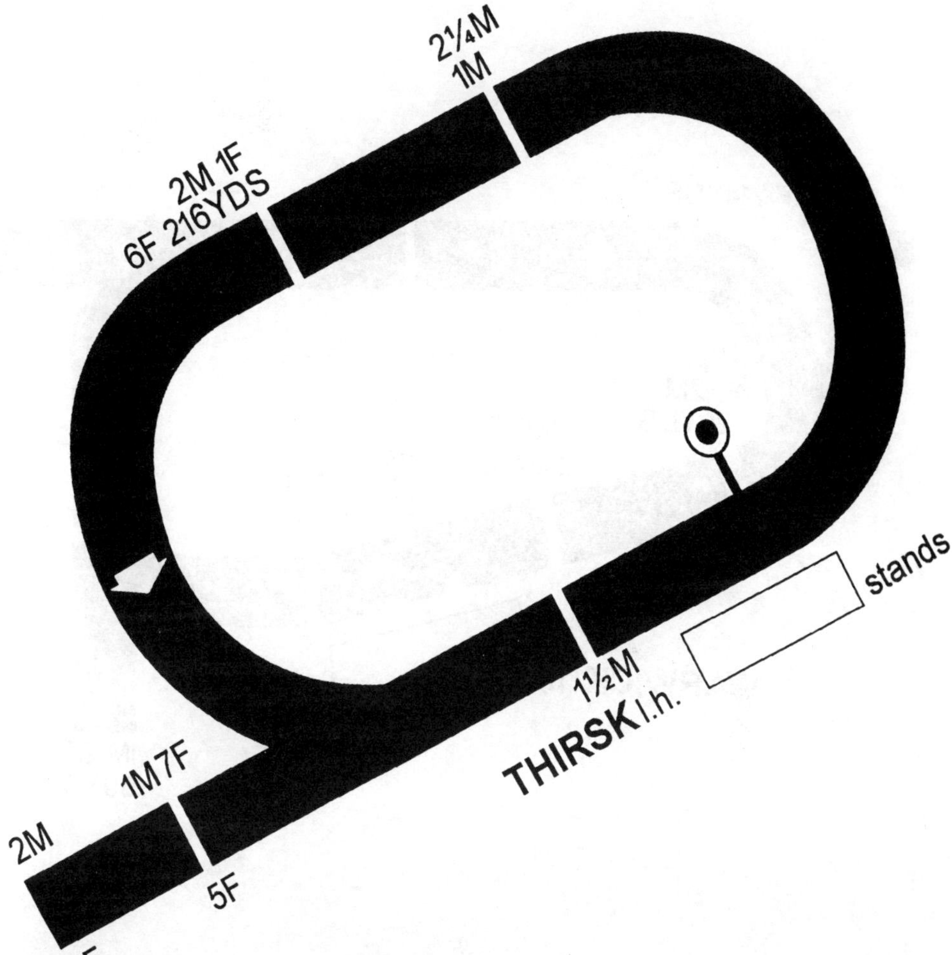

Thirsk invariably put the stalls on the stands' side (high) over sprint distances and for races over 1m 4f, which start in the straight. Both rails in the straight, which is about 26 metres wide and runs east, are permanent. The course used to use a towline, which meant watering was seriously affected by the prevailing south-westerly wind, but this year they will be using a hose reel and Briggs boom, which should even things out. No drainage work has been done as the course is sand and gravel-based, and they Vertidrain in winter.

Maximum runners: 5f (24), 6f (24), **7f** (14), **1m** (18), **1m 4f** (19), **2m** (24)

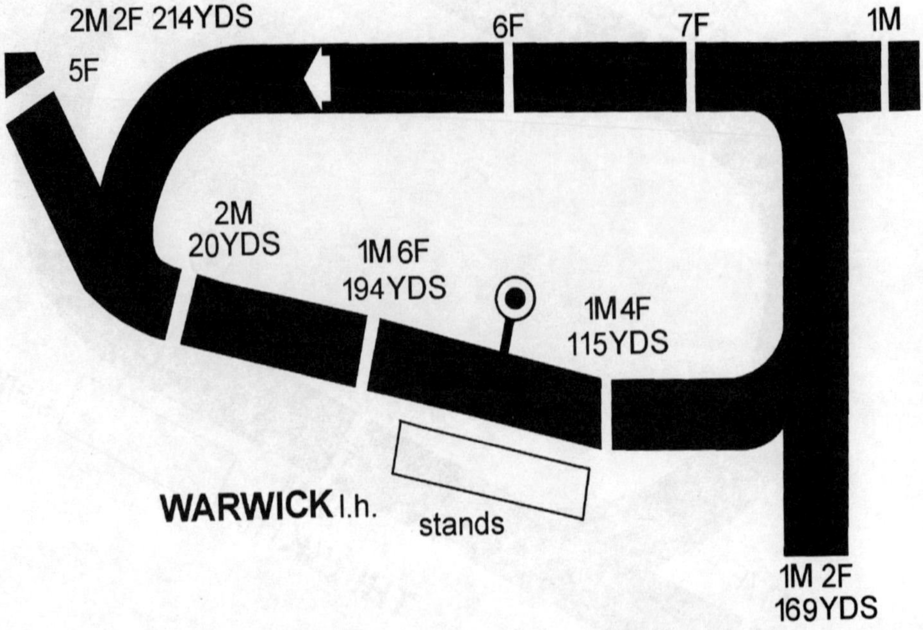

Warwick put the stalls on the inside rail (low) at all distances, and all rails are permanent. The five-furlong course starts off about 25 metres wide, narrowing to 14 metres at the bend into the straight. The straight runs east. The wind tends to have no effect on watering, which is done using an Upton irrigator, and the course Vertidrain once or twice a year.

Maximum runners: **5f** (20), **6f** (17), **6f 168y** (20), **7f** (20), **7f 164y** (20), **1m** (20), **1m 2f 110y** (20), **1m 2f 169y** (20), **1m 4f 56y** (13), **1m 4f 115y** (13), **1m 6f 135y** (14), **1m 6f 194y** (14), **1m 7f 181y** (19), **2m 20y** (19), **2m 2f 214y** (20)

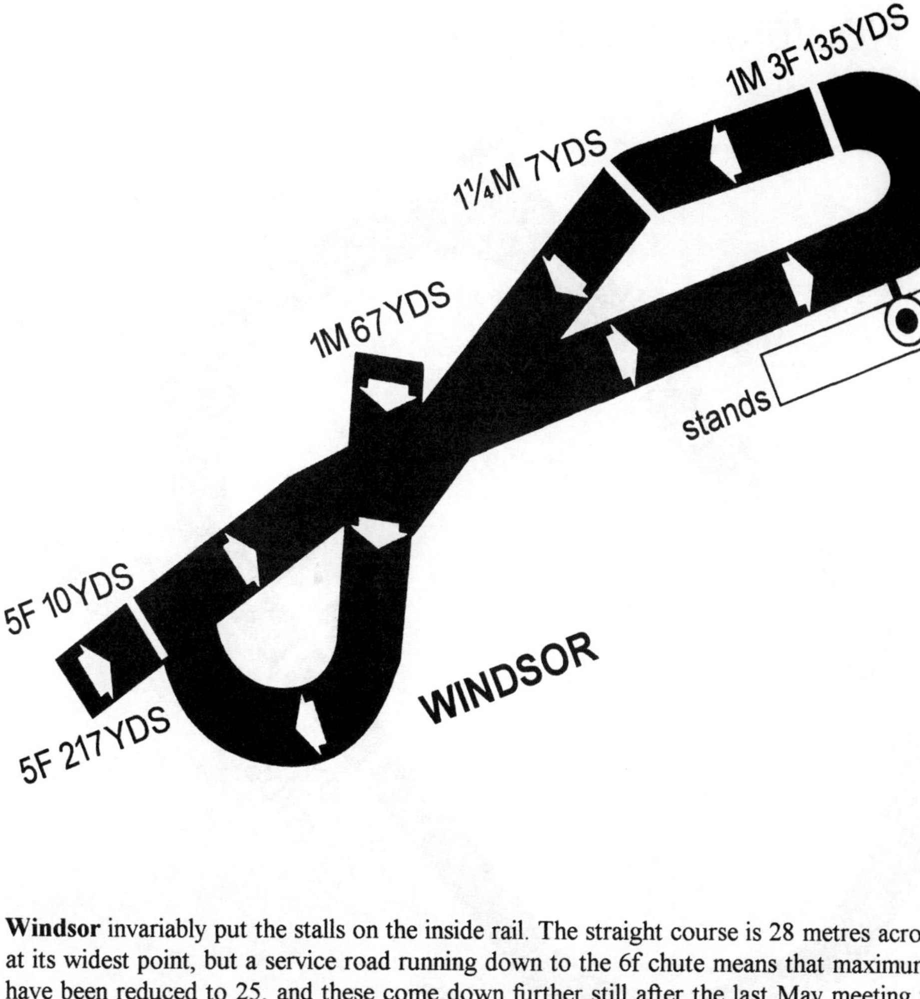

Windsor invariably put the stalls on the inside rail. The straight course is 28 metres across at its widest point, but a service road running down to the 6f chute means that maximums have been reduced to 25, and these come down further still after the last May meeting to 22. At this time, an extra rail, about 5-6 metres outside the normal line, is installed and kept there for about six meetings. Once that ground is worn, the rail is dropped to unveil a new strip of fresh ground. The straight course runs east. A towline is used, and adjustment can easily be made for any wind effect. The course has drained very freely since work took place prior to the '98 season, so no major work is needed now; the course is just regularly slitted, though Vertidraining may be done now that it has become part of Arena Group.

Maximum runners: **5f 10y** (25), **6f** (25), **1m 67y** (18), **1m 2f 7y** (22), **1m 3f 135y** (20)

WOLVERHAMPTON

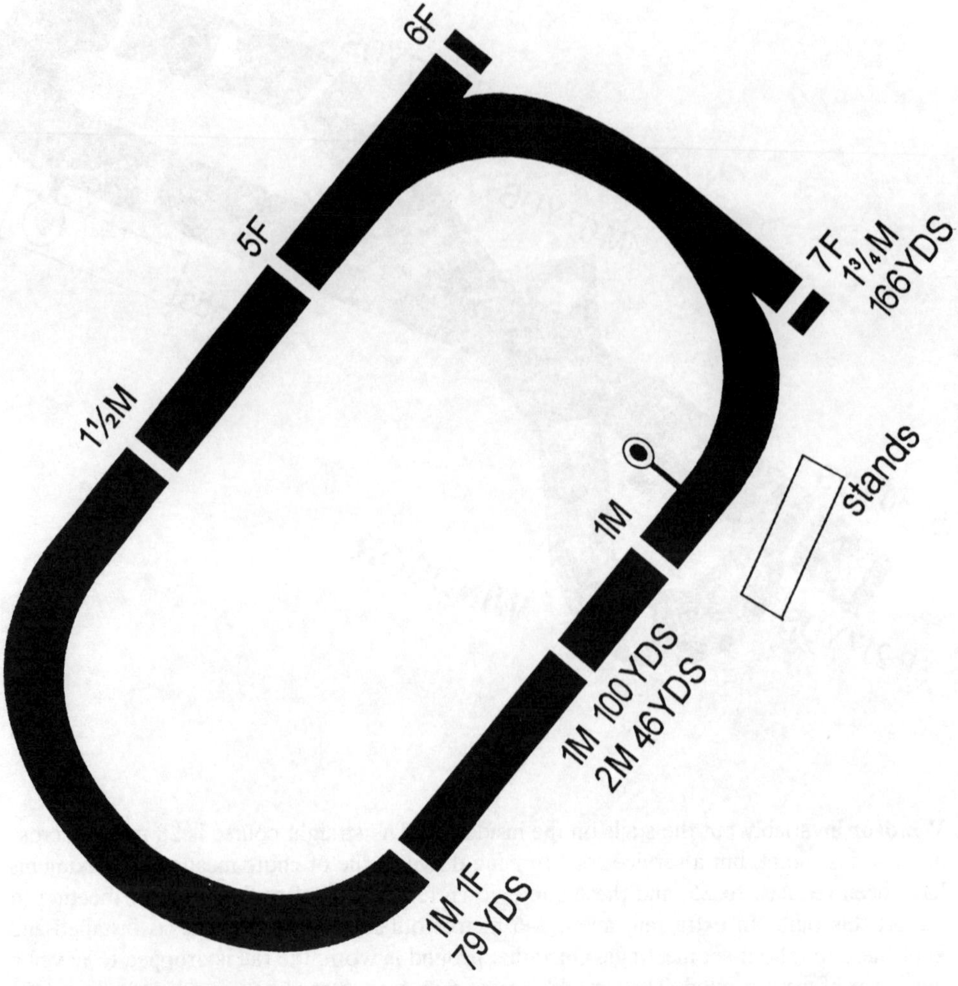

Wolverhampton all-weather seem to vary the position of the stalls frequently. Amateurs and apprentices do not race over seven furlongs.

Maximum runners: **5f** (13), **6f** (13), **7f** (12), **1m 100y** (13), **1m 1f 79y** (13), **1m 4f** (12), **1m 6f 166y** (12), **2m 46y** (13)

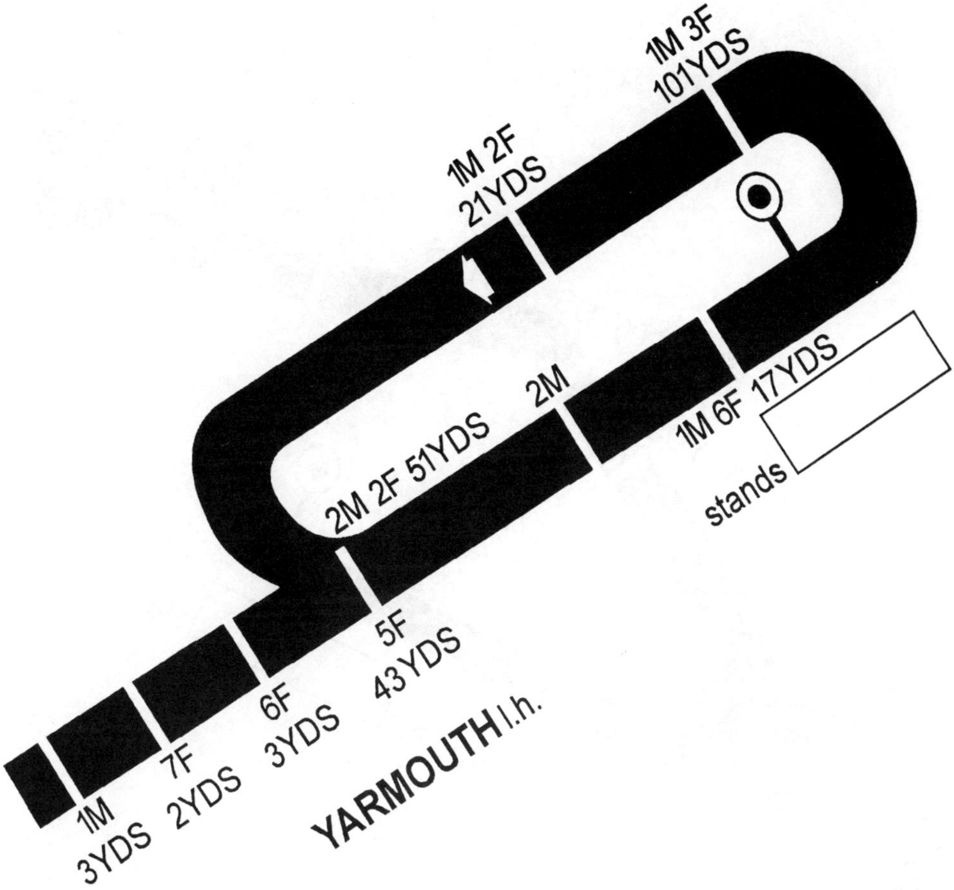

Yarmouth try to rotate the stalls' position on the straight course as much as possible, placing them either on the stands' rail (high) or the far rail (low). The ground often rides firm due to the course being based on sand, under between 4" and 8" inches of topsoil. Both rails in the straight are permanent. The straight course, which faces south, is about 22 metres wide. A Briggs boom irrigation system was brought in for the '99 season, replacing the old pop-up system, and this seems to have negated any draw bias.

Maximum runners: 5f 43y (20), 6f 3y (20), 7f 3y (20), 1m 3y (20), **1m 2f 21y** (17), **1m 3f 101y** (17), **1m 6f 17y** (20), **2m** (20), **2m 2f 51y** (20)

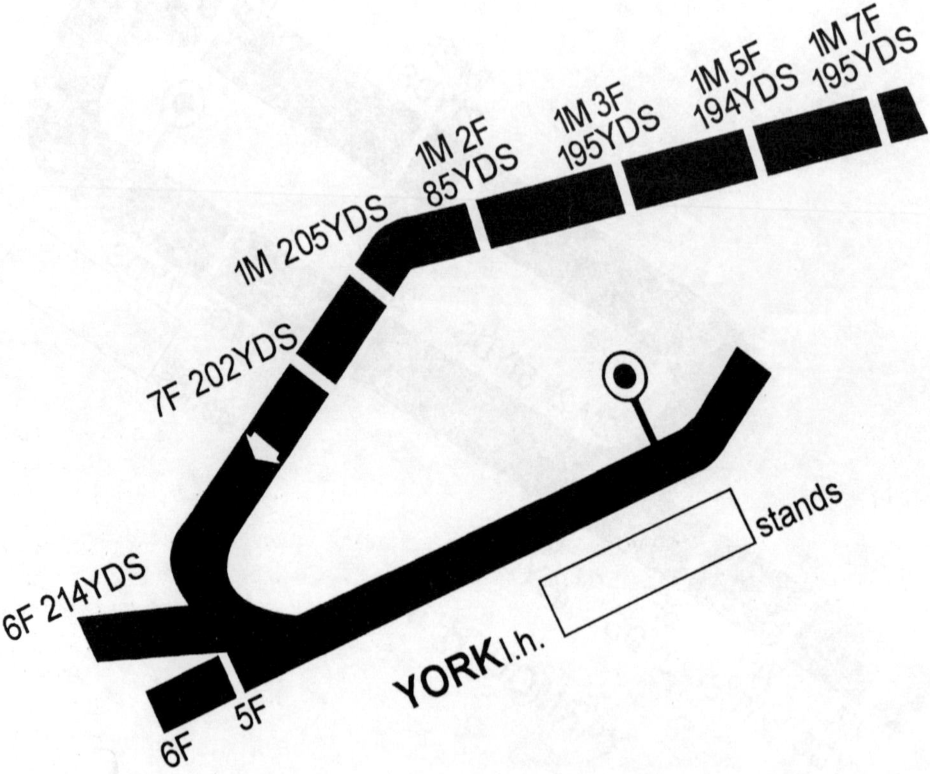

York usually put the stalls on the inside (low), although there have been cases of them going on the outside rail over 6f 214y. Both rails in the straight are permanent, but there is a false rail that can be used in the later stages of the season in order to preserve the ground. The course is about 34 metres wide for the first quarter-mile on the 6f 214y chute, 24-25 metres wide at the 6f start, narrowing down to 20 metres at finish. The course runs north, and there is a pop-up system used to water both sides of the straight. The prevailing wind is west, and watering is always done in the night when conditions are usually calmer.

Maximum runners: 5f (23), 6f (23), **6f 214y** (24), **7f 202y** (26), **1m 205y** (27),
1m 2f 85y (22), **1m 3f 195y** (22), **1m 5f 194y** (22), **1m 7f 195y** (22)

CHAPTER 3

A LOOK BACK AT 1999

This chapter looks at some of the major draw-affected races of the '99 season, and how the horses affected most by the draw went on to perform afterwards. Example races, as they appeared in Raceform Annual for 2000, are included for reference.

Sprint handicappers tend to go through much more clearly defined periods of either being in or out of form than other racehorses, possible because a majority of the races in which they compete are truly run, which leads to fewer hard-luck stories. And since most sprint handicaps are run on straight courses, the effect of the draw is often likely to provide a big clue as to into which category they fall.

A friend of mine used to swear by backing sprint handicappers with form figures along the lines of 000042, based on the theory that they had been out of form but were coming back, and that they were likely to have slipped down the handicap in the meantime. He enjoyed a fair amount of success using this method, which certainly has its merits, but such form figures are not guaranteed to tell the full story, since the 4 may have come in a field of five and the 2 in a match; or the 4 when he was first home up the unfavoured rail in a field of 20 and the 2 a short-head second, racing wide apart from the winner.

Herein lies another way of employing the effect of the draw, by effectively cancelling it. Clearly a race in which the result was affected by the draw cannot be treated in the same manner for analysis as a race which was not affected. The horses can not possibly have finished in the same position, or the same distance behind the winner, as on a level playing field.

Consequently, there is a need to establish what the result would have been had the draw not played a part on the outcome, and it is this analysis that pinpoints future potential punts. Try to imagine how the form figures would look had there been no draw bias.

Using the above set of form figures (000042) as an example, say the last nought was when the horse finished seventh overall but first home up the unfavoured stands' rail at

Beverley, beaten 3 lengths, it would be fair to assume he would have won from a high draw, so our adjusted form figures would become 000142. Say also that the 4 and 2 came when he finished first home on the unfavoured side at draw-affected courses, the form figures 000042 would become 000111. He would then become a horse to have a serious interest in on his next outing.

On the other side of the coin you have the horse flattered by having raced on the best ground. Form figures similar to 000001 are not uncommon in the world of sprint handicaps, but if that win came when he had the best of the draw and you assume that he would not have made the frame from a worse draw, then you can adjust your personal set of figures to 000000. When he goes off favourite for his next run under a penalty, your adjusted finishing positions will tell you that you have a favourite to oppose.

Both the above hypothetical sets of circumstances will affect the handicapping of a horse, since the handicapper can only rate races and the horses that ran in them on the bare result. He cannot allow for the effect of the draw, which is largely considered a subject open to conjecture, with the possible exception of Beverley, a course accepted as having a major bias.

According to *Raceform* handicapper David Dickinson, 8 lengths in a sprint handicap is worth somewhere in the region of 20lb. Courses such as Hamilton and Beverley often throw up races where the draw has that much of an effect, but while the race winner will be put up in the weights, the 'winner' on the unfavoured side will not, and he may even come down a couple of pounds:-

Hamilton, June 23, good, good to firm patches:-

2238 O'DONNELL FERGUSON OCEAN 11 H'CAP (0-60) (3-Y.O+) (Class F)
9-25 (9-27) **5f 4y** £3,761.25 (£1,140.00: £557.50: £266.25) Stalls: High GOING minus 0.42 sec per fur (F)

Form	Horse	Dist	Pos	SP	RR	SF
973^{9}	**Goretski (IRE)** ^{52} **(59)** (NTinkler) **6-9-13** JCarroll(17) (lw: cl up far side: led ½-wy: rdn & r.o)	—	**1**	5/2 ^{1}	66	49
1928^{10}	**Tinker's Surprise (IRE)** ^{12} **(40)** (JBalding) **5-8-8b** GBardwell(16) (chsd ldrs far side: hdwy 2f out: kpt on: nvr able to chal)	2	**2**	25/1	41	24
1722^{5}	**L A Touch** ^{19} **(41)** (MAPeill) **6-8-4**$^{(5)}$ DMernagh(13) (in tch far side: hdwy 2f out: kpt on wl fnl f)	1½	**3**	10/1	37	20
1750^{13}	**Southern Dominion** ^{19} **(54)** (MissJFCraze) **7-9-3b**$^{(5)}$ PGoode(8) (swvd rt s: racd far side & led: hung lft & racd centre: hdd ½-wy: kpt on)	nk	**4**	33/1	49	32
1284^{10}	**Skyers Flyer (IRE)** ^{37} **(42)** (RonaldThompson) **5-8-10** LNewton(1) (bhd stands' side tl r.o fnl 1½f: nrst fin)	nk	**5**	33/1	36	19
1854^{14}	**Superfrills** ^{14} **(48)** (MissLCSiddall) **6-9-2** LCharnock(18) (lw: racd far side: cl up: outpcd 2f out: no imp after)	1¼	**6**	16/1	38	21
1879^{3}	**William's Well** ^{13} **(53)** (MWEasterby) **5-9-0b**$^{(7)}$ SFinnamore(6) (chsd ldrs stands' side: no imp fnl 2f)	nk	**7**	10/1	42	25
2049^{2}	**Biff-Em (IRE)** ^{7} **(44)** (MissLAPerratt) **5-8-9**$^{(3)}$ RMullen(4) (chsd ldrs stands' side: no imp fnl 2f)	nk	**8**	6/1 ^{3}	32	15
936^{11}	**Sans Rivale** ^{54} **(41)** (DWChapman) **4-8-9** TWilliams(15) (in tch far side: outpcd ½-wy: no imp after)	½	**9**	14/1	27	10
1851^{13}	**Itch** ^{14} **(42)** (RBastiman) **4-8-10** NKennedy(11) (lw: racd far side: sn outpcd)	1¼	**10**	33/1	24	7
1979^{3}	**Danny Power (IRE)** ^{9} **(52)** (TDBarron) **3-9-0** CLowther(2) (led stands' side: rdn & no imp fr ½-wy)	¾	**11**	16/1	32	9
1988^{13}	**Just Dissident (IRE)** ^{9} **(42)** (RMWhitaker) **7-8-10** FLynch(7) (gd spd stands' side over 3f)	s.h	**12**	20/1	22	5
1854^{11}	**Gold Edge** ^{14} **(40)** (NTinkler) **5-8-8** KimTinkler(10) (s.i.s: racd far side: n.d)	1	**13**	16/1	17	—
1492^{5}	**Tempramental (IRE)** ^{28} **(54)** (DHaydnJones) **3-9-2b** AMackay(9) (s.i.s: a outpcd & bhd far side)	s.h	**14**	9/2 ^{2}	31	8
1879^{10}	**Distant King** ^{13} **(36)** (GPKelly) **6-8-4** GParkin(14) (racd far side: nvr wnt pce)	½	**15**	20/1	11	—
1755^{7}	**Hiltons Executive (IRE)** ^{18} **(45)** (EJAlston) **5-8-13** GDuffield(5) (racd stands' side: in tch 3f: sn n.d)	nk	**16**	16/1	19	2
1879^{8}	**Just Bob** ^{13} **(48)** (SEKettlewell) **10-9-2** DeanMcKeown(3) (lw: dwlt: racd stands' side: n.d)	1¼	**17**	14/1	18	1
1703^{11}	***Swan At Whalley*** ^{20} **(49)** (KARyan) **7-9-3** JFanning(12) (Withdrawn not under Starter's orders: ref to ent stalls)		**W**	14/1	—	—
				(SP 144.9%)	**17 Rn**	

58.9 secs (1.40) CSF £73.38 CT £390.68 TOTE £3.50: £1.80 £3.50 £3.10 £17.40 (£42.50) OWNER Mr P. D. Savill (MALTON) BRED Pierre Brichart

Although high numbers are more dominant at Hamilton when the going is testing, they are still favoured on faster ground, and the first three here, Goretski, Tinker's Surprise and L

A Touch all came from the top half-dozen stalls. In fact, five of the first six home raced on the far rail, the only exception being fifth-placed Skyers Flyer, who came home a length and a half to the good of the group up the stands' rail. He was beaten only 4 lengths total by the winner, and would probably have won from a high draw.

As a result of winning, Goretski was put up 6lb to 65. He went on to finish down the field on his next run. Meanwhile, Skyers Flyer was left on the same mark of 42 - and went on to win next time at 12/1 at Carlisle. This was just one of many examples of how handicapping on the bare result left the winner up the unfavoured side of a course on a winning mark.

American Cousin was a horse that served me particularly well during the '99 season, and one who was unlucky with the draw on more than one occasion. His **actual** form figures for the year were typical of a handicap sprinter, particularly his first six efforts:-

0000214215240

After taking a few runs to find his form, he had a good spell in early summer before gradually dropping off again, barring one decent second from a good draw at Hamilton.

Knocking out the effect of the draw from his runs, his figures would have been something along the lines of:-

0000114115440

So, instead of winning just twice, without being hampered by the draw he may well have won four. The two races that I had him winning that he actually didn't were both at Beverley, when he raced towards the unfavoured centre of the course:-

Beverley, June 22, good to firm:-

2194 CHESHIRE CHEESE MAIDEN APPRENTICE H'CAP (0-70) (3-Y.O+) (Class F)
4-45 (4-47) **5f** £2,189.50 (£622.00: £308.50) Stalls: High GOING minus 0.23 sec per fur (GF)

				SP	RR	SF
1704[12]	**Three Leaders (IRE)** [19] **(55)** (DNicholls) **3-8-9** DGlennon(15) (lw: a.p: nt clr run over 1f out: r.o ins fnl f to ld post)	—	**1**	100/30[1]	56	31
1649[14]	**American Cousin** [21] **(44)** (DNicholls) **4-8-4** CarolynBales(5) (lw: a.p: styd on to ld cl home: ct post)	s.h	**2**	16/1	45	26
1854[8]	**Tigi** [13] **(36)** (JJQuinn) **4-7-10b** RFowley(19) (led tl ct cl home)	hd	**3**	14/1	37	18
1950[13]	**Apples And Pears (IRE)** [10] **(53)** (MHTompkins) **3-8-7** PShea(17) (sn outpcd: hdwy over 1f out: styd on: nrst fin)	1½	**4**	9/2[2]	49	24
1413[9]	**Needwood Minstrel** [31] **(51)** (BCMorgan) **3-8-5** DHayden(18) (cl up tl wknd ins fnl f)	nk	**5**	8/1[3]	46	21
1777[7]	**Banningham Belle** [17] **(36)** (DShaw) **4-7-5b**[1](5) GSparkes(10) (rr div: hdwy over 1f out: styd on wl)	hd	**6**	12/1	30	11
1878[10]	**Against The Bill (IRE)** [12] **(45)** (TDEasterby) **3-7-13b** PHanagan(13) (b.off.hind: cl up: effrt 2f out: hung rt & nt qckn fnl f)	¾	**7**	9/1	37	12
1102[6]	**Palvic Lady** [45] **(62)** (CSmith) **3-9-2** RCody-Boutcher(11) (chsd ldrs: nt qckn appr fnl f)	2½	**8**	14/1	46	21
	Tong Road [243] **(45)** (BRCambidge) **3-7-8**(5) LisaWatson(9) (hld up: hdwy over 1f out: nvr rchd ldrs)	s.h	**9**	33/1	29	4
2004[6]	**Kissimmee Bay (IRE)** [7] **(43)** (NTinkler) **3-7-6**(5) JoannaBadger(2) (lw: bhd: hdwy 2f out: nvr nrr)	hd	**10**	20/1	27	2
1979[6]	**Rm Again** [8] **(42)** (RGuest) **3-7-10** MMathers(8) (in rr: wl bhd tl sme late hdwy)	s.h	**11**	9/1	25	—
1547[8]	**Now Is The Hour** [25] **(42)** (PSFelgate) **3-7-10** NicolaWright(6) (bhd tl sme late hdwy)	¾	**12**	16/1	23	—
1879[9]	**Scintilating Sound** [12] **(36)** (SRBowring) **4-7-5**(5) DAllan(3) (lw: b: outpcd fr ½-wy)	1	**13**	12/1	14	—
1975[15]	**Abstract (IRE)** [8] **(43)** (JSWainwright) **3-7-11b**[ow1] PaulCleary(1) (racd wd: outpcd fr ½-wy)	½	**14**	25/1	19	—
1724[12]	**Chillian** [18] **(44)** (MBrittain) **3-7-12** MSemple(12) (in tch over 3f: sn wknd)	nk	**15**	33/1	19	—
154[11]	**February** [150] **(41)** (JPSmith) **6-7-10t**(5)[ow5] SamanthaMcGinn(16) (sn outpcd & bhd)	2	**16**	100/1	10	—
1912[8]	**Red Shift (IRE)** [11] **(65)** (CREgerton) **4-9-11** LeanneMasterton(7) (lw: sn outpcd & bhd)	¾	**17**	10/1	31	12
	Quakeress (IRE) [668] **(68)** (JohnBerry) **4-9-9**(5) DWilliamson(14) (chsd ldrs over 3f: sn wknd)	1	**18**	20/1	31	12
1725[9]	**Silvano's Express** [18] **(42)** (MissJFCraze) **3-7-10** IGrantham(4) (sn bhd)	4	**19**	40/1	—	—

(SP 144.6%) **19 Rn**

64.5 secs (2.70) CSF £60.11 CT £686.85 TOTE £4.20: £1.90 £4.70 £3.80 £1.20 (£52.20) OWNER R J H Ltd (THIRSK) BRED Mrs M. Johnston

This was an amazing effort. To be beaten just a short-head from stall 5 of 19 on fast ground at Beverley (a handicap of around 6-8 lengths in my book compared to the 19 stall) under an apprentice who, no offence intended, looked no better than adequate, was extraordinary.

Four days later, American Cousin turned out again, this time under the stable's leading apprentice J.D.Smith, and off the same mark of 44. I headlined his chances in *Raceform On Saturday*, and made him a 15-point win bet (on a scale of 1-20). He was never in danger of defeat, winning easily at 3/1.

Before contemplating a bet on a horse who has turned in an eyecatching effort from a moderate draw, though, it is necessary to make sure he meets with the following set of criteria:-

1) **The ground is suitable** - the selection must have won or at least shown very good form on the prevailing ground.
2) **The trip is suitable** - the selection is not stepping up to seven furlongs for the first time having caught the eye over a sprint trip, unless he seems likely to be suited by it.
3) **The handicapper has not raised the rating a ridiculous amount** - the selection is not asked to race off a much higher mark than when it was noted. Anything more than a 3-4lb rise is pushing the limits.
4) **The race is similar in class to the time before** - the selection has not raised from, for example, a Class F handicap, to a Class C handicap.
5) **The selection has not been off the course for any length of time** - any longer than a six-week absence may suggest some sort of problem.
6) **Most importantly, the selection has a reasonable draw** - if the draw is again against him, he may again run above expectations, but is likely to be facing another impossible task.

Before placing a bet, it is also worth looking for other less obvious performance-affecting factors, such as the form of the trainer, which is particularly important, previous course form, the jockey (look for those who have shown in the past that they know where the best ground is - see pages 102-105, and those you have noted down as not possessing a great draw knowledge), and any other factors you may consider important in making a selection.

American Cousin met with all the requirements prior to winning at Doncaster:-

1) **The ground was suitable** - good to firm, the same as at Beverley.
2) **The trip was suitable** - he had been placed behind Lend A Hand over 6f at two.
3) **The handicapper had not raised the rating a ridiculous amount** - he ran off the same mark of 44.
4) **The race was similar in class to the time before** - he was up from Class F to Class E, so hardly a major jump. Class F to Class D would have been a potential off-putter.
5) **The selection had not been off the course for any length of time** - it had only been four days, and I firmly subscribe to the theory that sprinters are best when coming out again quickly.

6) **Most importantly, the selection had a reasonable draw** - this is not a significant factor at Doncaster as a rule, but if there was to be a bias, high numbers would have been marginally preferred, and he was drawn 10 of 15.

American Cousin (in front) twice ran well from desperate draws at Beverley

A little over three weeks later, it was a case of déjà vu, as American Cousin ran another cracking race from a moderate draw at Beverley.

Beverley, July 13, good to firm:-

2771 MAIN RING H'CAP (0-60) (3-Y.O+) (Class F)
4-45 (4-48) **5f** £3,116.00 (£938.00: £454.00: £212.00) Stalls: High GOING minus 0.40 sec per fur (F)

	Runner	Dist	Pos	SP	RR	SF
2491[4]	**Bollin Ann** 11 **(51)** (TDEasterby) **4-9-6** JFortune(18) (trckd ldrs: led 1f out: shkn up & r.o wl)	—	**1**	11/2[2]	55	38
2558[4]	**American Cousin** 8 **(51)** (DNicholls) **4-9-6** AlexGreaves(10) (lw: a chsng ldrs: kpt on fnl f)	2	**2**	4/1[1]	49	32
2515[9]	**High Carry** 10 **(54)** (NTinkler) **4-9-9** KimTinkler(15) (a chsng ldrs: n.m.r over 1f out: kpt on u.p)	nk	**3**	20/1	51	34
2692[3]	**Dekelsmary** 4 **(42)** (JBalding) **4-8-11t** JEdmunds(19) (lw: w ldr: led wl over 1f out: hdd 1f out: no ex)	hd	**4**	9/1	38	21
2685[2]	**Muja's Magic (IRE)** 4 **(43)** (KTIvory) **4-8-12v** KFallon(4) (racd wd: hdwy ½-wy: kpt on u.p fnl f: nrst fin)	1	**5**	6/1[3]	36	19
2520[13]	**Featherstone Lane** 10 **(43)** (MissLCSiddall) **8-8-12** DeanMcKeown(14) (sn pushed along: styd on fnl f: nrst fin)	nk	**6**	25/1	35	18
1654[4]	**Champagne N Dreams** 42 **(53)** (WWHaigh) **7-9-1**(7) JennyBenson(16) (hld up & bhd: hdwy on bit over 1f out: fin wl)	¾	**7**	20/1	43	26
2194[9]	**Tong Road** 21 **(43)** (BRCambidge) **3-8-7** JLowe(3) (s.i.s: swtchd rt s: hdwy 2f out: nvr nrr)	s.h	**8**	33/1	33	11
2111[5]	**Jackerin (IRE)** 25 **(58)** (BSRothwell) **4-9-10b**(3) RWinston(13) (lw: plld hrd: chsd ldrs 4f: wknd)	s.h	**9**	16/1	47	30

Form	Horse / details	Dist	Pos	SP	RR	SF
2348^{9}	**Lucky Uno** 16 **(48)** (CSmith) **3-8-9**(3) RFitzpatrick(12) (swtg: dwlt: nvr rchd ldrs)	hd	**10**	33/1	37	15
2583^{4}	**Plum First** 7 **(47)** (JSWainwright) **9-9-2** WSupple(6) (sn drvn along: nvr nr to chal)	1¼	**11**	14/1	32	15
1755^{9}	**Bow Peep (IRE)** 38 **(53)** (MWEasterby) **4-9-8** GParkin(8) (racd wd: sn pushed along: nvr trbld ldrs)	nk	**12**	16/1	37	20
2522^{7}	**Just Dissident (IRE)** 10 **(38)** (RMWhitaker) **7-8-7v** FLynch(17) (lw: chsd ldrs over 3f: sn wknd)	2	**13**	20/1	16	—
2554^{3}	**Superbit** 8 **(56)** (BAMcMahon) **7-9-11** KDarley(9) (lw: chsd ldrs tl wknd appr fnl f)	s.h	**14**	14/1	34	17
2558^{2}	**Skyers Flyer (IRE)** 8 **(48)** (RonaldThompson) **5-9-3** LNewton(5) (effrt ½-wy: nvr trbld ldrs)	½	**15**	12/1	24	7
2225^{13}	**At My Command (IRE)** 20 **(50)** (MWEasterby) **3-9-0** TLucas(1) (s.i.s: a bhd)	3½	**16**	33/1	15	—
2491^{6}	**Superfrills** 11 **(49)** (MissLCSiddall) **6-9-4** LCharnock(7) (racd wd: in tch tl outpcd fr ½-wy)	s.h	**17**	20/1	14	—
2522^{12}	**Tigi** 10 **(38)** (JJQuinn) **4-8-0b**(7) CCogan(11) (lw: in tch over 3f)	s.h	**18**	25/1	3	—
2522^{10}	**Bashful Brave** 10 **(38)** (JLEyre) **8-8-7v** RLappin(20) (led over 3f: wknd qckly)	nk	**19**	20/1	2	—
2491^{3}	**Kalar** 11 **(38)** (DWChapman) **10-8-7b** ACulhane(2) (lw: cl up 3f: wknd qckly)	2	**20**	14/1	—	—

(SP 139.5%) **20 Rn**

63.9 secs (2.10) CSF £24.19 CT £410.37 TOTE £7.20: £2.10 £2.10 £4.20 £2.10 (£17.60) Trifecta £689.80 OWNER Lady Westbrook (MALTON) BRED Sir Neil and Lady Westbrook

He had already won once having been out just four days previously, so had shown that he had the constitution to handle two quick races. History repeated itself and he hacked up at 7/2 having touched 9/2.

Newcastle, March 30, good to soft, good patches:-

513 {S} CORAL SPRINT H'CAP (0-85) (3-Y.O+) (Class D)
3-20 (3-21) **5f** £7,002.50 (£2,120.00: £1,035.00: £492.50) Stalls: Low GOING: 0.33 sec per fur (G)

Form	Horse / details	Dist	Pos	SP	RR	SF
366^{3}	**Tom Tun** 32 **(57)** (MissJFCraze) **4-8-5** TWilliams(4) (disp ld: led over 1f out: kpt on wl)	—	**1**	7/2 1	61	47
244^{3}	**Unshaken** 52 **(66)** (EJAlston) **5-9-0** KFallon(12) (lw: hdwy 2f out: n.m.r: styd on wl towards fin)	½	**2**	8/1 3	68	54
423^{2}	**Maiteamia** 20 **(60)** (SRBowring) **6-8-8b** JQuinn(1) (lw: disp ld tl hdd over 1f out: kpt on same pce)	nk	**3**	15/2 2	61	47
423^{6}	**Silk Cottage** 20 **(48)** (RBastiman) **7-7-10b** PFessey(8) (hdwy 2f out: styd on wl: nrst fin)	hd	**4**	20/1	49	35
277^{5}	**Young Bigwig (IRE)** 46 **(66)** (DWChapman) **5-9-0** ACulhane(3) (chsd ldrs: effrt over 1f out: nt qckn)	1½	**5**	8/1 3	62	48
	Gay Breeze 185 **(78)** (PSFelgate) **6-9-5**(7) SRighton(10) (cl up: effrt 2f out: no ex fnl f)	¾	**6**	12/1	72	58
	Goretski (IRE) 144 **(70)** (NTinkler) **6-9-4** JCarroll(6) (chsd ldrs: effrt 2f out: wknd ins fnl f)	1¼	**7**	16/1	60	46
	Mungo Park 162 **(77)** (MDods) **5-9-11** JWeaver(15) (lw: hld up & bhd: nvr able to chal)	s.h	**8**	10/1	67	53
	Cartmel Park 194 **(82)** (JBerry) **3-9-4** GCarter(11) (bhd tl sme hdwy fnl 2f)	hd	**9**	20/1	71	45
428^{12}	**Mukarrab (USA)** 17 **(49)** (DWChapman) **5-7-11** LCharnock(7) (lw: reard s: hdwy ½-wy: no imp)	1½	**10**	8/1 3	34	20
	Souperficial 151 **(52)** (DonEnricoIncisa) **8-8-0** KimTinkler(16) (a bhd)	2½	**11**	33/1	29	15
480^{12}	**Grey Kingdom** 4 **(80)** (MBrittain) **8-9-9**(5) DMernagh(5) (cl up 3f: wknd)	nk	**12**	33/1	56	42
	Sealed By Fate (IRE) 195 **(50)** (JSWainwright) **4-7-5v**(7) JMcAuley(13) (a bhd)	1	**13**	50/1	23	9
462^{3}	**Nifty Norman** 8 **(59)** (DNicholls) **5-8-7** FNorton(9) (gd spd 3f: btn whn hmpd over 1f out)	3	**14**	9/1	22	8
	Northern Svengali (IRE) 94 **(82)** (TDBarron) **3-9-4** OPears(14) (sn bhd)	nk	**15**	20/1	44	18
	Rose's Treasure (IRE) 199 **(71)** (BSRothwell) **3-8-7v** MFenton(2) (chsd ldrs: hmpd 2f out: sn btn)	1	**16**	33/1	30	4

(SP 125.1%) **16 Rn**

63.34 secs (4.54) CSF £25.64 CT £196.11 TOTE £4.00: £1.10 £2.10 £2.00 £8.50 (£21.00) Trifecta £158.50 OWNER Mrs O. Tunstall (YORK) BRED T. Tunstall

This unexceptional Newcastle event turned out to be one of the key races of the season, producing several subsequent winners, including Ayr Silver Cup winner Grey Kingdom, Maiteamia, Goretski and Cartmel Park. It was a day when the far-rail runners (low) were always well on top, and those drawn high were at a major disadvantage, as was often the way at Newcastle throughout the season.

At the time, Unshaken was noted as one to follow, *Raceform* race-reader Alan Amies' note-book comment leaving little doubt that this was a highly meritorious effort: "Unshaken ran a smashing race from his draw and looks in tremendous form." Unshaken went on to win from the best of the draw at Hamilton, and finished the season off almost a stone higher mark than that he raced from here.

Hamilton, April 10, heavy:-

637 BETTER BET WITH WILLIAM HILL H'CAP (0-85) (3-Y.O+) (Class D)
2-10 (2-11) **6f 5y** £5,914.00 (£1,792.00: £876.00: £418.00) Stalls: Low GOING: 1.28 sec per fur (HY)

Form	Horse / details	Dist	Pos	SP	RR	SF
513^{2}	**Unshaken** 11 **(68)** (EJAlston) **5-8-12** SSanders(17) (lw: trckd ldrs far side: led over 1f out: drvn out)	—	**1**	3/1 1	73	48
	Naissant 179 **(60)** (JSGoldie) **6-8-4** ACulhane(14) (chsd ldrs far side: outpcd 2f out: kpt on wl fnl f)	¾	**2**	14/1	63	38

524[5]	**San Michel (IRE)** [10] **(56)** (JLEyre) **7-8-0b** AMackay(16) (led far side after 2f tl over 1f out: no ex)	1½	**3**	10/1	55	30
513[15]	**Northern Svengali (IRE)** [11] **(80)** (TDBarron) **3-8-7**(5) KimberleyHart(15) (led far side 2f: a cl up: rdn 2f out: nt qckn fnl f)	nk	**4**	33/1	78	41
480[3]	**Jeffrey Anotherred** [15] **(77)** (MDods) **5-9-7** FLynch(13) (lw: prom far side: outpcd 2f out: kpt on fnl f)	2	**5**	9/2 [2]	70	45
486[8]	**Demolition Jo** [14] **(84)** (PDEvans) **4-9-9v**(5) NCallan(10) (b.off hind: chsd ldrs far side: nt qckn appr fnl f)	2½	**6**	14/1	70	45
157[7]	**Maydoro** [77] **(52)** (WMBrisbourne) **6-7-3**(7) PMQuinn(12) (sn outpcd far side: n.d)	7	**7**	100/1	20	—
509[8]	**Taffs Well** [12] **(59)** (BEllison) **6-8-3** NKennedy(11) (racd far side: nvr wnt pce)	½	**8**	14/1	25	—
577[3]	**Easter Ogil (IRE)** [5] **(81)** (IABalding) **4-9-11v** KFallon(4) (racd stands' side: edgd rt fr ½-wy: n.d)	11	**9**	5/1 [3]	18	—
	Mister Westsound [148] **(54)** (MissLAPerratt) **7-7-12b** RFfrench(3) (bit bkwd: chsd ldrs stands' side after 2f tl edgd rt & wknd fnl 2f)	1½	**10**	33/1	—	—
	Peter's Imp (IRE) [189] **(68)** (JBerry) **4-8-12** PFessey(6) (racd stands' side: n.d)	½	**11**	33/1	—	—
*428**	**Pips Song (IRE)** [28] **(70)** (DrJDScargill) **4-9-0** JQuinn(8) (racd stands' side: n.d)	3	**12**	13/2	—	—
483[6]	**Waterford Spirit (IRE)** [14] **(80)** (TDBarron) **3-8-12** OPears(5) (disp ld stands' side after 1f tl wl outpcd ½-wy)	1	**13**	33/1	1	—
	Mamma's Boy [159] **(67)** (JBerry) **4-8-4**(7) PBradley(9) (lw: disp ld stands' no ch w far side fr ½-wy)	1¾	**14**	16/1	—	—
585[17]	**Jacmar (IRE)** [5] **(63)** (MissLAPerratt) **4-8-7** CLowther(7) (bit bkwd: cl up stands' side tl wknd fnl 2½f)	4	**15**	33/1	—	—
491[6]	**Oriel Girl** [14] **(56)** (MJRyan) **4-8-0** GBardwell(1) (racd stands' side: lost tch fr ½-wy)	3	**16**	20/1	—	—
532[12]	**Suite Factors** [10] **(66)** (KRBurke) **5-8-10** DeanMcKeown(2) (disp ld stands' side tl wknd fr ½-wy)	1½	**17**	25/1	—	—
				(SP 132.5%)	**17 Rn**	

1m 19.7 (11.00) CSF £43.69 CT £296.01 TOTE £2.70: £1.10 £5.20 £3.50 £3.70 (£48.20) OWNER G G Sanderson & M Twentyman & A J Picton (PRESTON) BRED Stetchworth Park Stud Ltd

The result was never in doubt. Unshaken was always going best and only needed pushing out to hold on. The first runner home of the group to race up the stands' side, Easter Ogil, was beaten a total of about 25 lengths.

This was not a fluke by Hamilton standards, and any runner that races stands' side on soft ground here in the future will have approximately that much to find with the far-side group.

Unshaken (centre) was unluckily drawn at Newcastle, but ideally berthed at Hamilton

Hamilton, September 27, soft:-

4589 TOTE HAMILTON PARK 2-Y-O FINAL NURSERY (LORD HAMILTON OF DALZIEL TROPHY) H'CAP (2-Y.O) (Class C) 3-20 (3-23) **6f 5y** £10,698.75 (£3,240.00: £1,582.50: £753.75) Stalls: Low GOING: 0.31 sec per fur (G)

				SP	RR	SF
4401^{3}	**Golden Miracle (FR)** 9 **(77)** (MJohnston) **2-8-13** DHolland(16) (lw: trckd ldrs: led 1f out: hrd rdn & r.o)	—	**1**	4/1^{1}	77	24
2065^{4}	**Glenwhargen (IRE)** 103 **(60)** (MJohnston) **2-7-10** GBardwell(15) (cl up: led ½-wy tl hdd 1f out: kpt on nr fin)	½	**2**	20/1	59	6
4041^{9}	**Papagena (USA)** 27 **(64)** (CWThornton) **2-7-9**(5)ow4 DMernagh(14) (lw: a chsng ldrs: kpt on same pce fnl f)	3½	**3**	14/1	53	—
4401^{2}	**Dispol Jazz** 9 **(64)** (SEKettlewell) **2-8-0** LCharnock(12) (lw: chsd ldrs: swtchd rt 2f out: nt qckn fnl f)	¾	**4**	13/2^{3}	51	—
3899^{8}	**Aljazir** 33 **(63)** (EJAlston) **2-7-13**ow2 WSupple(11) (hdwy ½-wy: styd on: nvr able to chal)	s.h	**5**	14/1	50	—
4375^{*}	**Top of The Class (IRE)** 10 **(72)** (MartynWane) **2-8-8** NKennedy(8) (s.i.s: hdwy 2f out: styd on: nvr able to chal)	½	**6**	6/1^{2}	58	5
4401^{6}	**Horta (IRE)** 9 **(65)** (GCBravery) **2-8-1** RMullen(9) (lw: bhd: hdwy u.str.p over 1f out: no imp)	¾	**7**	10/1	49	—
4375^{4}	**College Maid (IRE)** 10 **(66)** (JSGoldie) **2-8-2** PFessey(1) (a.p: effrt & ch 2f out: sn btn)	1¼	**8**	16/1	47	—
4249^{13}	**Maron** 17 **(68)** (JBerry) **2-7-13**(5) PBradley(5) (hdwy whn n.m.r over 2f out: nvr trbld ldrs)	1¼	**9**	20/1	45	—
2944^{13}	**Sergeant Slipper** 70 **(61)** (CSmith) **2-7-6v**(5)ow1 JMcAuley(6) (dwlt: hdwy ½-wy: sn rdn & no imp)	3	**10**	66/1	30	—
3673^{10}	**Gain Time** 42 **(73)** (TDBarron) **2-8-9** CLowther(4) (bhd: rdn ½-wy: n.d)	hd	**11**	25/1	42	—
4375^{3}	**Sabre Lady** 10 **(85)** (MissLAPerratt) **2-9-7** KDarley(3) (lw: led after 1f tl hdd ½-wy: sn wknd)	nk	**12**	11/1	53	—
3467^{4}	**Howard's Lad (IRE)** 50 **(85)** (ISemple) **2-9-7** RWinston(7) (cl up tl rdn & wknd fnl 2f)	2½	**13**	16/1	47	—
2555^{10}	**Going Home (IRE)** 84 **(61)** (JLEyre) **2-7-11b1** DaleGibson(10) (in tch tl wknd fnl 2½f)	1¾	**14**	25/1	18	—
4543^{4}	**Shatin Beauty** 3 **(70)** (MissLAPerratt) **2-8-6** JFEgan(2) (lw: chsd ldrs over 3f: wknd)	5	**15**	14/1	14	—
4444^{5}	**Uncle Exact** 6 **(81)** (KARyan) **2-9-3** FLynch(13) (hdwy & in tch 2f out: sn btn & eased)	1¾	**16**	20/1	20	—
				(SP 120.3%)	**16 Rn**	

1m 15.7 (7.00) CSF £83.97 CT £669.28 TOTE £3.90: £1.10 £3.90 £5.70 £1.70 (£27.50) Trifecta £185.80 OWNER Maktoum Al Maktoum (MIDDLEHAM) BRED Gainsborough Stud Management Ltd

Later in the year, again on soft ground, none of the 16 runners stayed on the stands' rail, even though the stalls were placed on that side, but even so, the first three home came from the top three stalls.

Kempton, April 5, good:-

577 TRAVELLING THE TURF "RACECOURSE OF THE YEAR" H'CAP (0-85) (4-Y.O+) (Class D) 4-10 (4-18) **6f** £4,572.00 (£1,386.00: £678.00: £324.00) Stalls: High GOING minus 0.17 sec per fur (GF)

				SP	RR	SF
	Passion For Life 281 **(79)** (JAkehurst) **6-9-8** OPeslier(23) (mde all: clr over 1f out: pushed out)	—	**1**	13/2^{1}	85	72
109^{7}	**Rififi** 79 **(76)** (RIngram) **6-9-5** MRoberts(19) (b: hdwy on ins 2f out: chsd wnr fnl f: r.o wl)	nk	**2**	14/1	81	68
480^{8}	**Easter Ogil (IRE)** 10 **(81)** (IABalding) **4-9-10v** KFallon(21) (hdwy over 2f out: hrd rdn over 1f out: r.o fnl f)	¾	**3**	7/1^{2}	84	71
	Madmun (IRE) 202 **(75)** (MPTregoning) **5-9-4** RHills(10) (bhd 4f: hdwy over 1f out: r.o ins fnl f)	3	**4**	33/1	70	57
	Purple Fling 181 **(59)** (AJMcNae) **8-7-13**(3)ow2 RMullen(14) (hld up: rdn over 2f out: unable qckn)	½	**5**	33/1	53	40
480^{4}	**Vasari (IRE)** 10 **(73)** (WJMusson) **5-9-2** RPrice(5) (swtg: hld up: rdn over 2f out: one pce)	1	**6**	14/1	64	51
	Compradore 167 **(69)** (MBlanshard) **4-8-12** DaleGibson(15) (chsd ldrs: rdn over 2f out: one pce)	nk	**7**	20/1	59	46
	Blundell Lane (IRE) 210 **(72)** (APJarvis) **4-9-1** DSweeney(4) (a.p: rdn over 2f out: one pce)	hd	**8**	33/1	62	49
480^{15}	**Twice as Sharp** 10 **(85)** (PWHarris) **7-10-0** LDettori(20) (lw: a.p: chsd wnr over 2f out to 1f out: sn wknd)	¾	**9**	15/2^{3}	73	60
	Family Man 170 **(81)** (JRFanshawe) **6-9-10** RCochrane(9) (nvr nrr)	1¾	**10**	14/1	65	52
	Alpen Wolf (IRE) 170 **(72)** (WRMuir) **4-9-1** MartinDwyer(22) (prom over 4f)	nk	**11**	20/1	55	42
	Ivory Dawn 196 **(71)** (KTIvory) **5-8-11**(3) NPollard(18) (b: a mid div)	hd	**12**	33/1	53	40
	Deep Space (IRE) 191 **(84)** (EALDunlop) **4-9-13** PatEddery(16) (a mid div)	1½	**13**	7/1^{2}	62	49
	Golden Pound (USA) 151 **(62)** (MrsLStubbs) **7-8-5** SWhitworth(11) (nvr nrr)	nk	**14**	33/1	40	27
466^{14}	**King of Peru** 11 **(71)** (NPLittmoden) **6-9-0** TGMcLaughlin(2) (a mid div)	1¾	**15**	33/1	44	31
	Delta Soleil (USA) 205 **(76)** (VSoane) **7-9-0**(5) NCallan(17) (prom over 4f)	1½	**16**	20/1	45	32
	Contrary Mary 151 **(72)** (JAkehurst) **4-9-1** MHills(8) (bhd fnl 2f)	hd	**17**	33/1	41	28
	Bedevilled 315 **(75)** (MJHeaton-Ellis) **4-9-4** GBardwell(3) (bhd fnl 2f)	½	**18**	33/1	42	29
480^{9}	**Double Oscar (IRE)** 10 **(80)** (DNicholls) **6-9-9** AlexGreaves(12) (b: mid div over 4f)	1	**19**	12/1	45	32
	Buzzing (IRE) 299 **(62)** (RHannon) **4-8-5** DaneO'Neill(7) (dwlt: hdwy over 4f out: wknd over 2f out)	¾	**20**	33/1	25	12
428^{9}	**Juwwi** 23 **(68)** (JMBradley) **5-8-11** JFortune(13) (mid div over 4f)	1¼	**21**	14/1	27	14
	Carlton (IRE) 41 **(64)** (GLewis) **5-8-4b**(3) PDoe(1) (lw: a bhd)	hd	**22**	20/1	23	10
	Taoiste 254 **(80)** (MSSaunders) **6-9-9** RHughes(6) (b: prom over 3f)	5	**23**	25/1	26	13
				(SP 133.8%)	**23 Rn**	

1m 12.59 (1.59) CSF £73.99 CT £418.82 TOTE £7.90: £2.30 £3.50 £2.10 £8.70 (£41.10) OWNER Canisbay Bloodstock Ltd (EPSOM) BRED G. R. Smith (Thriplow) Ltd

This race marked the return of Kempton as a draw-affected course, especially given that the bias here has always been greater on softer ground in the past as opposed to this faster surface.

Passion For Life, drawn 23 of 23, was off a fair rating of 79 given his old form in Group races, and he was well backed to win from his plum draw. However, as a result of winning, he struggled in his subsequent outings. His form figures were typical of a sprint handicapper:-

fin position		**ran**	**off rating**	**draw**
1	of	23	79	v.good
3	of	17	85	v.good
11	of	17	85	poor
9	of	13	84	fair
10	of	13	82	fair
2	of	5	80	fair
7	of	14	79	fair
6	of	15	79	fair
1	of	19	78	fair *

** Passion For Life's draw at Salisbury on his last outing, 9 of 19, should not have been a factor, but Gary Hind took him to race alone up the far side, and this proved the decisive manoeuvre.*

As a result of winning from the best draw at Kempton, Passion For Life's rating was put up 6lb before his next outing at Sandown, which basically handicapped him out of it. Although again drawn very well there (18 of 17, one non-runner on soft ground), his penalty stopped him winning.

However, he did seemingly run well to finish third, which meant the handicapper was unable to drop him in the weights. This effectively stopped him featuring on any of his next three starts. After a few runs down the field, though, his ratings slipped back into the high 70s, and under an astute ride from Gary Hind he went in again at Salisbury.

Passion For Life remains in training this year, and starts the campaign on a mark of 83. Clearly suited by racing on the outside of a field, he will again be one to keep an eye on when dropping back into the high 70s.

Kempton, September 20, heavy:-

4431 ROADWAYS AND CAR PARKS H'CAP (0-75) (3-Y.O+) (Class E)
3-05 (3-10) **6f** £4,037.50 (£1,225.00: £600.00: £287.50) Stalls: High GOING: 0.21 sec per fur (G)

			SP	RR	SF
2644^{15} **Tartan Lass** 74 **(73)** (RGuest) **4-9-13** TQuinn(26) (racd far side: a.p: led over 1f out: drvn out)	—	**1**	12/1	76+	51
3551^{6} **Top Banana** 40 **(59)** (HCandy) **8-8-6**(7) NicolaWright(20) (racd far side: a.p: rdn over 2f out: chsd wnr over 1f out: unable qckn)	1½	**2**	20/1	58	33
4272^{8} **Almasi (IRE)** 9 **(74)** (CFWall) **7-10-0** RMullen(21) (lw: racd far side: hdwy over 2f out: rdn over 1f out: one pce fnl f)	1	**3**	12/1	70	45
3956^{22} **Double March** 23 **(66)** (HCandy) **6-9-6** WRyan(24) (b: racd far side: hdwy over 1f out: r.o ins fnl f)	3	**4**	9/1 2	54	29
3737^{2} **Dolphinelle (IRE)** 33 **(67)** (RHannon) **3-9-5** RHughes(19) (lw: racd far side: mid div whn rdn over 2f out: hdwy over 1f out: nvr nrr)	1¾	**5**	16/1	51	24
3938^{4} **Night Life (IRE)** 24 **(69)** (MLWBell) **3-9-2**(5) CCarver(13) (racd far side: a.p: rdn over 2f out: wknd ins fnl f)	1¼	**6**	12/1	49	22
4412^{5} **Brevity** 2 **(64)** (DSasse) **4-9-1t**(3) PDoe(9) (lw: racd stands' side: prom over 4f)	4	**7**	14/1	34	9
4233* **Juwwi** 11 **(74)** (JMBradley) **5-9-7**(7) DarrenWilliams(14) (lw: racd far side: s.s: hdwy over 1f out: nvr nrr)	2	**8**	12/1	38	13
3744^{20} **Double-O** 33 **(66)** (WJarvis) **5-8-13b**(7) DMcGaffin(18) (racd far side: led over 4f)	nk	**9**	20/1	30	5
3416^{4} **Montendre** 45 **(58)** (RJHodges) **12-8-12** KFallon(17) (lw: racd far side: nvr nrr)	¾	**10**	10/1 3	20	—
3938* **Kilmeena Lad** 24 **(73)** (EAWheeler) **3-9-6**(5) SCarson(25) (racd far side: prom over 4f)	2½	**11**	8/1 1	28	1
3953^{11} **Vasari (IRE)** 23 **(63)** (WJMusson) **5-9-3** RPrice(23) (racd far side: prom over 3f)	½	**12**	12/1	17	—
3810^{12} **At Large (IRE)** 31 **(73)** (JARToller) **5-9-13b** SWhitworth(7) (racd stands' side: a mid div)	nk	**13**	25/1	26	1
3651^{12} **Supreme Angel** 37 **(67)** (MPMuggeridge) **4-9-7b** TSprake(16) (racd far side: nvr nrr)	¾	**14**	14/1	18	—
4121^{13} **Cold Climate** 17 **(62)** (BobJones) **4-8-13**(3) ADaly(10) (racd stands' side: nvr nrr)	1¼	**15**	20/1	9	—

				SP	RR	SF
3571[7]	**Stand Tall** 39 **(73)** (LadyHerries) **7-9-13** JReid(2) (racd stands' side: bhd fnl 3f)	1	**16**	14/1	18	—
4352[9]	**Oriel Girl** 4 **(55)** (MJRyan) **4-8-9** PMcCabe(12) (racd far side: prom over 2f)	2	**17**	20/1	—	—
2734[13]	**Sharp Hat** 72 **(66)** (TJEtherington) **5-9-6** MRoberts(8) (racd stands' side: bhd fnl 2f)	2½	**18**	20/1	—	—
3420[5]	**Diamond Geezer (IRE)** 45 **(67)** (RHannon) **3-8-12**(7) PFitzsimons(3) (racd stands' side: prom over 3f)	¾	**19**	25/1	—	—
*4154**	**Santandre** 16 **(61)** (RHollinshead) **3-8-13** RFfrench(5) (lw: racd stands' side: bmpd s: a bhd)	6	**20**	20/1	—	—
3900[3]	**Rogue Spirit** 26 **(75)** (PWHarris) **3-9-10**(3) NPollard(6) (racd stands' side: bmpd s: a bhd)	8	**21**	14/1	—	—
311[3]	**Wild Thing** 214 **(61)** (RHannon) **3-8-6**(7) RSmith(15) (racd far side: bhd fnl 4f)	10	**22**	33/1	—	—
				(SP 140.4%)	**22 Rn**	

1m 15.85 (4.85) CSF £227.00 CT £1,577.70 TOTE £20.30: £5.20 £5.60 £4.50 £3.60 (£538.50) Trifecta Not won; £1,033.90 to Warwick 21/9/1999 OWNER Matthews Breeding and Racing (NEWMARKET) BRED Matthews Breeding and Racing Ltd
IN-FOCUS: **The far side was undoubtedly the place to be with 11 of the first 12 coming from that side.**

In a field of 22 (four non-runners), 11 of the first 12 home raced up the far side, and the first four home all came from stalls in the 20s. The first one home up the stands' side was Brevity, who beat the next one on his flank by about 6 lengths. Brevity went on to run next time on the all-weather, so couldn't be backed there, as it usually pays to avoid outliers on their next start if they switch surfaces.

All horses that race both on turf and all-weather have two ratings, one for each surface. While it is often the case that a horse who turns in an eyecatching effort from a poor draw on turf is simply improving, there have been enough cases in the past where they've gone on to fail on the sand to put me off backing them when they switch. Although I am prepared to make the occasional exception. If a three-year-old turns in an eyecatching effort early in the season on turf, the chances are that he is just improving, so I would back him as long as he already has some experience of the sand. I would never back an all-weather debutant, however.

Brevity had one more run back on turf, actually off a 1lb lower mark than at Kempton (63), but ran as though over the top. He remains in training in 2000, and starts the campaign on a handy rating of 61.

The two sprint handicaps at Kempton that traditionally attract large fields, scheduled in 2000 for April 24 and September 18, are worth keeping a very close eye on, especially if the ground comes up soft.

Folkestone, April 20, soft:-

765 NORMAN POOLE MEMORIAL MAIDEN STKS (I) (3-Y.O) (Class D)
4-00 (4-04) **7f (straight)** £3,110.75 (£926.00: £440.50: £197.75) Stalls: Low GOING: 1.14 sec per fur (S)

				SP	RR	SF
297[6]	**Rainbow Romeo (IRE)** 63 **(55)** (JRPoulton) **3-9-0** RCochrane(4) (bhd whn swtchd far side 5f out: hdwy to ld over 3f out: clr over 2f out: rdn: r.o wl)	—	**1**	14/1	70	13
	Cinnamon Lady 182 **(68)** (DMorris) **3-8-9** NDay(9) (led over 3f: swtchd far side 2f out: unable qckn)	6	**2**	4/1 3	51	—
531[8]	**Count Frederick** 20 (JRJenkins) **3-9-0** JFortune(5) (rdn 3f out: hdwy 2f out: swtchd far side wl over 1f out: r.o one pce)	1¾	**3**	33/1	52	—
	Trois 163 (LMCumani) **3-9-0** RFfrench(8) (w'like: bit bkwd: bhd whn rdn 3f out: nvr nr to chal)	17	**4**	7/2 2	13++	—
	Scenic Lady (IRE) 202 (LADace) **3-8-9** TGMcLaughlin(3) (chsd ldrs over 3f)	½	**5**	66/1	7	—
	Democracy (IRE) 328 (RHannon) **3-9-0** RHughes(6) (bit bkwd: a.p: rdn over 2f out: eased whn btn over 1f out)	7	**6**	6/4 1	—	—
	Talaud (IRE) (IABalding) **3-8-9**(5) ANicholls(1) (str: scope: bit bkwd: prom over 5f)	2½	**7**	7/1	—	—
	Cabbage Crusader 175 (PLGilligan) **3-8-6**(3) APolli(7) (bkwd: prom 2f)	20	**8**	66/1	—	—
488[11]	**Petrus (IRE)** 24 **(74)** (CEBrittain) **3-9-0** PRobinson(2) (w ldr over 3f: wknd over 2f out)	1¼	**9**	10/1	—	—
				(SP 116.4%)	**9 Rn**	

1m 38.2 (15.20) CSF £63.18 TOTE £23.90: £2.80 £1.60 £4.10 (£19.90) OWNER Mr Eric Perry (LEWES) BRED Brendan Ryan and Islanmore Stud
IN-FOCUS: **This race categorically showed that the far side was the place to be. However, with the first three ending up racing there the form for this race should be treated with a great deal of caution.**
Rainbow Romeo (IRE), who showed very little in the past, only won this thanks to a masterful ride from Cochrane, who was the only jockey appearing to realise that there was a big advantage by going to the far side instead of staying in the centre. The combination easily moved to the front at halfway and stormed clear much to the delight of Cochrane who turned round to his fellow riders and made a gesture which quite clearly showed what he thought of them. (14/1: 8/1-16/1)

The earlier 16-runner maiden had already been turned into a procession by Mexican Rock, who raced up the far side, but in this smaller field most jockeys seemed content to race towards the stands' side until it was too late. Not Ray Cochrane, though.

Cochrane had clearly made up his mind before the race exactly what he was going to do; he was going to let the rest go off in front, hopefully towards the centre or stands' side, drop in behind and go over to the far rail without being seen. And that was exactly what he did, allowing a couple of furlongs for things to settle down and then tacking over. He won by 6 lengths.

Cochrane is not averse to making this sort of move, occasionally unsuccessfully, although more often than not it pays off. He was the first to successfully go over to the far rail at Lingfield on soft ground a good few years ago (see 'jockeys to follow' pages 102-105).

Sandown, April 23, good to soft, soft patches:-

825 BOW STREET MEDIAN AUCTION MAIDEN STKS (2-Y.O F) (Class E)
4-40 (4-47) **5f 6y** £3,566.25 (£1,080.00: £527.50: £251.25) Stalls: High GOING: 0.62 sec per fur (GS)

				SP	RR	SF
697[9]	**Never Diss Miss** [9] (RJRWilliams) **2-8-11** RHills(12) (hdwy on ins over 2f out: led over 1f out: rdn out)	—	**1**	20/1	79	35
622[3]	**Charming Lotte** [15] (PShakespeare) **2-8-11** CRutter(9) (lw: led over 3f: unable qckn)	3½	**2**	15/2 [3]	68	24
	Divine Prospect (IRE) (APJarvis) **2-8-11** DSweeney(10) (cmpt: outpcd: hdwy on ins over 1f out: r.o wl ins fnl f)	hd	**3**	25/1	68	24
	Royal Ivy (BWHills) **2-8-11** MHills(5) (b: w'like: s.s: n.m.r over 2f out: hdwy over 1f out: r.o wl ins fnl f)	1¼	**4**	15/2 [3]	64	20
	Kalindi (MRChannon) **2-8-11** TQuinn(11) (w'like: bit bkwd: a.p: rdn over 2f out: wknd ins fnl f)	2	**5**	9/4 [1]	57	13
	Big Movie Star (BJMeehan) **2-8-11** PatEddery(13) (leggy: w ldr over 3f)	½	**6**	7/2 [2]	56	12
647[14]	**Magic Babe** [11] (DRCElsworth) **2-8-8**(3) NPollard(3) (s.i.s: outpcd: hdwy fnl f: r.o)	1	**7**	40/1	52	8
	Chorus (BRMillman) **2-8-11** TSprake(14) (str: bit bkwd: s.s: nvr nr to chal)	hd	**8**	9/1	52	8
629[5]	**Kigema (IRE)** [14] (CNAllen) **2-8-11** JWeaver(2) (spd over 3f)	1½	**9**	40/1	47	3
	Southern Mist (WGMTurner) **2-8-11** JFEgan(8) (str: bit bkwd: prom 2f)	½	**10**	16/1	46	2
622[7]	**Berkeley Dido (IRE)** [15] (MLWBell) **2-8-11** MFenton(6) (bhd fnl 2f)	1¾	**11**	14/1	40	—
476[3]	**Santiburi Girl** [28] (JRBest) **2-8-11** LDettori(7) (bhd fnl 2f)	3½	**12**	16/1	29	—
	Fox Star (IRE) (RHannon) **2-8-11** DaneO'Neill(4) (leggy: a bhd)	nk	**13**	9/1	28	—

(SP 128.4%) **13 Rn**

66.93 secs (6.73) CSF £154.59 TOTE £42.00: £7.70 £2.00 £6.20 (£73.50) OWNER Mr Tim Fenner (NEWMARKET) BRED Highclere Stud Ltd

IN-FOCUS: **Sandown's first sprint race of the new season once again demonstrated how vital it is to have a high draw when the stalls are on the far side for the bias is more marked the softer the ground.**

Even with the stalls on the far rail, it proved essential to be drawn high here. Interestingly, the first three home were the three biggest-priced in the top five stalls, but looking back to the year Croft Pool won a heavily draw-affected Temple Stakes ('97) the principals there were also big prices.

On the straight course here, jockeyship plays a large part on the outcome, with those able to secure a position hard up against the far rail often seeming to bring improvement from their mounts.

Beverley, May 8, good, good to soft patches:-

1097 LA FEMME LADIES' H'CAP (0-70) (3-Y.O+) (Class E)
2-50 (2-50) **7f 100y** £3,194.00 (£962.00: £466.00: £218.00) Stalls: High GOING: 0.09 sec per fur (G)

				SP	RR	SF
942[5]	**Komlucky** [8] **(41)** (KARyan) **7-9-9** MissERamsden(15) (lw: trckd ldrs: effrt over 2f out: styd on to ld cl home)	—	**1**	9/2 [1]	42	33
731[12]	**Miss Eliminator** [22] **(46)** (JLHarris) **4-9-11**(3) MrsMMorris(16) (led: clr 2f out: wknd & ct cl home)	nk	**2**	33/1	46	37
941[10]	**Mai Tai (IRE)** [8] **(48)** (DWBarker) **4-9-13**(3) MrsCWilliams(10) (chsd ldrs: effrt 3f out: one pce fnl 2f)	2½	**3**	12/1	43	34
450[9]	**Copper Cookie** [50] **(35)** (MJPolglase) **4-8-10**(7) MissLMO'Brien(11) (bhd tl styd on wl fnl 2f: nrst fin)	1¼	**4**	50/1	27	18
71[7]	**Tilaal (USA)** [117] **(43)** (MDHammond) **7-9-4**(7) MrsAHammond(9) (t: dwlt: bhd tl styd on wl fnl 2f)	1¼	**5**	12/1	33	24
852[2]	**Tom** [12] **(35)** (CWFairhurst) **4-9-3v** MrsSBosley(12) (n.m.r appr st: hmpd 2f out: nvr trbld ldrs)	s.h	**6**	11/2 [3]	25	16

				SP	RR	SF
	Silver Secret ^{192} **(48)** (SGollings) **5-9-13**$^{(3)}$ MissEJJones(7) (dwlt: nvr nrr)	nk	**7**	14/1	37	28
*925**	**Takhlid (USA)** ^{9} **(67)** (DWChapman) **8-11-7** MissRClark(5) (swtg: rr div: effrt & hmpd appr st: hdwy 2f out: nvr rchd ldrs)	1¾	**8**	5/1 ^{2}	52	43
905^{5}	**Mutabari (USA)** ^{10} **(52)** (MrsSLamyman) **5-10-6v** MrsLPearce(13) (chsd ldrs tl wknd over 1f out)	nk	**9**	9/2 ^{1}	37	28
942^{7}	**Time of Night (USA)** ^{8} **(47)** (JLEyre) **6-10-1** MissDianaJones(2) (in tch tl wknd fnl 2½f)	2½	**10**	9/1	26	17
729^{4}	**Celandine** ^{22} **(63)** (AndrewTurnell) **6-10-10**$^{(7)}$ MissSThomas(8) (b.nr hind: in tch tl outpcd fnl 2f)	1	**11**	8/1	40	31
923^{8}	**Breezed Well** ^{9} **(43)** (BRCambidge) **13-9-6**$^{(5)ow8}$ MrsHNoonan(3) (n.d)	1¼	**12**	33/1	17	—
792^{6}	**Risky Way** ^{17} **(55)** (BSRothwell) **3-9-11** MissAElsey(4) (bhd: hdwy 7f out: wknd over 2f out)	s.h	**13**	16/1	29	8
447^{3}	**Melomania (USA)** ^{51} **(40)** (PHowling) **7-9-3**$^{(5)}$ CarolineHaddow(14) (chsd ldrs: hung rt 2f out: sn wknd)	nk	**14**	12/1	14	5
906^{17}	**Allrighthen** ^{10} **(53)** (TWall) **3-9-2**$^{(7)ow3}$ MissCHurst(1) (racd wd: a bhd)	5	**15**	16/1	16	—
	Tigi ^{262} **(36)** (JJQuinn) **4-8-13**$^{(5)}$ MissSHiggins(6) (chsd ldrs tl wknd fnl 3f)	8	**16**	25/1	—	—
				(SP 142.7%)	**16 Rn**	

1m 38.5 (7.40) CSF £166.85 CT £1,627.94 TOTE £6.00: £1.50 £9.80 £3.20 £11.30 (£126.00) OWNER Hambleton Racing Partnership (HAMBLETON) BRED T. Barratt

At some courses it is possible for poorly-drawn runners to get across to a favoured rail if the jockey is prepared to take the risk, but not so at Beverley over 7f 100y. Here, the runners encounter a long right-hand bend not long after the start, which is why those horses drawn well that race prominently enjoy such an advantage. That was clearly the case here, and Emma Ramsden was never going to come off the fence on board the winner Komlucky.

Beverley, May 8, good, good to soft patches:-

1100 WILLIAM HILL H'CAP (0-80) (3-Y.O+) (Class D)
4-30 (4-32) **5f** £4,744.00 (£1,432.00: £696.00: £328.00) Stalls: High GOING: 0.09 sec per fur (G)

				SP	RR	SF
748^{14}	**Black Army** ^{19} **(69)** (JMPEustace) **4-9-6** JTate(20) (cl up: led over 1f out: all out)	—	**1**	12/1	72	48
826^{8}	**Legs Be Frendly (IRE)** ^{15} **(69)** (KMcAuliffe) **4-9-6b** WSupple(19) (lw: a.p: hdwy u.p over 1f out: hung rt: styd on towards fin)	nk	**2**	16/1	71	47
969^{5}	**Nifty Norman** ^{7} **(57)** (DNicholls) **5-8-5**$^{(3)}$ JDSmith(14) (s.s: gd hdwy 2f out: styng on wl whn hmpd ins fnl f)	3	**3**	9/1 ^{3}	49	25
969^{10}	**Piggy Bank** ^{7} **(65)** (MWEasterby) **3-8-7** TLucas(18) (led tl hdd over 1f out: no ex)	2	**4**	20/1	51	18
905^{11}	**Bowlers Boy** ^{10} **(71)** (JJQuinn) **6-9-8** AMcGlone(15) (effrt ½-wy: styd on: nrst fin)	nk	**5**	12/1	56	32
855^{6}	**Ashover Amber** ^{12} **(64)** (TDBarron) **3-8-6** DeanMcKeown(11) (chsd ldrs: rdn 2f out: r.o one pce)	nk	**6**	25/1	48	15
855^{5}	**Colonel Sam** ^{12} **(65)** (JAGlover) **3-8-7** NDay(17) (chsd ldrs over 3f: grad wknd)	¾	**7**	12/1	47	14
996^{8}	**Pigeon** ^{5} **(72)** (DWBarker) **4-9-9** TWilliams(12) (chsd ldr: rdn 2f out: wknd fnl f)	s.h	**8**	16/1	54	30
905^{15}	**Young Bigwig (IRE)** ^{10} **(64)** (DWChapman) **5-9-1** ACulhane(6) (lw: bhd: hdwy 2f out: nvr nr to chal)	2½	**9**	16/1	38	14
875^{8}	**Mousehole** ^{11} **(61)** (RGuest) **7-8-12** CLowther(10) (bhd: sme hdwy over 1f out: n.d)	4	**10**	14/1	22	—
919^{3}	**D'Marti** ^{9} **(65)** (CBBBooth) **4-8-11**$^{(5)}$ DMernagh(13) (lw: prom over 3f)	s.h	**11**	10/1	26	2
969^{12}	**Bilko** ^{7} **(74)** (DNicholls) **5-9-11** AlexGreaves(9) (n.d)	2½	**12**	16/1	27	3
996^{3}	**Ajnad (IRE)** ^{5} **(57)** (RFMarvin) **5-8-8b** SRighton(16) (b.hind: chsd ldrs: hrd rdn ½-wy: grad wknd)	hd	**13**	3/1 ^{1}	9	—
964^{6}	**Maladerie (IRE)** ^{7} **(69)** (MDods) **5-9-6v** FLynch(5) (rdn ½-wy: nvr trbld ldrs)	hd	**14**	16/1	21	—
826^{9}	**Anstand** ^{15} **(75)** (MSSaunders) **4-9-12** DSweeney(2) (s.i.s: n.d)	2½	**15**	25/1	19	—
855^{8}	**Moocha Cha Man** ^{12} **(68)** (BAMcMahon) **3-8-10** JBramhill(1) (racd wd: n.d)	1¾	**16**	40/1	6	—
919^{2}	**Dominelle** ^{9} **(65)** (TDEasterby) **7-9-2** KDarley(7) (lw: racd wd: outpcd fr ½-wy)	1¼	**17**	7/2 ^{2}	—	—
	Sammal (IRE) ^{219} **(72)** (JAGlover) **3-8-7**$^{(7)}$ RCody-Boutcher(3) (racd wd: outpcd fr ½-wy)	2	**18**	50/1	—	—
	Quite Happy (IRE) ^{316} **(71)** (MHTompkins) **4-9-8** SDrowne(8) (sn bhd)	hd	**19**	25/1	—	—
				(SP 146.2%)	**19 Rn**	

65.7 secs (3.90) CSF £191.15 CT £1,708.43 TOTE £19.20: £3.80 £3.30 £2.40 £2.70 (£57.30) OWNER Mr K. J. Mercer (NEWMARKET) BRED K. J. Mercer

A typical big-field Beverley handicap sprint where, although the percentages were not in the favour of the punter, it was essentially possible to ignore 7/2 second-favourite Dominelle and a good few others, which made things more manageable. Although warm favourite Ajnad was never going that well, Shashi Righton didn't make the best use of his high draw.

The winner, Black Army, predictably struggled after this success:-

fin position		**ran**	**off rating**	**draw**
1	of	19	69	v.good
14	of	18	75	good

8	of	13	74	fair
5	of	15	73	good
3	of	15 (AW)	72	fair
18	of	18	72	fair

Magic Of Love showed she was a filly of real ability at Beverley

Beverley, July 27, good to firm:-

3163 FAMILY DAY MAIDEN AUCTION STKS (2-Y.O F) (Class F)
4-45 (4-48) **5f** £2,495.00 (£695.00: £335.00) Stalls: High GOING minus 0.58 sec per fur (F)

				SP	RR	SF
	Magic of Love (MLWBell) **2-8-7** MFenton(2) (w'like: scope: lw: trckd ldrs: rdn to ld wl ins fnl f)	—	**1**	5/1 3	86+	40
2901 7	**Kilbrannan Sound** 10 (BAMcMahon) **2-8-3** JFEgan(8) (cl up: led 2f out tl wl ins fnl f: kpt on)	½	**2**	13/8 1	80	34
2624 6	**Lunalux** 20 (CSmith) **2-8-3** JTate(3) (led 3f: r.o one pce)	4	**3**	12/1	68	22
2895 5	**Desert Safari (IRE)** 10 (EJAlston) **2-8-3** WSupple(6) (lw: chsd ldrs: rdn 2f out: no imp)	2	**4**	12/1	61	15
	Thirty Six Cee (AWCarroll) **2-8-0** DaleGibson(9) (leggy: sn outpcd & bhd: hdwy 2f out: styd on)	¾	**5**	11/1	56	10
2676 6	**Harmonize** 18 (MartynWane) **2-8-0** AWhelan(10) (in tch: sn pushed along: kpt on: no imp)	2	**6**	14/1	49	3
	Super Kim (PLGilligan) **2-8-2**ow2 GDuffield(1) (neat: s.i.s: outpcd & bhd tl styd on fnl f)	2	**7**	50/1	45	—
2770 2	**Double Fault (IRE)** 14 (TDEasterby) **2-8-7** KDarley(4) (sn pushed along & nvr trbld ldrs)	1¼	**8**	8/1	46	—
2729 2	**Blue Line Lady (IRE)** 17 (RAFahey) **2-8-1**(3)ow1 RWinston(5) (sn pushed along & nvr able to chal)	¾	**9**	5/2 2	41	—
1134 8	**Margarita Mou** 78 (CSmith) **2-7-9**(5) JMcAuley(11) (s.i.s: a outpcd & bhd)	8	**10**	50/1	11	—
2562 9	**Jenin** 22 (JWPayne) **2-8-0** JQuinn(7) (in tch tl wknd fnl 2f)	6	**11**	25/1	—	—
				(SP 132.6%)		**11 Rn**

62.1 secs (0.30) CSF £13.88 TOTE £7.40: £2.00 £1.50 £4.60 (£8.60) Trifecta £370.50; £172.21 to Goodwood 28/7/1999 OWNER Mrs Maureen Buckley (NEWMARKET) BRED Mrs C. S. Knowles

There was a word going around for Magic Of Love before she made her debut at Beverley, but she seemed to have little chance from a low draw against the favourite, Kilbrannan Sound, who had run well from a less-than-ideal stall in the Weatherbys Super Sprint.

Despite racing wide of the rail for most of the way and looking on the green side, she won nicely, and I marked her down as a filly worth following. She finished her season by winning the valuable Tattersalls Auction Stakes at Newmarket.

Windsor, May 10, good, good to firm patches:-

1138 BONUSPRINT H'CAP (0-80) (3-Y.O) (Class D)
6-45 (6-48) **6f** £4,201.50 (£1,272.00: £621.00: £295.50) Stalls: High GOING minus 0.20 sec per fur (GF)

				SP	RR	SF
1005^{*}	**Pandjojoe (IRE)** 7 **(62)** (RAFahey) **3-8-6** 6x GHind(25) (a.p: led over 1f out: r.o wl)	—	**1**	7/4 1	74+	37
924^{*}	**Night Life (IRE)** 11 **(63)** (MLWBell) **3-8-7** JQuinn(14) (a.p: r.o wl ins fnl f)	3	**2**	10/1 3	67	30
702^{9}	**Kilmeena Lad** 25 **(72)** (EAWheeler) **3-8-11**(5) SCarson(18) (lw: a.p: hrd rdn fnl f: r.o)	nk	**3**	14/1	75	38
	Tina's Royale 208 **(69)** (HCandy) **3-8-13** CRutter(19) (led tl over 1f out: r.o)	1½	**4**	20/1	68	31
650^{4}	**Milady Lillie (IRE)** 28 **(59)** (KTIvory) **3-8-0**(3) ADaly(13) (b: b.hind: a.p: rdn 2f out: one pce)	½	**5**	20/1	57	20
1013^{17}	**Prince of Aragon** 7 **(61)** (KTIvory) **3-8-5** AMcGlone(16) (b: b.hind: a.p: one pce fnl 2f)	1¼	**6**	33/1	56	19
	My Man Friday 218 **(57)** (WRMuir) **3-8-1** MartinDwyer(1) (gd spd 4f)	3	**7**	50/1	44	7
314^{5}	**Diamond Geezer (IRE)** 81 **(60)** (RHannon) **3-7-11**(7) LNewman(8) (nrst fin)	s.h	**8**	14/1	46	9
724^{4}	**Uzy** 24 **(66)** (IABalding) **3-8-10** KFallon(12) (mid div: styd on fnl 2f)	2	**9**	12/1	47	10
257^{*}	**Deviletta (USA)** 90 **(75)** (JHMGosden) **3-9-5** LDettori(9) (lw: s.s: hdwy 3f out: one pce fnl 2f)	1¼	**10**	7/1 2	53	16
	Franklin-D 287 **(60)** (JRJenkins) **3-8-4** SDrowne(15) (a mid div)	1¼	**11**	33/1	34	—
1030^{8}	**Cappella (IRE)** 6 **(73)** (RHannon) **3-9-3** DaneO'Neill(24) (nvr nr to chal)	hd	**12**	14/1	47	10
	Langans Figurine (IRE) 262 **(63)** (MJFetherston-Godley) **3-8-7** TSprake(20) (no hdwy fnl 2f)	s.h	**13**	25/1	37	—
685^{14}	**Montague Tigg (IRE)** 26 **(68)** (NTinkler) **3-8-12** WRyan(11) (a mid div)	s.h	**14**	25/1	42	5
	Our Bandbox 244 **(59)** (SMellor) **3-8-3** RFfrench(6) (lw: nvr on terms)	hd	**15**	40/1	33	—
	Tempramental (IRE) 217 **(58)** (DHaydnJones) **3-8-2** AMackay(7) (a bhd)	2½	**16**	25/1	25	—
1013^{15}	**Pisces Lad** 7 **(69)** (SDow) **3-8-13** GCarter(23) (s.s: a bhd)	½	**17**	33/1	35	—
533^{3}	**Gali** 40 **(67)** (CAHorgan) **3-8-11** DHolland(21) (a bhd)	¾	**18**	20/1	31	—
401^{3}	**Indian Swinger (IRE)** 67 **(65)** (JMPEustace) **3-8-9** JTate(17) (bhd fnl 3f)	¾	**19**	20/1	27	—
863^{7}	**Wry Ardour** 13 **(55)** (AGNewcombe) **3-7-13** FNorton(2) (s.s: a bhd)	1¾	**20**	25/1	12	—
	Giffoine 227 **(75)** (SDow) **3-9-2**(3) PDoe(22) (a bhd)	s.h	**21**	25/1	32	—
760^{9}	**Startoo** 21 **(65)** (RFJohnsonHoughton) **3-8-9** SWhitworth(3) (prom tl wknd over 2f out)	2	**22**	25/1	17	—
	Top Tarn (IRE) 245 **(55)** (CFWall) **3-7-13** NCarlisle(5) (lw: prom over 2f)	nk	**23**	33/1	6	—
842^{6}	**Petrovna (IRE)** 16 **(77)** (PLGilligan) **3-9-7** SSanders(10) (mid div tl wknd 3f out: eased fnl f)	10	**24**	20/1	1	—
				(SP 148.7%)	**24 Rn**	

1m 13.0 (2.90) CSF £15.14 CT £218.49 TOTE £2.80: £1.30 £3.50 £2.70 £3.90 (£9.50) OWNER Mr J. Dixon (MALTON) BRED Seamus Byrne Jnr

Pandjojoe had already won in the style of a very well-handicapped horse at Newcastle the week before, and was a warm order here from his draw in stall 25 and with a jockey likely to make the most of it on board. The first six home all came from the top half of the draw. My Man Friday and Diamond Geezer were the first two home among the low numbers, and the two went on to meet on their next outings at Lingfield.

High numbers had looked favoured at the previous Lingfield meeting, so, while My Man Friday again looked drawn out of it in 2, everything looked set up for Diamond Geezer to go well from 18 of 18. He was backed in from an early 8/1 down to 4/1 favouritism, but only managed fourth behind three other well-drawn horses.

Lingfield, May 25, good to firm:-

1456 NEWMARKET V EPSOM RODEO BULL CONTEST H'CAP (0-65) (3-Y.O) (Class F)
3-00 (3-03) **6f** £2,540.60 (£706.60: £339.80) Stalls: High GOING minus 0.43 sec per fur (F)

				SP	RR	SF
1284^{16}	**Sounds Lucky** 8 **(58)** (NPLittmoden) **3-8-9**(5) CCarver(16) (chsd ldrs: rdn to ld over 1f out: r.o wl)	—	**1**	33/1	62	40
739^{3}	**Bread Winner** 38 **(59)** (IABalding) **3-9-1b** MHills(13) (hdwy 2f out: hrd rdn over 1f out: r.o wl ins fnl f)	1¾	**2**	6/1 2	58	36
1328^{18}	**James Dee (IRE)** 6 **(65)** (APJarvis) **3-9-0**(7) SClancy(15) (a.p: led over 2f out tl over 1f out: unable qckn)	nk	**3**	12/1	63	41
1138^{8}	**Diamond Geezer (IRE)** 15 **(58)** (RHannon) **3-9-0** DaneO'Neill(18) (a.p: rdn over 2f out: ev ch over 1f out: one pce)	¾	**4**	4/1 1	54	32

				SP	RR	SF
1013^{13}	**Cedar Wells (USA)** ^{22} **(58)** (GLewis) **3-9-0** NDay(12) (lost pl over 3f out: rallied fnl f: r.o)	2	**5**	8/1 ^{3}	49	27
1238^{16}	**Pansy** ^{10} **(62)** (HMorrison) **3-9-4** SSanders(6) (dwlt: outpcd: hdwy over 1f out: nvr nrr)	1½	**6**	25/1	49	27
1138^{7}	**My Man Friday** ^{15} **(55)** (WRMuir) **3-8-11** MartinDwyer(2) (chsd ldrs: bmpd 5f out: rdn over 2f out: sn wknd)	nk	**7**	25/1	41	19
1013^{19}	**Bayonet** ^{22} **(65)** (RFJohnsonHoughton) **3-9-7b** JFortune(19) (led over 3f)	½	**8**	8/1 ^{3}	50	28
1290^{11}	**Pipsisewa (IRE)** ^{8} **(62)** (DRCElsworth) **3-9-1**(3) NPollard(8) (b.hind: dwlt: swtchd rt 5f out: shkn up over 2f out: nt clr run over 1f out: stdy hdwy fnl f: nvr nrr)	nk	**9**	12/1	46	24
1138^{11}	**Franklin-D** ^{15} **(55)** (JRJenkins) **3-8-11** SDrowne(14) (nvr nr to chal)	hd	**10**	20/1	39	17
	Breeds Hill ^{267} **(62)** (CFWall) **3-9-4t** GHind(5) (hmpd & lost pl 5f out: nvr nrr)	1	**11**	20/1	43	21
855^{11}	**La Paola (IRE)** ^{29} **(63)** (BJMeehan) **3-8-12b**^{1}(7) GHannon(17) (lw: s.i.s: hdwy 5f out: rdn over 2f out: sn wknd)	½	**12**	16/1	43	21
1189^{17}	**Lady Lazarus** ^{12} **(60)** (MBlanshard) **3-9-2** JQuinn(10) (b.hind: lw: a bhd)	2½	**13**	33/1	33	11
589^{5}	**Thrifty** ^{50} **(61)** (MJRyan) **3-9-3** PMcCabe(7) (a bhd)	nk	**14**	11/1	33	11
1138^{13}	**Langans Figurine (IRE)** ^{15} **(58)** (MJFetherston-Godley) **3-9-0** TSprake(9) (mid div tl wknd & hmpd over 1f out)	1¼	**15**	25/1	27	5
1177^{4}	**Dolly Day Dream (IRE)** ^{13} **(58)** (KTIvory) **3-8-7v**(7) CCatlin(20) (b: spd 4f)	¾	**16**	10/1	25	3
749^{5}	**Aston Eyre** ^{36} **(59)** (AGJuckes) **3-9-1** GBardwell(1) (prom 4f)	nk	**17**	33/1	25	3
500^{11}	**Westside Flyer** ^{57} **(57)** (AKelleway) **3-8-13** MRoberts(3) (a bhd)	8	**18**	25/1	2	—
1102^{7}	***Princess Mo*** ^{17} **(56)** (PatMitchell) **3-8-12** JTate(11) (Withdrawn not under Starter's orders: ref to ent stalls)		**W**	16/1	—	—

(SP 134.8%) **18 Rn**

1m 10.45 (1.45) CSF £188.72 CT £2,333.75 TOTE £21.10: £2.80 £2.00 £4.60 £1.40 (£47.20) OWNER Mr Paul Dixon (NEWMARKET) BRED T. Barratt

Although My Man Friday and Pansy both ran well enough to finish first and second home of the low numbers, there was nothing in either performance to warrant backing them next time out. The bias clearly favoured high numbers, but the overall performance of runners down the centre previously suggested they had not achieved anything out of the ordinary.

Ripon, July 17, good to firm:-

2928 BERNADETTE MCWILLIAMS MEMORIAL MAIDEN H'CAP (0-70) (3-Y.O+) (Class E)
4-00 (4-01) **6f** £3,215.00 (£965.00: £465.00: £215.00) Stalls: Low GOING minus 0.50 sec per fur (F)

				SP	RR	SF
2810^{U}	**Bank House (IRE)** ^{3} **(42)** (GPKelly) **4-8-4b**^{1}**t** TLucas(8) (led 5f out: clr fnl f: eased nr fin)	—	**1**	14/1	51+	40
2383^{6}	**Bedevilled** ^{19} **(66)** (TDBarron) **4-10-0** CLowther(16) (racd alone far side: a.p: outpcd fnl f)	5	**2**	6/1 ^{3}	62	51
2222^{2}	**Trapper Norman** ^{24} **(49)** (CSmith) **7-8-8**(3) NCallan(6) (chsd ldrs: drvn along thrght: kpt on ins fnl f)	¾	**3**	5/1 ^{2}	43	32
2678^{2}	**Impaldi (IRE)** ^{8} **(44)** (BEllison) **4-8-6** NKennedy(1) (led 1f: styd on same pce appr fnl f)	½	**4**	6/1 ^{3}	36	25
2755^{7}	**Young Rosein** ^{5} **(44)** (MrsGSRees) **3-7-8**(7) AngelaHartley(17) (lw: outpcd tl styd on ins fnl f: nvr nrr)	1¼	**5**	16/1	33	17
2303^{4}	**September Harvest (USA)** ^{22} **(56)** (MrsSLamyman) **3-8-13** TWilliams(7) (lw: outpcd tl r.o ins fnl f: nrst fin)	1	**6**	10/1	42	26
2459^{9}	**Now Is The Hour** ^{16} **(40)** (PSFelgate) **3-7-6**(5)ow1 JMcAuley(11) (s.i.s: sn prom: wknd over 1f out)	¾	**7**	25/1	24	8
2753^{3}	**Ballymorris Boy (IRE)** ^{5} **(52)** (JPearce) **3-8-9** RPrice(14) (nvr trbld ldrs)	1	**8**	9/1	34	18
2321^{14}	**Vosburgh** ^{21} **(51)** (PCalver) **3-8-5**(3) RWinston(10) (chsd ldrs over 4f)	1	**9**	14/1	30	14
2452^{11}	**Blazing Billy** ^{17} **(38)** (CADwyer) **4-7-9**(5)ow4 DMernagh(12) (prom: rdn 2f out: sn btn)	¾	**10**	33/1	15	—
2638^{6}	**Smoke Signal (IRE)** ^{9} **(67)** (MJohnston) **3-9-10** JFanning(15) (lw: a outpcd)	1¼	**11**	4/1 ^{1}	41	25
2132^{17}	**Prime Surprise** ^{29} **(39)** (DWBarker) **3-7-5**(5) IonaWands(13) (lw: s.i.s: effrt u.p over 2f out: n.d)	hd	**12**	33/1	12	—
2585^{10}	**Ban Gardai (IRE)** ^{11} **(58)** (EJAlston) **4-9-6** LCharnock(5) (swtg: prom: rdn ½-wy: sn lost pl)	nk	**13**	20/1	31	20
	Waltham Skylark ^{287} **(43)** (KAMorgan) **4-8-5**ow2 DeanMcKeown(9) (bit bkwd: chsd ldrs 4f)	s.h	**14**	33/1	16	5
2456^{12}	**Found At Last** ^{16} **(60)** (MissSEHall) **3-9-3** DaleGibson(4) (a outpcd)	5	**15**	33/1	19	3
2379^{14}	**Banningham Belle** ^{19} **(40)** (DShaw) **4-7-9**(7)ow5 PFitzsimons(3) (b: a outpcd)	11	**16**	20/1	—	—
2506^{6}	**Indian Dance** ^{15} **(68)** (JWHills) **3-9-11t** ACulhane(2) (s.i.s: a outpcd)	1	**17**	6/1 ^{3}	—	—

(SP 143.0%) **17 Rn**

1m 10.9 (-0.10) CSF £94.68 CT £470.76 TOTE £40.70: £5.20 £2.70 £1.30 £2.10 (£145.50) Trifecta £633.20; £802.77 to 19/7/1999 OWNER Mr G. P. Kelly (SHERIFF HUTTON) BRED Kevin Doyle

With 17 runners on fast ground, it seemed certain that a decent-sized group would head off for the far rail, but the only one to go over was Bedevilled from stall 16 under Carl Lowther, and he finished a clear second.

Looking at the race beforehand, it seemed that there were not many 'draw jockeys' in the top half dozen or so stalls but, given that the field was only six off the maximum (Young Rosein in 17 was three-quarters of the way across the course), I was fairly certain the field would split pretty much into two equal groups. But these are jockeys we're talking about!

Angela Hartley is a tidy enough rider, but to bring a horse drawn 17 in a six-furlong event at Ripon across the slower centre of the track to race up the stands' rail was not the smartest move of all time. So for the filly to finish a never-nearer fifth was a fine effort.

Nottingham, August 13, good to firm, firm patches:-

3624 MANSFIELD BREWERY H'CAP (0-75) (3-Y.O) (Class E)
2-30 (2-30) **6f 15y** £3,643.20 (£1,015.20: £489.60) Stalls: High GOING minus 0.13 sec per fur (G)

Form	Horse	Dist	Pos	SP	RR	SF
2759^{3}	**Venika Vitesse** ^{32} **(68)** (TDBarron) **3-9-0** CLowther(4) (a.p centre: led wl over 1f out: hld on wl nr fin)	—	1	7/1^{3}	69	46
3375*	**Moocha Cha Man** ^{9} **(71)** (BAMcMahon) **3-9-3b** ^{6x} KDarley(12) (lw: hld up: hdwy 2f out: chsd wnr fnl f: nt pce to chal)	½	**2**	7/1^{3}	71	48
3217^{10}	**Adelphi Boy (IRE)** ^{15} **(75)** (MCChapman) **3-9-7** TSprake(10) (chsd ldrs: effrt & hrd rdn over 1f out: fin wl)	½	**3**	11/1	73	50
2928^{5}	**Young Rosein** ^{27} **(53)** (MrsGSRees) **3-7-6**$^{(7)ow3}$ AngelaHartley(16) (lw: a.p stands' side: ev ch 1f out: kpt on wl cl home)	s.h	**4**	33/1	51	28
2571^{10}	**My Man Friday** ^{39} **(50)** (WRMuir) **3-7-10** NKennedy(18) (a.p stands' side: rdn over 1f out: r.o)	hd	**5**	14/1	48	25
3081^{4}	**Top of The Pops (IRE)** ^{21} **(62)** (CWThornton) **3-8-8** DeanMcKeown(8) (hdwy 2f out: kpt on u.p fnl f)	nk	**6**	20/1	59	36
3286^{4}	**Bollin Roberta** ^{13} **(67)** (TDEasterby) **3-8-13** RWinston(7) (mde most tl wl over 1f out: wknd ins fnl f)	¾	**7**	12/1	62	39
2564^{7}	**Dim Ofan** ^{39} **(72)** (BPalling) **3-9-1**$^{(3)}$ GFaulkner(5) (prom centre over 4f)	hd	**8**	16/1	67	44
3401^{13}	**Seven Springs (IRE)** ^{8} **(56)** (RHollinshead) **3-8-2** WSupple(6) (chsd ldrs centre: rdn over 1f out: nt pce to chal)	1¾	**9**	25/1	46	23
3420^{3}	**Blue Star** ^{7} **(71)** (NPLittmoden) **3-8-10v**$^{(7)}$ CCogan(14) (lw: chsd ldrs: rdn 2f out: no imp)	s.h	**10**	8/1	61	38
3068^{10}	**Colonel Sam** ^{21} **(56)** (JAGlover) **3-8-2b^{1}** GDuffield(9) (swtg: sn prom: rdn over 1f out: wknd appr fnl f)	1¾	**11**	16/1	42	19
2525^{16}	**Natural Pearl** ^{41} **(52)** (JJQuinn) **3-7-12v**^{1ow2} FNorton(2) (nvr trbld ldrs)	s.h	**12**	33/1	37	14
2755^{10}	**Tapaua (IRE)** ^{32} **(58)** (MDods) **3-8-4** FLynch(17) (racd stands' side: nvr on terms)	s.h	**13**	12/1	43	20
3401^{15}	**College Music (IRE)** ^{8} **(53)** (MBrittain) **3-7-8**$^{(5)}$ DMernagh(13) (outpcd)	s.h	**14**	33/1	38	15
3076^{9}	**Pandjojoe (IRE)** ^{21} **(73)** (RAFahey) **3-9-5** JCarroll(15) (prom stands' side: rdn over 2f out: wknd qckly appr fnl f)	4	**15**	5/1^{2}	48	25
3013^{13}	**My Emily** ^{23} **(73)** (GLMoore) **3-9-2**$^{(3)}$ JDSmith(11) (in tch: rdn over 2f out: sn wknd)	2	**16**	9/2^{1}	42	19
3401^{7}	**The Rain Lady** ^{8} **(50)** (PDEvans) **3-7-10** MHenry(1) (swtg: racd alone far side: rdn along ½-wy: nvr on terms)	6	**17**	50/1	4	—
				(SP 132.5%)	**17 Rn**	

1m 14.4 (2.90) CSF £50.87 CT £529.00 TOTE £9.90: £1.90 £3.30 £2.50 £6.10 (£48.60) Trifecta £154.00 OWNER Mr Kevin Shaw (THIRSK)
BRED Snowdrop Stud Co Ltd
LONG HANDICAP My Man Friday 7-8 Natural Pearl 7-1 Young Rosein 7-1 The Rain Lady 7-0
2928 Young Rosein won the race on the stands side and showed she is coming to hand. That first success could be just around the corner. (33/1)
1138 My Man Friday made the majority of the running under the stands rail, and did not go down without a fight. This was his first real sign of ability, and there should be a small race within his compass. (14/1)

A little over a month later, Young Rosein reappeared at Nottingham and would have been one to back had she not been running from 9lb out of the handicap. Again though, she ran an eyecatching race up what turned out to be the unfavoured side of the course, and she was kept as a horse to follow.

Next time at Musselburgh, she had everything in her favour:-

1) **The ground was suitable** - good to firm, good patches, almost identical to at Ripon and Nottingham.
2) **The trip was suitable** - up to seven furlongs, a trip she had been crying out for having stayed on strongly at the finish on both previous outings over six.
3) **The handicapper had not raised the rating a ridiculous amount** - she had effectively run off a mark of 53 at Nottingham, given that she was out of the handicap, and was back down 1lb on 52 here.
4) **The race was similar in class to the time before** - Class E, the same as her two previous races.
5) **The selection had not been off the course for any length of time** - 13 days - anything around two weeks is about ideal.
6) **Most importantly, the selection had a reasonable draw** - 13 of 14, and high numbers are, if anything, slightly favoured at Musselburgh over seven furlongs.

Also in Young Rosein's favour was that Angela Hartley had been replaced by George Duffield, and she responded to a more aggressive ride.

Having been offered at 8/1 by William Hill in the morning, Young Rosein opened on course at 6/1 and remained steady at that price. This is the sort of punting opportunity that may come along only once or twice a year but, when they arrive, the feeling of not being able to see defeat is unbelievable.

Leicester, June 12, good to soft, soft patches:-

1950 MERCURY RACE NIGHT H'CAP (0-70) (3-Y.O+ F & M) (Class E)
9-15 (9-16) **5f 218y** £3,071.00 (£856.00: £413.00) Stalls: Centre GOING: 0.21 sec per fur (G)

Form	Horse	Dist	Pos	SP	RR	SF
1681*	**Nightingale Song** ^{10} **(41)** (LMontagueHall) **5-8-5** MHenry(13) (a.p: led over 2f out: clr appr fnl f: just hld on)	—	**1**	11/1	47	18
1755^{5}	**Windy Gulch (USA)** ^{7} **(59)** (MJohnston) **4-9-9** JCarroll(16) (hld up: hdwy over 2f out: rdn over 1f out: r.o strly towards fin)	nk	**2**	10/1	64	35
1703^{4}	**Mill End Quest** ^{9} **(50)** (MWEasterby) **4-9-0** LDettori(18) (lw: hld up: hdwy over 2f out: kpt on: nt pce to chal)	3	**3**	11/2^{2}	47	18
1661^{7}	**Selkirk Rose (IRE)** ^{10} **(50)** (JGGiven) **4-9-0** JFanning(1) (b: bhd: hdwy 2f out: rdn & r.o wl ins fnl f)	¾	**4**	16/1	45	16
1755^{6}	**Petite Danseuse** ^{7} **(43)** (DWChapman) **5-8-7** ACulhane(5) (lw: hdwy wl over 1f out: nrst fin)	¾	**5**	9/1	36	7
1597^{9}	**Grace** ^{12} **(54)** (JMBradley) **5-8-11**$^{(7)}$ DarrenWilliams(7) (lw: hdwy stands' side 2f out: kpt on wl ins fnl f)	¾	**6**	10/1	45	16
1649^{6}	**Bunty** ^{11} **(43)** (CADwyer) **3-7-13** JQuinn(8) (bhd: hdwy u.p 2f out: nt rch ldrs)	4	**7**	20/1	24	—
1417^{6}	**Kustom Kit Kate** ^{21} **(52)** (SRBowring) **4-9-2b** DaleGibson(17) (b: lw: led over 3f out tl over 2f out: rdn & wknd over 1f out)	¾	**8**	12/1	31	2
1801^{3}	**Cappella (IRE)** ^{5} **(68)** (RHannon) **3-9-10** DaneO'Neill(11) (mid div: effrt & rdn over 2f out: no imp)	1	**9**	7/1	44	7
1302^{6}	**Afrietino** ^{25} **(47)** (MrsNMacauley) **5-8-11** DeanMcKeown(4) (prom stands' side 4f)	s.h	**10**	33/1	23	—
1132^{4}	**Mariana** ^{33} **(44)** (TTClement) **4-8-8v**^{ow3} TGMcLaughlin(20) (nvr nr ldrs)	¾	**11**	40/1	18	—
1725^{11}	**Princess Belfort** ^{8} **(32)** (BDLeavy) **6-7-10** JBramhill(12) (swtchd lft s: chsd ldrs: rdn 3f out: sn lost tch)	nk	**12**	100/1	5	—
1724^{2}	**Apples And Pears (IRE)** ^{8} **(53)** (MHTompkins) **3-8-9** RHills(14) (in tch: effrt & rdn 2f out: sn outpcd)	nk	**13**	13/2^{3}	25	—
1755^{3}	**Oriel Girl** ^{7} **(56)** (MJRyan) **4-9-6v** PMcCabe(3) (hld up: a in rr)	½	**14**	9/2^{1}	27	—
1598^{9}	**Miss Bananas** ^{12} **(39)** (CNKellett) **4-8-3** NCarlisle(19) (a bhd & outpcd)	3	**15**	20/1	2	—
866^{11}	**Blushing Victoria** ^{46} **(50)** (JAGlover) **4-9-0** SSanders(6) (lw: s.s: a bhd)	s.h	**16**	25/1	13	—
1691^{8}	**College Music (IRE)** ^{10} **(54)** (MBrittain) **3-8-5**$^{(5)}$ DMernagh(15) (led over 2f: rdn along ½-wy: grad wknd)	3	**17**	10/1	9	—
1687^{9}	**Absolutely Abstone** ^{10} **(32)** (WMBrisbourne) **5-7-3b**$^{(7)}$ PMQuinn(10) (s.s: hdwy after 2f: wknd over 2f out)	½	**18**	66/1	—	—
				(SP 139.8%)	**18 Rn**	

1m 16.3 (6.30) CSF £113.72 CT £640.32 TOTE £18.30: £3.40 £2.10 £1.80 £3.30 (£111.60) OWNER Mr Stephen Bayless (EPSOM) BRED A. Bromley

By this point on the card (this was the last race of the evening) the ground was looking pretty cut up, and they finished fairly strung out. High numbers had previously looked favoured on a faster surface here, but this race showed that they also held the upper hand on dead ground.

Those racing down the centre of the track looked in control from some way out and I took my eye off the stands'-rail bunch at about the two-furlong point, only to notice Selkirk Rose finishing well on that side at the line. Next time, Selkirk Rose ran at Nottingham. She had everything in her favour and won at 11/1:-

1) **The ground was suitable** - her only previous win had been on good to firm, so good, good to firm patches looked ideal.
2) **The trip was suitable** - six furlongs again.
3) **The handicapper had not raised her rating a ridiculous amount** - actually down 1lb from 50 to 49.
4) **The race was similar in class to the time before** - down a grade from Class E to Class F.
5) **She had not been off the course for any length of time** - nine days.
6) **Most importantly, she had a reasonable draw** - 17 of 20 with pace on her side guaranteed from Bee Health Boy in 19. I tend to have a marginal preference for high numbers here when pondering a bet.

Royal Ascot, June 16, good to firm:-

2042 {S} ROYAL HUNT CUP H'CAP (3-Y.O+) (Class B)
4-20 (4-26) **1m (straight)** £68,850.00 (£25,650.00: £12,450.00: £5,250.00: £2,250.00: £1,050.00) Stalls: High GOING minus 0.12 sec per fur (G)

				SP	RR	SF
1565^{3}	**Showboat** ^{18} **(92)** (BWHills) **5-8-6**$^{(3)}$ NPollard(30) (lw: racd far side: hdwy 3f out: led over 1f out: comf)	—	**1**	14/1	108	89
1183^{6}	**Plan-B** ^{35} **(96)** (JHMGosden) **4-8-13** WRyan(31) (racd far side: hld up: hdwy over 3f out: r.o u.p appr fnl f: no ch w wnr)	6	**2**	14/1	100	81
456^{7}	**Refuse To Lose** ^{88} **(92)** (JMPEustace) **5-8-9** JTate(29) (racd far side: led tl over 1f out: kpt on u.p fnl f)	hd	**3**	20/1	96	77
$1896a^{3}$	**Raheen (USA)** ^{15} **(95)** (RAFahey) **6-8-12** MRoberts(19) (racd stands' side: hld up in rr: gd hdwy 2f out: nrst fin)	2	**4**	33/1	95	76
1608^{5}	**Yarob (IRE)** ^{16} **(82)** (DNicholls) **6-7-8**$^{(5)}$ ANicholls(4) (a.p stands' side: led over 3f out tl ins fnl f)	½	**5**	25/1	81	62
1183^{*}	**Sugarfoot** ^{35} **(107)** (NTinkler) **5-9-10** MJKinane(6) (racd stands' side: mid div: hmpd 4f out: hdwy 2f out: rdn & r.o wl fnl f)	hd	**6**	14/1	106	87
1565^{4}	**Family Man** ^{18} **(87)** (JRFanshawe) **6-8-4** OUrbina(2) (prom stands' side: rdn over 1f out: one pce)	hd	**7**	25/1	85	66
1600^{*}	**Wild Sky (IRE)** ^{16} **(85)** (MJHeaton-Ellis) **5-8-2vt** ^{5x} FNorton(16) (mid div: effrt over 2f out: nt pce to chal)	s.h	**8**	33/1	83	64
1576^{*}	**King Darius (IRE)** ^{18} **(89)** (RHannon) **4-8-6**^{ow1} ^{5x} RHughes(23) (racd far side: hdwy 2f out: nt rch ldrs)	nk	**9**	16/1	87	68
$520a^{7}$	**Free To Speak (IRE)** ^{80} **(100)** (DKWeld,Ireland) **7-9-3b** PJSmullen(27) (chsd ldrs far side: hrd rdn over 2f out: grad wknd)	nk	**10**	33/1	97	78
1614^{9}	**Peartree House (IRE)** ^{16} **(88)** (WRMuir) **5-8-5** PatEddery(17) (chsd ldrs stands' side: rdn over 2f out: wknd over 1f out)	s.h	**11**	33/1	85	66
1614^{3}	**Persiano** ^{16} **(98)** (JRFanshawe) **4-9-1** RCochrane(9) (racd far side: nvr rchd ldrs)	hd	**12**	10/1 ^{3}	95	76
1614^{10}	**Gulf Shaadi** ^{16} **(87)** (MissGayKelleway) **7-8-4**^{ow1} SSanders(7) (racd stands' side: n.d)	1	**13**	50/1	82	63
1339^{4}	**Topatori (IRE)** ^{27} **(82)** (MHTompkins) **5-7-13** GBardwell(13) (racd stands' side: nvr rch ldrs)	¾	**14**	40/1	75	56
1730^{12}	**Abajany** ^{12} **(85)** (MRChannon) **5-8-2** SDrowne(15) (racd stands' side: nvr trbld ldrs)	½	**15**	33/1	77	58
1111^{11}	**Consort** ^{39} **(90)** (MrsAJPerrett) **6-8-7** DHolland(14) (dwlt: a in rr)	¾	**16**	20/1	81	62
1614^{*}	**Lonesome Dude (CAN)** ^{16} **(103)** (SirMichaelStoute) **4-9-6v** ^{7x} GaryStevens(26) (sn chsng ldr far side: rdn & wknd wl over 1f out)	1¼	**17**	12/1	91	72
1676^{2}	**Silk St John** ^{14} **(94)** (MJRyan) **5-8-11** PMcCabe(12) (racd stands' side: hdwy over 3f out: wknd fnl 2f)	½	**18**	33/1	81	62
1450^{5}	**Sick As A Parrot** ^{22} **(83)** (CADwyer) **4-7-11v**$^{(3)}$ PDoe(11) (racd stands' side: n.d)	1	**19**	66/1	68	49
1458^{*}	**China Red (USA)** ^{22} **(92)** (JWHills) **5-8-9** ^{5x} MHills(32) (prom far side over 5f)	3	**20**	33/1	71	52
1803^{*}	**No Extras (IRE)** ^{9} **(83)** (GLMoore) **9-7-7**$^{(7)}$ ^{5x} RBrisland(22) (swtg: racd far side: rdn ½-wy: a bhd)	2	**21**	33/1	58	39
1959^{5}	**Gift of Gold** ^{4} **(85)** (ABailey) **4-8-2** ^{5x} AMackay(28) (chsd ldrs far side over 5f)	nk	**22**	33/1	60	41
1345^{*}	**Oriental** ^{27} **(94)** (JHMGosden) **4-8-11** LDettori(5) (racd stands' side: ıdn over 3f out: no imp)	hd	**23**	13/2 ^{1}	69	50
1757^{10}	**Wuxi Venture** ^{11} **(86)** (SPCWoods) **4-8-3** RHills(21) (racd far side: a bhd)	5	**24**	66/1	51	32
1402^{4}	**Rich In Love (IRE)** ^{25} **(93)** (CACyzer) **5-8-10** GMosse(1) (w ldrs stands' side over 4f: wknd over 2f out)	nk	**25**	25/1	57	38
1730^{*}	**Scene (IRE)** ^{12} **(81)** (JAGlover) **4-7-12** ^{7x} MHenry(8) (lw: mde most stands' side over 4f: wknd over 2f out)	¾	**26**	25/1	43	24
1614^{5}	**Pantar (IRE)** ^{16} **(100)** (IABalding) **4-9-3** KFallon(24) (chsd ldr far side: drvn along ½-wy: wknd over 2f out)	1	**27**	9/1 ^{2}	60	41
1608^{4}	**Captain Scott (IRE)** ^{16} **(93)** (JAGlover) **5-8-10** JFortune(18) (lw: racd far side: in tch to ½-wy: sn wknd)	3	**28**	20/1	47	28
950^{10}	**Hornbeam** ^{46} **(97)** (JRJenkins) **5-9-0** OPeslier(20) (w ldrs stands' side 5f)	½	**29**	66/1	50	31
1183^{8}	**Latalomne (USA)** ^{35} **(94)** (BEllison) **5-8-8**$^{(3)}$ RWinston(10) (prom to ½-wy: sn lost tch)	¾	**30**	66/1	46	27
1730^{11}	**Mount Holly (USA)** ^{12} **(81)** (KMahdi) **5-7-12t** JQuinn(3) (chsd ldrs stands' side: rdn 3f out: sn wknd)	¾	**31**	50/1	31	12
1444^{5}	**Blakeset** ^{23} **(84)** (RHannon) **4-8-1** JFEgan(25) (b.hind: lost tch over 3f out)	1	**32**	66/1	32	13
				(SP 136.0%)	**32 Rn**	

1m 38.59 (-0.41) CSF £137.33 CT £1,989.94 TOTE £22.00: £4.70 £3.30 £5.30 £11.80 (£125.10) Trifecta £16,581.80 OWNER Mr R. D. Hollingsworth (LAMBOURN) BRED R. D. Hollingsworth

In a field of 32, three of the first four home came from the top four stalls, but it was a bias not to be repeated over the remainder of the week. This was not the first time high numbers had held the upper hand in the big-field mile handicaps at Royal Ascot; stall 30 has always fared particularly well for some reason.

The far side often does best at the Festival meetings when the rail is pushed back.

Ascot, August 7, good, good to firm patches:-

3444 {S} TOTE INTERNATIONAL H'CAP (3-Y.O+) (Class B)
3-05 (3-09) **7f** £86,000.00 (£32,000.00: £15,500.00: £6,500.00: £2,750.00: £1,250.00) Stalls: High GOING minus 0.10 sec (G)

				SP	RR	SF
2072^{2}	**Russian Revival (USA)** ^{51} **(114)** (JHMGosden) **6-9-7** LDettori(25) (swtg: racd far side: mde all: rdn out)	—	**1**	9/1 ^{1}	122	99
2467^{5}	**Mubrik (IRE)** ^{37} **(100)** (JHMGosden) **4-8-7** RHills(26) (swtg: racd far side: a.p: chsd wnr over 2f out: rdn over 1f out: unable qckn)	2	**2**	14/1	103	80
2700^{5}	**Peculiarity** ^{28} **(105)** (BSmart) **3-8-6** JStack(6) (swtg: racd stands' side: a.p: hrd rdn over 1f out: one pce)	1	**3**	40/1	106	77
3216^{2}	**Showboat** ^{9} **(106)** (BWHills) **5-8-13** RCochrane(1) (swtg: racd stands' side: rdn & hdwy over 1f out: r.o wl ins fnl f)	¾	**4**	14/1	105	82
3223^{2}	**Swallow Flight (IRE)** ^{9} **(100)** (GWragg) **3-8-1** MRoberts(8) (racd stands' side: a.p: rdn over 3f out: one pce)	nk	**5**	9/1 ^{1}	99	70
3233^{*}	**Petrus (IRE)** ^{8} **(95)** (CEBrittain) **3-7-7**$^{(3)}$ ^{3x} ANicholls(27) (racd far side: a.p: rdn wl over 1f out: one pce)	nk	**6**	25/1	93	64
2644^{*}	**Grangeville (USA)** ^{30} **(98)** (IABalding) **4-8-5** KFallon(4) (lw: racd stands' side: a.p: rdn 2f out: one pce)	nk	**7**	10/1 ^{2}	95	72

				SP	RR	SF
3117*	**Cretan Gift** 13 **(96)** (NPLittmoden) **8-8-3v**ow1 MFenton(2) (racd stands' side: bhd whn nt clr run on ins over 2f out: hdwy over 1f out: r.o ins fnl f)	½	**8**	16/1	92	69
2700^{3}	**Sugarfoot** 28 **(107)** (NTinkler) **5-9-0** MJKinane(21) (lw: racd far side: a.p: rdn over 2f out: one pce)	1¼	**9**	20/1	100	77
2743*	**Tajasur (IRE)** 27 **(103)** (JLDunlop) **4-8-10** TQuinn(10) (swtg: racd stands' side: hdwy over 1f out: one pce)	nk	**10**	11/1^{3}	96	73
3117^{7}	**Young Josh** 13 **(90)** (ACStewart) **4-7-11** MartinDwyer(24) (swtg: racd far side: a mid div)	¾	**11**	40/1	81	58
3261^{20}	**Silca Blanka (IRE)** 7 **(90)** (AGNewcombe) **7-7-11** AWhelan(15) (b: racd far side: hdwy on ins 3f out: wknd over 1f out)	s.h	**12**	50/1	81	58
2877^{7}	**Late Night Out** 22 **(105)** (WJarvis) **4-8-12** MTebbutt(5) (racd stands' side: a mid div)	s.h	**13**	50/1	96	73
3223^{3}	**Indian Lodge (IRE)** 9 **(98)** (MrsAJPerrett) **3-7-13** JQuinn(9) (racd stands' side: hdwy over 2f out: wknd over 1f out)	hd	**14**	12/1	89	60
3100^{3}	**Sunstreak** 14 **(101)** (CFWall) **4-8-8** PatEddery(16) (racd far side: a mid div)	1¾	**15**	11/1^{3}	88	65
3095^{5}	**Dilkusha (IRE)** 14 **(94)** (BJMeehan) **4-7-12**(3)ow4 RMullen(3) (racd stands' side: nvr nrr)	1¼	**16**	66/1	78	55
3131^{6}	**Nomore Mr Niceguy** 13 **(91)** (EJAlston) **5-7-12**ow1 WSupple(7) (racd stands' side: prom over 4f)	s.h	**17**	50/1	75	52
3131^{2}	**Ho Leng (IRE)** 13 **(100)** (MissLAPerratt) **4-8-7** DaneO'Neill(22) (racd far side: a mid div)	hd	**18**	16/1	83	60
7076a^{0}	**Bartex (FR)** 62 **(91)** (TClout,France) **5-7-12** YFukunaga(20) (racd far side: nvr nrr)	1¼	**19**	66/1	72	49
	Matin De Printemps (FR) 20 **(91)** (HVandePoele,France) **5-7-12** AurelienMalenfant(17) (lw: racd far side: a bhd)	3½	**20**	33/1	64	41
2344^{5}	**Cool Edge (IRE)** 42 **(100)** (MHTompkins) **8-8-7** GBardwell(23) (racd far side: bhd fnl 2f)	2½	**21**	50/1	67	44
2877^{2}	**Caballero** 22 **(103)** (CEBrittain) **3-8-4** DHolland(18) (swtg: racd far side: mid div over 5f)	1¼	**22**	33/1	67	38
3036a^{6}	**Cubism (USA)** 25 **(103)** (JWHills) **3-8-4** MHenry(13) (swtg: racd far side: a bhd)	2	**23**	40/1	62	33
2543^{3}	**Therhea (IRE)** 35 **(92)** (BRMillman) **6-7-10**(3) PDoe(11) (racd stands' side: a bhd)	½	**24**	40/1	50	27
2910^{4}	**Ettrick** 21 **(100)** (ACStewart) **3-8-1**ow2 GCarter(12) (swtg: racd stands' side: bhd fnl 2f)	2	**25**	14/1	54	25
3087*	**Refuse To Lose** 14 **(98)** (JMPEustace) **5-8-5** 3x JTate(14) (swtg: racd far side: prom over 4f)	2	**26**	20/1	47	24
2543^{8}	**Jo Mell** 35 **(101)** (TDEasterby) **6-8-8** JWeaver(19) (racd far side: prom over 4f)	1¾	**27**	12/1	46	23

(SP 132.7%) **27 Rn**

1m 26.93 (-0.07) CSF £103.78 CT £4,424.10 TOTE £9.80: £2.50 £3.00 £9.90 £4.10 (£39.10) Trifecta £10,855.30; £9,326.41 to Ascot 8/8/1999 OWNER Maktoum Al Maktoum (NEWMARKET) BRED Swettenham Stud

There was an amazing amount of confidence behind Russian Revival in the morning prior to this race, with him being backed down from around the 16/1 mark to 9s at the off.

Although it wasn't publicised in the racing press, it again turned out that the far rail had been moved out to unveil a fresh strip of ground, and that proved decisive. Showboat was on the wrong side this time, but not for the first time went close to winning on the unfavoured flank in a big race here. He seems to run his best races at Ascot.

Newmarket July, July 6, good:-

2574 {S} H & K COMMISSIONS BOOKMAKERS H'CAP (0-80) (3-Y.O+) (Class D)
2-35 (2-36) **1m (July)** £8,350.00 (£2,500.00: £1,200.00: £550.00) Stalls: Low GOING minus 0.55 sec per fur (F)

				SP	RR	SF
2117^{2}	**Muyassir (IRE)** 18 **(69)** (PJMakin) **4-9-3** SSanders(17) (trckd ldrs stands' side: hdwy to ld ent fnl f: drvn out)	—	**1**	10/1^{2}	72	55
2173^{2}	**Iron Mountain (IRE)** 15 **(72)** (NACallaghan) **4-9-6** KFallon(20) (lw: chsd ldrs stands' side: led wl over 1f out: hdd ent fnl f: kpt on wl)	½	**2**	10/1^{2}	74	57
2124^{5}	**Redswan** 18 **(66)** (SCWilliams) **4-9-0t** WRyan(16) (lw: racd stands' side: hdwy & ev ch ins fnl f: kpt on)	½	**3**	11/1^{3}	67	50
2347^{3}	**Topton (IRE)** 10 **(67)** (PHowling) **5-9-1b** JQuinn(11) (hld up stands' side: hdwy & ev ch ent fnl f: sn rdn & btn)	1½	**4**	16/1	65	48
1647^{14}	**Derryquin** 35 **(63)** (PLGilligan) **4-8-11b**1 JFEgan(19) (led & wnt clr stands' side: hdd wl over 1f out: no ex)	4	**5**	66/1	53	36
1600^{12}	**King of Tunes (FR)** 36 **(70)** (JJSheehan) **7-9-4** JStack(18) (swtg: chsd ldrs stands' side: rdn over 2f out: r.o one pce)	1	**6**	33/1	58	41
2247^{4}	**Ben Gunn** 13 **(72)** (PTWalwyn) **7-9-6** MJKinane(14) (swtg: hld up stands' side: hdwy 3f out: sn rdn: btn appr fnl f)	1	**7**	8/1^{1}	58	41
2243*	**Dilkusha (IRE)** 13 **(75)** (BJMeehan) **4-9-9** TQuinn(13) (racd stands' side: effrt 3f out: no imp)	¾	**8**	10/1^{2}	60	43
2257^{4}	**Adulation (USA)** 13 **(76)** (PWChapple-Hyam) **5-9-10** JFortune(15) (lw: bhd stands' side: effrt 3f out: no imp)	½	**9**	20/1	60	43
2350^{4}	**Tipperary Sunset (IRE)** 9 **(65)** (JJQuinn) **5-8-8**(5) ANicholls(12) (lw: in tch stands' side: outpcd fnl 2½f)	1	**10**	20/1	47	30
2223^{2}	**Three Angels (IRE)** 13 **(74)** (MHTompkins) **4-9-8** SDrowne(1) (lw: racd far side: styd on fnl 3f: no ch w stands' side)	4	**11**	16/1	48	31
1592^{3}	**Bobbydazzle** 36 **(73)** (DrJDScargill) **4-9-7** JMurtagh(2) (w ldr far side: rdn & no imp fnl 3f)	1¼	**12**	20/1	44	27
2439^{2}	**Weetman's Weigh (IRE)** 6 **(77)** (RHollinshead) **6-9-11** LDettori(7) (lw: led far side tl ins fnl f: no ch w stands' side)	2½	**13**	10/1^{2}	43	26
2470*	**Saifan** 5 **(65)** (DMorris) **10-8-13v** 5x NDay(6) (racd far side: bhd fnl 3f)	6	**14**	25/1	19	2
2346^{7}	**Minetta** 10 **(71)** (MLWBell) **4-9-5** MFenton(10) (lw: in tch stands' side over 4f)	hd	**15**	16/1	25	8
2224^{4}	**Indium** 13 **(76)** (WJMusson) **5-9-10** GCarter(8) (lw: trckd ldrs far side: effrt 3f out: n.d)	½	**16**	10/1^{2}	29	12
1732^{7}	**High Hoyland** 32 **(74)** (RHannon) **3-8-13** DaneO'Neill(3) (s.i.s: racd far side: a bhd)	hd	**17**	16/1	27	1
2445^{2}	**Samara Song** 6 **(66)** (IanWilliams) **6-9-0** JWeaver(5) (racd far side: hmpd after 1½f: n.d)	2	**18**	14/1	15	—
2124^{4}	**Far Removed (IRE)** 18 **(76)** (MrsVCWard) **4-9-7**(3) NPollard(4) (lw: racd far side: nvr trbld ldrs)	nk	**19**	12/1	24	7
1414^{15}	**Final Dividend (IRE)** 45 **(74)** (MJFetherston-Godley) **3-8-13** MHills(9) (racd far side: n.d)	3½	**20**	25/1	15	—

(SP 129.2%) **20 Rn**

1m 37.31 (0.11) CSF £91.05 CT £676.82 TOTE £12.50: £2.90 £2.80 £2.30 £3.10 (£81.30) Trifecta £1,037.00 OWNER Mr William Otley (MARLBOROUGH) BRED Barronstown Stud and Katom

This was not the first time high numbers had been favoured at the July Meeting - the stands' rail was also on top when Ho Leng won the '98 Bunbury Cup from stall 20 of 20, beating runners drawn 18, 16, 15, 19 and 17. It's a bias that becomes more accentuated the faster the ground, and the Newmarket turf is often at its fastest for these three days.

The huge bias favouring high numbers in '99 was, at the time, put down to the grass being longer on the far rail, and it prompted the stalls being moved from their advertised position of low (far side) to the stands' side in a bid to cancel the bias for the remainder of the card, a completely unsatisfactory move.

It is down to the course to ensure the most level playing field possible, and that would presumably include making sure that grass has been cut for one of the biggest meetings of the year! If the stalls have been advertised as low, they should remain low for the entire meeting whatever happens. Courses must realise that not all punters place their bets race by race, and anyone who had banked on a high bias prior to racing got a raw deal. This was one step away from staggering the stalls as they do in greyhound racing.

Grangeville won Newmarket's Bunbury Cup from stall 20, as had Ho Leng a year earlier

The stalls were positioned down the centre for the Bunbury Cup and, although the field were inclined to head for the centre strip, those that raced towards the stands' side of centre were again favoured.

There had been a wholesale tipping line-inspired gamble on Grangeville the Monday before the race, which at the time I thought was a risky move without knowing the draw, but whoever was behind it got lucky as he was allocated stall 20 of 20. He won very easily.

Goodwood, July 30, firm, good to firm patches:-

3233 {S} BONUSPRINT H'CAP (0-100) (3-Y.O) (Class C)
2-15 (2-20) **7f** £19,300.00 (£5,800.00: £2,800.00: £1,300.00) Stalls: High GOING minus 0.25 sec per fur (GF)

Form	Horse / details	Dist	Pos	SP	RR	SF
2832*	**Petrus (IRE)** 16 **(79)** (CEBrittain) **3-7-13**(5) ANicholls(16) (a.p: led over 2f out: edgd lft ins fnl f: rdn out)	—	1	11/1	88	47
2503^{7}	**Diamond Decorum (IRE)** 28 **(80)** (PDEvans) **3-8-5** JFEgan(15) (b: lw: chsd ldrs: rdn over 2f out: chsd wnr over 1f out: unable qckn)	1½	2	20/1	86	45
2625^{2}	**Elmhurst Boy** 23 **(78)** (SDow) **3-8-0v**^{1}(3) PDoe(12) (swtg: plld hrd: a.p: nt clr run over 2f out tl over 1f out: nt clr run on ins fnl f: r.o)	½	3	33/1	82	41
2964^{2}	**Bon Ami (IRE)** 10 **(92)** (JBerry) **3-9-3** KDarley(14) (w ldr: led over 4f out tl over 3f out: ev ch over 2f out: one pce)	1½	4	16/1	93	52
2644^{9}	**Achilles Star** 22 **(89)** (KRBurke) **3-9-0** JWeaver(1) (lw: bhd whn rdn 3f out: hdwy over 1f out: r.o ins fnl f)	s.h	5	16/1	90+	49
3089^{2}	**Zucchero** 6 **(74)** (DWPArbuthnot) **3-7-13b** JQuinn(8) (b: b.hind: chsd ldrs: rdn over 2f out: wknd ins fnl f)	1½	6	5/1 ^{2}	72	31
2578*	**Juno Marlowe (IRE)** 24 **(96)** (PWHarris) **3-9-7** TQuinn(11) (led over 2f: led again over 3f out tl over 2f out: hrd rdn over 1f out: eased whn btn fnl f)	nk	7	14/1	93	52
2490*	**Pulau Tioman** 28 **(96)** (MAJarvis) **3-9-7** PRobinson(13) (a.p: rdn over 2f out: wknd ins fnl f)	s.h	8	8/1 ^{3}	93	52
2498*	**Daytime** 28 **(84)** (RHannon) **3-8-9** RHughes(9) (lw: rdn over 3f out: hdwy & nt clr run over 1f out: swtchd lft: 9th & btn whn nt clr run ins fnl f)	nk	9	100/30 ^{1}	80	39
2577^{10}	**Princely Dream (IRE)** 24 **(86)** (RAFahey) **3-8-11v**^{1} JFortune(6) (bhd whn nt clr run 3f out: nvr nrr)	s.h	10	20/1	82	41
1394^{4}	**Buona Sera** 69 **(72)** (WRMuir) **3-7-11** MartinDwyer(3) (bhd: rdn over 3f out: nvr nrr)	1	11	33/1	66	25
2334^{13}	**Fearby Cross (IRE)** 34 **(86)** (JDBethell) **3-8-11** KFallon(2) (s.i.s: bhd whn rdn over 2f out: hdwy over 1f out: eased whn btn ins fnl f)	nk	12	16/1	79	38
3130^{7}	**Route Sixty Six (IRE)** 5 **(80)** (GLMoore) **3-8-5** MRoberts(5) (sme hdwy over 1f out: sn wknd)	1¾	13	12/1	69	28
2577^{7}	**Maple (IRE)** 24 **(83)** (DRCElsworth) **3-8-5**(3) NPollard(4) (b.hind: hdwy 4f out: wknd 2f out)	4	14	25/1	63	22
1727^{17}	**My Petal** 56 **(83)** (RHannon) **3-8-8** DaneO'Neill(10) (prom over 3f)	nk	15	33/1	62	21
2577^{6}	**Midhish Two (IRE)** 24 **(86)** (PMitchell) **3-8-8**(3) RMullen(7) (bhd fnl 3f)	9	16	20/1	45	4

(SP 118.1%) **16 Rn**

1m 26.54 (1.74) CSF £195.03 CT £3,4C2.22 TOTE £14.80: £2.80 £5.50 £5.40 £3.10 (£163.10) Trifecta £2,010.90 OWNER Mr C. E. Brittain (NEWMARKET) BRED Anamoine Ltd

Unlike in previous seasons, Goodwood moved the far (inside) rail before racing on the Friday of the Glorious meeting rather than the Saturday, which meant the fresh strip of ground did not have as much of an effect on Stewards' Cup day. However, it did see high numbers massively favoured on the Friday. The jockeys on the first four in the above seven-furlong handicap all did the sensible thing and raced prominently from their high draws towards the inside rail all the way. All those that tried to come from off the pace wider out never had a chance.

Goodwood, July 31, good to firm:-

3261 {S} VODAFONE STEWARDS' CUP H'CAP (3-Y.O+) (Class B)
3-50 (3-55) **6f** £51,500.00 (£15,500.00: £7,500.00: £3,500.00) Stalls: Low GOING minus 0.17 sec per fur (GF)

Form	Horse / details	Dist	Pos	SP	RR	SF
2743^{2}	**Harmonic Way** 20 **(92)** (RCharlton) **4-8-6t** RHughes(8) (racd stands' side: in rr 3f: gd hdwy over 1f out: led ins fnl f: rdn out)	—	1	12/1 ^{3}	99	69
2339*	**Halmahera (IRE)** 35 **(107)** (IABalding) **4-9-7** KDarley(10) (racd stands' side: rdn over 2f out: hdwy over 1f out: r.o wl ins fnl f)	1½	2	16/1	110	80
3117^{3}	**Literary Society (USA)** 6 **(92)** (JARToller) **6-8-6** SWhitworth(28) (lw: racd far side: hdwy 2f out: ev ch ins fnl f: unable qckn)	nk	3	16/1	94++	64
2879^{4}	**Twice as Sharp** 15 **(91)** (PWHarris) **7-8-5**ow1 PatEddery(6) (racd stands' side: a.p: led over 1f out tl ins fnl f: one pce)	½	4	33/1	92	62
2701^{4}	**Sylva Paradise (IRE)** 21 **(82)** (CEBrittain) **6-7-10v** GBardwell(4) (swtg: racd stands' side: lost pl 3f out: rallied over 1f out: r.o ins fnl f)	hd	5	33/1	83	53
3117^{12}	**Brave Edge** 6 **(94)** (RHannon) **8-8-1**(7) RSmith(2) (racd stands' side: lost pl 3f out: rallied 1f out: r.o)	s.h	6	40/1	95	65
2743^{6}	**Loch Laird** 20 **(84)** (MMadgwick) **4-7-9**(3)ow2 PDoe(11) (racd stands' side: hrd rdn & hdwy over 1f out: r.o ins fnl f)	¾	7	66/1	83	53
3049^{W}	**Levelled** 8 **(95)** (MRChannon) **5-8-9** SDrowne(7) (racd stands' side: bhd whn rdn over 2f out: hdwy fnl f: r.o)	½	8	50/1	92	62
2941^{7}	**Cadeaux Cher** 12 **(90)** (BWHills) **5-8-4**ow1 RCochrane(3) (lw: racd stands' side: outpcd: hdwy fnl f: r.o)	nk	9	12/1 ^{3}	86	56
2643^{10}	**Superior Premium** 23 **(110)** (RAFahey) **5-9-5**(5) DMernagh(5) (lw: racd stands' side: a.p: rdn over 2f out: ev ch over 1f out: wknd ins fnl f)	nk	10	33/1	106	76
2644^{10}	**Deep Space (IRE)** 23 **(95)** (EALDunlop) **4-8-9** GCarter(17) (racd far side: hdwy 2f out: r.o ins fnl f)	nk	11	20/1	90	60
2105^{26}	**Perryston View** 43 **(96)** (PCalver) **7-8-10b** GDuffield(1) (racd stands' side: led: rdn over 2f out: hdd over 1f out: sn wknd)	1½	12	33/1	87	57
3213^{8}	**Iris May** 3 **(82)** (JBerry) **4-7-10** PFessey(30) (racd far side: a.p: rdn over 2f out: wknd ins fnl f)	1¼	13	33/1	69	39
3101^{2}	**Double Oscar (IRE)** 7 **(82)** (DNicholls) **6-7-5b**(5) ANicholls(21) (b: racd far side: hdwy 1f out: wknd fnl f)	2	14	12/1 ^{3}	64	34
3049^{2}	**Magic Rainbow** 8 **(86)** (MLWBell) **4-7-11**(3)ow1 RMullen(26) (racd far side: a.p: hrd rdn 2f out: wknd fnl f)	nk	15	12/1 ^{3}	67	37

				SP	RR	SF
2900^{2}	**Night Shot** 14 **(106)** (IABalding) **4-9-6** KFallon(24) (racd far side: a mid div)	¾	**16**	13/2^{2}	85	55
2701*	**Night Flight** 21 **(101)** (RAFahey) **5-9-1** 7x LDettori(23) (lw: racd far side: a.p: rdn over 2f out: wknd fnl f)	s.h	**17**	12/1^{3}	80	50
1967*	**Pepperdine (IRE)** 49 **(94)** (DNicholls) **3-8-3** SSanders(25) (racd far side: hdwy over 2f out: wknd over 1f out)	½	**18**	9/2^{1}	72	37
2879^{9}	**Cauda Equina** 15 **(82)** (MRChannon) **5-7-5**(5) RBrisland(27) (racd far side: a mid div)	¾	**19**	50/1	58	28
2445*	**Silca Blanka (IRE)** 31 **(87)** (AGNewcombe) **7-8-1** 3x JQuinn(29) (b: racd far side: prom 4f)	s.h	**20**	40/1	63	33
2577^{11}	**Amazing Dream (IRE)** 25 **(98)** (RHannon) **3-8-7** DaneO'Neill(12) (lw: racd stands' side: prom 4f)	hd	**21**	50/1	73	38
2577^{5}	**Champagne Rider** 25 **(89)** (KMcAuliffe) **3-7-12** FNorton(15) (racd far side: a bhd)	nk	**22**	40/1	64	29
2743^{3}	**Primo Lara** 20 **(98)** (PWHarris) **7-8-12** AClark(22) (racd far side: prom 4f)	½	**23**	25/1	71	41
2964*	**Red Lion** 11 **(99)** (JWPayne) **3-8-8** 3x RHills(20) (racd far side: dwlt: bhd fnl 2f)	½	**24**	25/1	71	36
3061^{6}	**Coastal Bluff** 8 **(95)** (NPLittmoden) **7-8-2b**(7) CCogan(9) (b.hind: racd stands' side: s.s: a bhd)	¾	**25**	40/1	65	35
1568^{14}	**Now Look Here** 63 **(90)** (BAMcMahon) **3-7-13**ow1 RFfrench(14) (racd far side: a bhd)	nk	**26**	50/1	59	24
2879^{6}	**Double Bounce** 15 **(83)** (HMorrison) **9-7-11**ow1 CRutter(18) (racd far side: dwlt: a bhd)	½	**27**	66/1	51	21
2701^{7}	**Tussle** 21 **(97)** (MLWBell) **4-8-11** OPeslier(19) (racd far side: bhd fnl 2f)	s.h	**28**	12/1^{3}	65	35
2964^{7}	**Price of Passion** 11 **(88)** (DWPArbuthnot) **3-7-4**(7)ow1 LNewman(13) (lw: racd far side: bhd fnl 3f)	nk	**29**	66/1	55	20
2941^{3}	**Indian Spark** 12 **(90)** (JSGoldie) **5-8-4** JFEgan(16) (racd far side: bhd fnl 3f)	1¾	**30**	33/1	52	22
				(SP 141.6%)	**30 Rn**	

1m 10.3 (0.50) CSF £158.21 CT £2,873.17 TOTE £16.20: £3.80 £4.70 £4.30 £7.50 (£108.10) Trifecta £4,880.90 OWNER Mrs Alexandra Chandris (BECKHAMPTON) BRED Mrs J. Chandris

The work carried out at Goodwood to break up the faster ground on the far rail paid dividends, but ultimately only served to swing the bias full circle, as low numbers enjoyed a definite advantage in the Stewards' Cup (although in the other sprints handicaps run during the week, when the stalls did not stretch right across the track, there seemed no noticeable bias - Zuhair won twice, once racing down the centre, once up the stands' rail).

Back to the Stewards' Cup, credit had to go to *Raceform On Saturday*'s Mike Cattermole, who was asked by connections to choose winner Harmonic Way's stall and who went for stall 8. Literary Society ran a cracking race down the far side to beat his group by the best part of 3 lengths, but unfortunately he went on to run next time in a listed race at Newmarket, where he bumped into a genuine Group 1-class opponent in Arkadian Hero. Thus he became a no-bet.

Epsom, August 30, good:-

4013 {S} TOTE BOOKMAKERS SPRINT H'CAP (0-105) (3-Y.O+) (Class B)
2-35 (2-37) **5f** £17,425.00 (£5,275.00: £2,575.00: £1,225.00) Stalls: High GOING minus 0.31 sec per fur (GF)

				SP	RR	SF
3762*	**Emma Peel** 12 **(101)** (BJMeehan) **3-9-13** LDettori(10) (lw: racd stands' side: rdn & hdwy 1f out: str run to ld wl ins fnl f: r.o wl)	—	**1**	13/2^{1}	104	66
3762^{5}	**Angie Baby** 12 **(73)** (RIngram) **3-7-6**(7) ABeech(13) (racd stands' side: a.p: unable qckn ins fnl f)	1¾	**2**	8/1^{2}	70	32
3825^{10}	**Batchworth Belle** 9 **(92)** (EAWheeler) **4-9-1**(5) SCarson(12) (racd stands' side: dwlt: hdwy wl over 1f out: edgd lft 1f out: one pce)	nk	**3**	10/1^{3}	88	52
3237^{4}	**Johayro** 31 **(73)** (JSGoldie) **6-8-1** JLowe(5) (racd stands' side: a.p: rdn over 1f out: one pce ins fnl f)	hd	**4**	14/1	69	33
3962^{12}	**Kilcullen Lad (IRE)** 2 **(74)** (RIngram) **5-7-9v**(7)ow2 PFitzsimons(9) (racd stands' side: bhd tl gd hdwy fnl f: r.o wl)	s.h	**5**	10/1^{3}	70	34
3166^{13}	**Repertory** 34 **(100)** (MSSaunders) **6-10-0** RPrice(3) (racd far side: led: rdn over 1f out: hdd wl ins fnl f: sn wknd)	½	**6**	10/1^{3}	94	58
3794^{2}	**Passion For Life** 10 **(79)** (JAkehurst) **6-8-7** DSweeney(11) (racd stands' side: a.p: rdn over 2f out: one pce)	nk	**7**	8/1^{2}	72	36
3732^{5}	**Iris May** 12 **(76)** (JBerry) **4-7-13**(5) PBradley(6) (racd stands' side: prom over 3f)	¾	**8**	12/1	67	31
3622^{4}	**Miss Hit** 17 **(72)** (DRCElsworth) **4-7-11**(3)ow3 ADaly(14) (lw: racd stands' side: nvr nrr)	nk	**9**	10/1^{3}	62	26
3956^{13}	**Levelled** 2 **(92)** (MRChannon) **5-9-6** TQuinn(4) (lw: racd far side: a.p: hrd rdn over 1f out: wknd ins fnl f)	¾	**10**	8/1^{2}	80	44
3762^{7}	**Henry Hall (IRE)** 12 **(96)** (NTinkler) **3-9-8** KimTinkler(8) (racd stands' side: chsd ldrs over 3f)	s.h	**11**	16/1	84	46
3264*	**Aurigny** 30 **(90)** (SDow) **4-9-1**(3) PDoe(7) (racd stands' side: s.s: hdwy over 2f out: wknd ins fnl f)	hd	**12**	12/1	77	41
3101*	**Antonia's Double** 37 **(77)** (JBerry) **4-8-5** PFessey(1) (b.hind: lw: s.s: swtchd stands' side 4f out: a bhd)	s.h	**13**	12/1	64	28
3264^{2}	**Crowded Avenue** 30 **(90)** (PJMakin) **7-9-4** SSanders(2) (racd far side: a.p: hrd rdn over 1f out: wknd fnl f)	10	**14**	10/1^{3}	45	9
				(SP 127.7%)	**14 Rn**	

55.37 secs (1.17) CSF £54.75 CT £361.52 TOTE £4.10: £2.10 £3.40 £4.00 (£24.10) Trifecta £972.90 OWNER Mr Arthur Smith (UPPER LAMBOURN) BRED Arthur E. Smith

For a long way it looked as though Repertory was bang in contention racing towards the far rail, but in the final furlong, the energy preserved by racing up the faster stands' side showed, as that group pulled away.

Zuhair won twice at Goodwood, once up the stands' side, once down the middle

Thirsk, September 4, firm:-

4148 IRWIN MITCHELL MAIDEN H'CAP (0-60) (3-Y.O+) (Class F)
5-30 (5-31) **5f** £3,013.75 (£910.00: £442.50: £208.75) Stalls: High GOING minus 0.71 sec per fur (HD)

Form	Horse / details	Dist	Pos	SP	RR	SF
3801^{6}	**Beveled Hawthorn** ^{15} **(26)** (DNicholls) **4-7-5**(5) IonaWands(18) (swtg: mde most stands' side: hung lft most of wy: drvn out)	—	**1**	$10/1^{3}$	28	14
3624^{11}	**Colonel Sam** ^{22} **(54)** (JAGlover) **3-9-9b** LNewton(16) (lw: a chsng wnr: kpt on u.p fnl f: nvr able to chal)	1¼	**2**	$5/1^{2}$	52	37
3633^{8}	**Carmarthen (IRE)** ^{22} **(52)** (KRBurke) **3-9-0**(7) DarrenWilliams(3) (led centre: rdn 2f out: no ex ins fnl f)	¾	**3**	$10/1^{3}$	48	33
3753^{2}	**Record Time** ^{17} **(53)** (EJAlston) **3-9-8** WSupple(5) (prom centre: hdwy 2f out: nt qckn ins fnl f)	1¼	**4**	$2/1^{1}$	45	30
3871^{7}	**Defiance** ^{11} **(40)** (APJames) **4-8-10b** JStack(14) (chsd ldrs: nt qckn appr fnl f)	2	**5**	12/1	25	11
3291^{9}	**Little Cinnamon** ^{33} **(55)** (JLEyre) **3-9-3b¹**(7) RCody-Boutcher(10) (outpcd tl hdwy ½-wy: styd on u.str.p fnl 2f)	nk	**6**	20/1	39	24
3868^{11}	**Chok-Di** ^{11} **(42)** (MrsMReveley) **3-8-11** ACulhane(7) (chsd ldrs: one pce fnl 2f)	s.h	**7**	$10/1^{3}$	26	11
3949^{11}	**Silvano's Express** ^{7} **(34)** (MissJFCraze) **3-8-3b** NCarlisle(6) (chsd ldrs centre: rdn ½-wy: grad wknd)	nk	**8**	25/1	17	2
3845^{17}	**Lady Lauren** ^{13} **(43)** (GWoodward) **3-8-12** SDWilliams(1) (lw: s.i.s: nvr bttr than mid div)	s.h	**9**	20/1	26	11
3768^{16}	**Westwood View** ^{16} **(50)** (JJQuinn) **3-9-5b¹** GParkin(11) (sn outpcd)	nk	**10**	12/1	32	17
3753^{7}	**Fine And Rosy** ^{17} **(27)** (MDods) **4-7-11**ow1 NKennedy(19) (sn drvn along: lost tch fr ½-wy)	1	**11**	16/1	6	—
3257^{14}	**Coeur du Lion** ^{36} **(40)** (DNicholls) **3-8-6b¹**(3) JDSmith(4) (gd spd centre over 3f)	hd	**12**	25/1	19	4
2807^{7}	**Miss Hamouse (IRE)** ^{52} **(34)** (JParkes) **3-7-10**(7) PHanagan(17) (n.d)	2	**13**	25/1	6	—
3914^{7}	**Lemon Strip** ^{9} **(40)** (BPalling) **3-8-4**(5) DMernagh(8) (cl up centre tl hrd rdn & wknd fnl 2½f)	¾	**14**	14/1	10	—
3948^{15}	**Burning Love** ^{8} **(30)** (BWMurray) **4-7-7**(7) JennyBenson(13) (n.d)	nk	**15**	50/1	—	—
3674^{11}	**Precious Years** ^{19} **(40)** (LRLloyd-James) **4-8-10** KDarley(12) (dwlt: a bhd)	½	**16**	20/1	7	—
3948^{16}	**Cool Katie** ^{8} **(30)** (KARyan) **3-7-13** PFessey(15) (n.d)	nk	**17**	25/1	—	—
3855^{8}	**Rm Again** ^{12} **(36)** (RGuest) **3-8-5b** SDrowne(9) (sn bhd)	½	**18**	12/1	1	—

(SP 144.5%) **18 Rn**

58.4 secs (0.40) CSF £57.00 CT £518.47 TOTE £26.70: £4.10 £1.80 £3.20 £1.40 (£64.60) Trifecta Not won; £533.52 to 6/9/1999 OWNER Mrs Margaret Dunning (THIRSK) BRED C. J. Sexton

There was a big word for Carmarthen here, but he looked drawn out of it, even in such a desperate affair. Beveled Hawthorn had shown nothing previously, while runner-up Colonel Sam had looked a difficult ride, but both took advantage of the faster strip right under the stands' rail.

David Nicholls enjoyed an amazing year with his sprinters

Other 1999 races of note

Race 500	**Hamilton** - Sharp Edge Boy won from stall 11 of 12 on soft ground at 25/1. The race had looked open beforehand, as is often the way with these early-season 3-y-o only handicaps.
Race 582	**Newcastle** - This was one of the rare occasions during the season when the stands' rail rode faster than the far side, despite there being some cut in the ground.
Race 614	**Ripon** - Every so often, the bias favouring high numbers here seems to all but disappear, and it will often continue that way for two or three meetings. It pays to scale down bets during these periods.
Race 650	**Windsor** - High numbers were clearly favoured, and the first one home from the middle to low stalls, Achilles Star, went on to score next time at 14/1. In races with 20+ runners here on fast ground, it normally pays to concentrate only on the top ten.
Race 665	**Newmarket July** - Low numbers were at a definite advantage at the Craven meeting, particularly so in this race. Black Silk ran well to finish second from stall 13, and was unfortunate to bump into another outlier, Achilles Star, on his next start.
Race 711	**Ripon** - Ivory's Grab Hire finished second having raced towards the centre, and would probably have won had he raced nearer either flank. It may be harsh to say given Ken Ivory's record with sprinters, but he would be one of the trainer's whose representatives I'd be less inclined to back when they are drawn that awkward six or seven stalls off a favoured rail.
Race 730	**Thirsk** - After rain had fallen persistently during the afternoon, it seemed the one place not to be was the stands' rail, and the first and second home were the only two to race down the centre. In the following handicap, although the winner was drawn high, all the runners kept away from the rails, edging instead towards the centre.
Race 742	**Thirsk** - With the ground well and truly opened up from the previous day, the far rail rode much faster, so Tom Tun ran a cracking race to beat the others up the stands' side by 2 lengths and more. He won next time at 7/2.
Race 872	**Windsor** - The ground was described as good to soft, but the top two, under two 'draw' jockeys, both stayed stands' side and finished first and second. However, the third home, drawn 1, was right there at the finish. Yielding ground seems to be point at which the biases are negated here.
Races 1004-10	**Newcastle** - Low numbers were clearly better off in the sprints, but not in the 1m 3y event. For some reason, the straight mile course rarely seems to mirror the sprint biases.

Race 1225 **Thirsk** - On soft ground, George Duffield was keen to get over to the far rail as quickly as possible and it proved the decisive move of the race, although he did have to endure a stewards' enquiry for chopping Oriel Star off in his rush.

Race 1289 **Windsor** - Given that high numbers had enjoyed a major advantage in the earlier sprints, it was surprising to see Pat Eddery race wide on Turtle's Rising.

Race 1428 **Hamilton** - The ground was given as soft, good to soft patches, but it looked dead and high numbers did not enjoy the same sort of advantage in the sprints as on genuinely soft ground.

Race 1490 **Folkestone** - Jimmy Fortune went straight to the far rail aboard Miss Money Spider and the result was never in doubt. Front-runners that manage to get hard on the far rail here often do well.

Race 1510 **Yarmouth** - The wind had been fresh the previous couple of days, and with the sun drying out already-firm ground, high numbers were well on top.

Race 1663 **Beverley** - Richard Quinn, in his anxiety to get straight over to the far side from stall 2 of 7, caused a bit of crowding among most of the field, allowing the winner a free run up the far rail.

Race 1801 **Windsor** - On soft ground, the stands' rail was not the place to be, but all bar the top four or five stalls raced in a bunch pretty much down the middle.

Race 1849 **Beverley** - On soft ground, only two jockeys in a field of 11 raced hard up the favoured stands' rail, Alan Mackay on the winner Step Ahead and Michael Tebbutt on Late Night Lady (sixth).

Race 1854 **Beverley** - On the same card, Pleasure won the handicap sprint, finishing 2½ lengths ahead of the runner-up on the far rail. The approximate advantage enjoyed by low numbers on this ground would be around 3 lengths.

Race 1992 **Windsor** - On good to firm ground, high numbers predictably enjoyed the edge, the first four coming from stalls 21, 1, 18 and 20. The clear outlier Cold Climate was unsuited by the drop back to five furlongs next time, but continued to run well from moderate draws before finally coming good at Newmarket.

Race 2004 **Thirsk** - On fast ground, high numbers were clearly favoured, so E B Pearl's effort to finish a little over a length off the winner having raced down the centre, under a jockey described as a 'passenger' by *Raceform* Race-reader Walter Glynn, was meritorious. She ran disappointingly next time on the all-weather before going on to win an uncompetitive selling handicap at Redcar off a mark just 1lb higher than that off which she ran at Thirsk.

Race 2105 **Royal Ascot** - Showboat had made it look as though the far rail was favoured in the Hunt Cup, but the finish of the Wokingham was fought out by two horses drawn in the bottom four.

Race 2269 **Newcastle** - Although the official going was given as good, the race times suggested it was nearer firm, and consequently the winner of the handicap sprint coming up the stands' rail was not too big a surprise.

Race 2496 **Salisbury** - On dead ground, Richard Quinn always had the measure of the small group to race on the far rail, on board Ellway Prince, but he gave up some way out as the stands' side were well in front.

Race 2644 **Newmarket July** - High numbers had looked sure to be favoured judging by previous results at the meeting and that was the case, even though the field rather converged towards the centre.

Race 2819 **Folkestone** - Jimmy Fortune staged a repeat performance on Miss Money Spider, heading straight for the far rail from stall 7 of 13 and making it all. It was a touch surprising to see Richard Quinn come stands' side from stall 5.

Race 3063 **Newmarket July** - There were a few meeting staged here over the summer where the one place not to be was the far rail, the majority of winners coming wide down the outside of the field.

Race 3076 **Thirsk** - On very fast ground (this was a course record) Johayro was allowed an uncontested lead up the stands' rail, and horses can be hard to peg back here when that is the case.

Races 3146 & 9 **Windsor** - On good to firm ground, high numbers were well on top in sprints, the top five stalls in a field of 15 filling the first five positions in the former, and the top five filling five of the first six positions in the latter.

Race 3156 **Yarmouth** - Lee Newman went it alone down the centre, while the rest stayed far side, on Mezzoramio and won easily.

Race 3538 **Beverley** - Gay Breeze looked to have a fine chance beforehand, but Alex Greaves seemed content to just race towards the far rail rather than try to ensure getting right on it.

Race 3542 **Hamilton** - Although the runners did not form two definite groups, those racing far side of centre still finished comfortably in front of those nearer the stands' rail.

Race 3665 **Ripon** - A classic example of a race where the best horse did not win because of his draw. Trajan finished over 5 lengths ahead of the rest to come up the stands' side, but Laund View Lady, on the opposite flank, was always in control.

Race 3739 **Kempton** - A group of seven raced on the stands' side in a field of 17 and the first of them home came tenth, almost 14 lengths behind the winner.

Race 3744 **Leicester** - In a field of 20 (one non-runner), the first five home were drawn 18, 16, 20, 17 and 21. Of the low numbers, James Dee, from stall 2, won up the stands' side, about 4 lengths off the winner, and he went on to win on the all-weather next time at 12/1.

Race 4027 **Ripon** - Usually the stands' rail rides faster than the centre, but that was not the case here, with all the principals going straight down the middle.

Race 4068a **Curragh** - Every year the Tattersalls Breeders Stakes, a race that invariably attracts a large field, shows a distinct draw advantage, which depends entirely on which part of the course is in use. When the race is staged on the 'Curragh side' those that race hard against the stands' rail from low stalls are favoured. However, if racing is staged on the far side as was the case in '99, high numbers have a massive advantage. The problem is finding out beforehand, as press coverage over here leaves much to be desired, and the Curragh, in my experience, are not the best at giving out that kind of information before the actual day of the meeting. Halland Park Girl showed herself a very useful juvenile come the end of the season and, in hindsight, 7/1 was a knocking price given her high draw. Ginola's Magic, the 15/8 favourite, never had a hope racing up the stands' rail, particularly as he had played up badly before the start. The first runner home up the stands' rail, Contact, went on to win at a big price next time. This is definitely a race to keep a close eye on in future.

Race 4131 **Epsom** - Paul Bradley gave Tuscan Dawn a masterful ride, never leaving the stands' rail from stall 14 of 14 on a front-runner.

Race 4167 **Hamilton** - Although the ground was riding fast, the far rail was still the place to be and this was one occasion when a plan came together perfectly. David Chapman had presumably asked Kimberley Hart to go straight for the far rail and try to make it all, and bully Another Nightmare (who hates not having an uncontested lead) out of it.

Races 4285-6 **Nottingham** - This was one of only a couple of meetings during the year (see also race 4989) when the stands' rail was clearly riding much faster than the centre, and high numbers dominated both sprints. It always pays to keep an eye on the first sprint of the card here just in case a bias appears on one side.

Race 4325 **Beverley** - The ground looked to have been over-watered, which meant that low numbers held the upper hand. This is not something that can be picked up before racing starts.

Race 4419 **Newbury** - High numbers were favoured, as was the case in another big-field straight race here during '99, the Weatherbys Super Sprint.

Race 4656 **Newmarket July** - The course had already staged a lot of racing and the strip of ground by the far rail seemed less cut up.

CHAPTER 4

BEATING THE BOOKMAKER

It is no more than ten years ago that the larger bookmakers were actually offering 25% and 33% bonuses on top of tricast dividends, but that quickly went out of the window as the layers' knowledge of the draw came more up to speed.

Tricasts and the BOLA report

In early 1996, it was decided by BOLA (the Betting Office Licensees' Association) that the need was there to change the formula for calculating tricast, and later forecast, dividends to eradicate the effect of the draw. A press release dated February 1, 1996, stated:

'A new horserace tricast designed to eliminate problems associated with the stalls draw in certain races is to be introduced from February 5 (1996). The new formula, which is the result of extensive research, will produce returns which are increased, reduced or remain unaltered according to the stalls position of the placed horses.........

Overall, there will be lower returns when placed horses are drawn together, but higher returns in the majority of cases. The new formula will more accurately reflect the true chances of any combination of runners in a race.........

In these races, the stall position (draw) of the runners may impact the result favouring one side of the course or the other. This may be aggravated by other factors such as the state of the going, watering methods and a horse following the pace of a race.'

This 33-page report showed, in-depth, the new formula for calculating tricast dividends and effectively ended my favoured method of punting, to perm four, five or six horses in a combination tricast in likely draw-affected races.

Basically, reductions are now made when the first three come home from the same third in the draw (ie, in an 18-runner race, the first three all come from stalls 1-6 or all from stalls 13-18 (it was decided the middle segment of runners could not be favoured by the draw)). Here are a few examples of how the new formula affects tricast dividends in an 18-runner straight course handicap (it applies at every course, even those recognised as having no notable draw bias):-

Stalls of placed runners	Starting price	Old Dividend	New Dividend	% +/-
1-2-3	12/1 25/1 6/1	£1,791.31	£1,142.38	-36.23%
2-4-6	25/1 50/1 20/1	£20,212.10	£9,621.56	-52.4%
2-8-17	25/1 10/1 7/1	£1,767.76	£1,811.74	+2.49%
1-14-18	12/1 14/1 20/1	£2,998.57	£3,073.17	+2.49%

Essentially, the bigger the prices of the placed runners in races where the draw played a part, the greater the deduction from tricast returns. The reductions go well over 50%, a figure not compensated for by the increases on the occasions when the first three horses home are drawn apart from each other, normally only 1% or 2%.

Although the report shows that, in an 11-runner handicap, where there are 165 different possible three-horse combinations, 38 tricasts would remain the same, 119 would show an increase and only 8 would result in a decrease, the increases are minimal while the reductions potentially huge. Consequently, tricasts are no longer a viable punting method for draw followers.

Computer straight forecast

At about the same time as BOLA brought in the new formula for calculating tricast dividends, they brought in a separate formula to calculate 'fairer' computer straight forecasts (CSF's).

This formula is equally as complicated as the one employed for working out tricast returns and now incorporates such factors as the bookmakers' betting margins and the number of what are described as 'rags'.

'Rags' are deemed to be any runners a long way off the price of the favourite in a race, the likes of 50/1 shots in a race where the favourite may be 6/4. Effectively, the bigger the gap between the price of the favourite and that of the outsider(s) in a race, the lower the CSF seems to become in comparison to what it would have been before the new calculating formula came into existence.

It used to be considered that a decent rough guide to working out what the CSF was likely to return was to add a point onto the starting price of the runner-up, then to multiply that figure by the SP of the winner, and knock off the point again, similar to the formula used for working out returns on doubles. For example, if the winner was returned 4/1 and the runner-up 5/1, the CSF would be somewhere in the region of £23.00 (4 x 6 (5+1) - 1) = 23. This approach was shown to be fairly accurate in returns from several pre-1996 races:-

1995 Talented Ting (11/2) beat Sarmatian (10/1) in a field of 12 at Hamilton where the favourite was returned at 2/1. The straight forecast paid £60.69.

It should have been approximately 5½ (11/2) x 11 (10/1 + 1) = £60.50 - 1 = £59.50, so the dividend was good.

1995 Pallium (7/2 Fav) beat Arc Lamp (5/1) in a field of 10 at Ripon. The straight forecast paid £19.73.

It should have been approximately 3½ x 6 - 1 = £20.00, so the return was good.

1995 Sharp Prospect (8/1) beat Set Table (9/1) in a field of 23 at Doncaster. The straight forecast paid £73.45.

It should have been approximately 8 x 10 - 1 = £79.00, so the dividend was fair.

In,

1999 Don Puccini (10/1) beat Halland Park Girl (6/1) in a field of 25 at Newbury where the favourite returned at 9/2. The straight forecast paid £58.15

It should have been approximately 10 x 7 - 1 = £69.00, so the return was poor.

1999 Westcourt Magic (4/1 Fav) beat Sotonian (20/1) in a field of 11 at Chester, where third-placed Caution would have made the first two but for being drawn in stall 10. The straight forecast paid £84.36.

It should have paid approximately 4 x 21 - 1 = £83.00, so the dividend was good.

1999 Kalar (8/1) beat Tancred Times (8/1) in a field of 23 at Ripon, where the favourite returned at 7/1 and the draw was a major factor. The straight forecast paid £64.53.

It should have been approximately 8 x 9 - 1 = £71.00, so the dividend was fair.

Interestingly, the CSF's in the last two example races above show that forecasts are not affected by draw biases (also the case in 1999's other draw-bias races). Therefore, the straight forecast is a bet that remains of interest.

When Don Puccini beat Halland Park Girl at Newbury, the draw did not play a major part in the outcome of the race, but since the spread in price between the favourite (9/2) and the outsiders (100/1 x 3) was so great, the dividend was lower than it would have been using the old method of calculation.

Conversely, at Ripon, the range was not so great, with Petite Danseuse returning 7/1 favourite, and the outsiders (x2) only 50/1 shots. This lower gap between the favourite's and outsiders' starting prices is particularly common in sprint handicaps, given their often competitive nature, so the CSF's within them will normally stand up, even when there is a draw advantage.

When Westcourt Magic beat Sotonian on bad ground at Chester, third-placed Caution looked as though he could have gone close to winning had he not been drawn so badly. So, even in a race where the draw played a part, the CSF return was very healthy given the competitive nature of the race.

Westcourt Magic won on very soft ground at Chester

Tote trio - later trifecta

When I wrote *The Effects of the Draw*, the Tote were operating the trio bet in competition to the tricast, but the trio was replaced last year by the new trifecta.

I must confess to not often betting the old trio, as the pools rarely reached a high enough level to justify playing. Also, the pools that were carried forward from the previous day almost always went on to a race unlikely to show a draw bias.

So far, the new trifecta, which is identical to a tricast in that it involves six bets to cover the six possible permutations - A-B-C, A-C-B, B-A-C, B-C-A, C-A-B and C-B-A - doesn't seem to be attracting a fantastic level of interest. The Tote started by only offering the bet on one race each day, invariably the showcase race, but have now extended it to cover every race. This is not a bet I advise taking an interest in unless the pools begin to regularly reach a more worthwhile level.

Tote exacta

Not long after the Tote switched from the trio to the trifecta, they also switched from the long-established dual forecast to the new exacta.

The beauty of the old dual forecast was that it offered an alternative to the straight forecast, and often paid the better of the two (remembering it only had to exceed half the CSF figure as it covered first and second in either order), but the exacta is identical to the computer straight forecast. The early indications are that it is paying fairly well.

As with all pool bets, the problem for the draw follower is that the more punters who start to focus on horses' draws, the lower the dividends will become. It is too early to say whether this is a bet worth playing, and until it has been possible to look at a few dividends from draw-affected races, it is perhaps best to hold fire.

Win singles

Any bookmaker will tell you the bet he least likes taking is the win single. The percentages on his side are poor (returning around the 80% mark of stakes invested), so it is a bet never pushed by the marketing boys. Think about it, how often do you see the 10% or 20% bonuses offered on Yankees, Round Robins and Lucky 15s offered on win singles?

Win singles are now my only way of betting on horseracing following the down-scaling of the old tricast dividends. Basically, everything taking place at the moment on-course is encouraging the punter to follow the win single route.

Since the pitch auctions took place in '99, it has not been uncommon to see books verging on being under-round on-course, thanks to the increased competition, and easily the best way in which to bet now is tax-free, at the track.

Clearly, not everyone is in a position to be able to go on-course and bet tax-free every day, but the upsurge in the number of internet bookmakers offering tax-free bets from far-flung locations means it is now possible for anyone who is on-line to bet without the crippling 9% reduction.

Interestingly, the on-line bookmaker that I used during 1999 seemed to stop offering early prices on as many sprint handicaps as the season wore on, so it remains to be seen what will be available on this front during 2000.

For those without internet access, it is now possible to bet by account with only a 3% reduction through Victor Chandler in Gibraltar, and more will doubtless follow. Things have never been so good for the punter (with the exception of the tricast!) and the possibility of making a long-term profit, for those prepared to specialise in one area and bet only win singles has never been so good.

Implementing a bank system

I recommend implementing a bank system and keeping exact records throughout the season (which helps maintain discipline). Start with a bank of £1,000, £500, £100, whatever you like, whatever amount you are prepared to plough in for the season.

Then rate your selections either on a scale of 1-5 (5 being a banker bet), or on a scale of 1-20 (the scale I now use for *SprintLine* recommendations - see Chapter 5).

Using a £1,000 bank as an example, if you decide to employ the 1-5 scale, make a one-point selection £25, a two-point selection £50, and so on up to a five-point selection being

£125. When the bank doubles to £2,000, double your stakes, so a one-point selection becomes £50, etc. Double your stakes again when you reach £4,000, or halve them if your bank goes back to below £1,000.

If ranking selections on a scale of 1-20, make a one-point selection £5, up to a 20-point selection at £100. If you decide to join the *SprintLine* service (details on page 111), you will be working on the 1-20 scale, so if you decide your bank at the start of the year is to be £200, a one-point selection would be £2, up to a 20-point selection being £40. Last year, it would have been possible to have started with a bank as low as that, and comfortably cover the amount required to join *SprintLine*, and more.

Making a selection

It is imperative to watch as much racing as possible and to have access to either a daily or weekly results section. I used to find the best way in which to calculate selections (before being able to watch every race live) was to cross out all races which do not show any sign of a draw bias in the weekly results section of *Raceform Update*, and then to start sifting through looking for outliers. Write down the selections on a 'rolling list' and award them a rating either on a scale 1-5, or 1-20, whichever way you decide to go. It is unlikely that this list will ever contain more than about ten selections, and each selection will normally be scratched after being backed once.

Watch for

* *Any horse that wins his side or runs exceptionally well when the field splits into more than one group*
* *Any horse that runs well when racing alone*
* *Any horse that runs unexpectedly poorly from a good draw. These are invariably worth opposing next time*

Beware of

* *Any horse that seems to run well on the unfavoured side on more than one occasion during a season*
* *Any horse switching from turf to all-weather or vice versa*

When to scratch selections

If a selection goes on to win next time, it should then almost always come off the list, but what to do if he does not have everything in his favour next time is down to the individual. If he does not have the ground in his favour for his next run, or he has gone up 4lb or more in the weights, he will become a no-bet, so a decision then has to be made as to whether or not to keep him on the list.

If a selection does not have his ideal conditions for his next run, you should still be looking for him to run well in order to show that he remains in the sort of form that led to him being picked in the first place. If he runs a poor race without having an obvious excuse, delete him.

The 'rogues gallery'

This was a topic I touched on in *The Effects of the Draw*, and one that has increased in my thinking since that time. Time and again, a horse will seem to have run well from the worst of the draw on more than one occasion, but then not go on to perform when conditions are in his favour next time. Every year, two or three examples of this enigma become apparent. Certainly, two stick in my mind from the '97 season, both juveniles, Happy Days and Quiz Master, and in '99, My Man Friday was a classic example.

My Man Friday first came to my attention when finishing seventh in a field of 24 at Windsor in May, finishing easily first of the low numbers on a day when those drawn high enjoyed a definite edge. Next time he was again drawn out of it at Lingfield in stall 2 on the one day of the season that high numbers were noticeably on top. Again, he ran a cracker to finish seventh, despite taking a bump not long after the start.

So on to Windsor after a fair break, when he again didn't have a draw but ran all right, despite finishing only tenth of 18. Next up at Nottingham, he turned out to not have a draw in stall 18, when second on his side to Young Rosein, a filly I had had my eye on after she had run well from a desperate draw at Ripon. That was the fifth time in five outings he had had the worst of the draw, and all it had served to do was stop him making the frame, so keeping his handicap mark down.

Next time, he had no chance at the weights in a Newmarket claimer (receiving just 4lb, instead of the 23lb he would have in a handicap, from favourite Compensation). Yet again he ran a cracker to finish third, beaten less than a length. Finally, it was all systems go at Epsom in early September. Back in a handicap and off the same mark as at Newmarket, he was in a race in which the draw was unlikely to have much of an effect. I managed to get on at 8/1 in the morning. After an on-course plunge, he started the 4/1 second-favourite and could not have been beaten if repeating his Newmarket form. So what happened? Well, not to put too fine a point on it, he dogged it.

Some put it down to him not handling the bend, others even thought he had run a promising race! But the facts were, in his first seven races of the season, My Man Friday had run well six times out of six from a poor draw (raced pretty much alone at Newmarket) but then, when he had an outstanding chance, he ran badly. This is something I've seen so many times in the past.

I know for a fact that shrewd sprint handicapper trainer David Chapman feels that some horses just will not put it in when they're racing in a crowd, and these are the type we have to be aware of. In *The Effects of the Draw*, I wrote:

> *'On more than one occasion in the recent past, David Chapman-trained sprinters drawn low have switched over to race on the far rail (at Thirsk) when most thought that the stands' rail would be much quicker. His representatives are always worth noting under such conditions.'*

Less than a month later his Young Bigwig, drawn seemingly unfavourably in stall 1 of 15 at Thirsk, won at 25/1. This was not down to him racing on the best ground, being well handicapped or anything else, it was largely down to the fact that he was able to race away from the main bunch, and consequently gave it full effort. There are plenty of these characters around in the world of sprint handicapping. Mr Chapman said as much when I spoke to him, commenting: "If I've got two or three like that in my stable, then I can't believe nobody else has too."

These rogues just will not put it all in if they are crowded, racing on the left-outside, or right-outside of a field, or anything else they don't like - it's down to the individual's quirk. Horses like Young Bigwig, Red Charger and Wishbone Alley are three that spring immediately to mind from 1999.

The problem here is that there are not too many trainers around who would readily admit that one of their horses has a questionable attitude, or perhaps they might call it a 'slight kink'. It's simply a case of getting to know the horses and their thoughts on the game, which is why specialising on sprinting and watching as many races as possible is so important.

As a rule of thumb, for the purposes of keeping these dodge-pots off your list, it will usually pay not to continue following a horse once it runs well from a poor draw for a second time.

Course specialists

This has never been a method of punting that's held much appeal to me but, while going back through the five-furlong results for the past couple of years, it became clear that Beverley is one track that has to be considered a specialists' course, particularly for sprinters.

Time and again, runners that cropped up as outliers at Beverley returned to show the run was no fluke, often irrespective of what they had achieved in the interim. A couple of Beverley specialists could be back there in 2000:

Muja's Magic is one I will be keeping a very close eye on. She used to be considered something of a Brighton specialist, but her two efforts at Beverley suggest that the next time she returns, she will be something to bet on if in any sort of form (and with any sort of draw!). She caught my eye in the race won by Bollin Ann (1999, Race 2771), finishing only 3+ lengths behind the winner from an impossible draw, and receiving the comment in-running: "raced wide, headway halfway, kept on under pressure final furlong, nearest finish." Unfortunately, next time, she ran in a claimer, so couldn't take advantage of what was a fair handicap mark and thus became unbackable using the criteria laid out on page 64. However, six weeks after her first run at Beverley, Muja's Magic returned to the Yorkshire course off the same mark of 43. Despite being out of the handicap, Chris Catlin's 7lb claim countered that problem, and she fairly bolted up at 33/1.

American Cousin's performances at Beverley speak for themselves. In three runs, he has twice finished a close second, despite having absolutely impossible draws. He remains lowly enough rated to contest races at the course in 2000 and should be watched if returning.

Where to back selections

Once a selection has been made and you have decided how much to invest, after checking that he meets all the requirements (and possibly scaling down the stake if he doesn't quite meet them all) all that is left, other than to actually race, is where and how to back him.

As has already been stipulated, the only way to back a selection is in a win single. Then it is just a case of whether to take starting price tax-free if the internet route is a possibility, or to take the best early price.

A majority of draw-based selections come from and go on to run next time in sprint handicaps, races that off-course bookmakers tend to price up in the mornings. Shopping around for the best morning prices is, more often than not, the best way to go, even accounting for tax deductions, as most of the value tends to be found early. So try to make sure you have access to as many of the bigger bookmakers as you can.

The bigger firms have to be seen to be competitive in the *Racing Post's Pricewise*, *Raceform On Saturday's Steamers* and other such columns, normally betting to around 135% in the larger-field races, which suits our purposes as it would not be unusual to see a big-field sprint handicap's over-round ending up at 150%+.

So many times in the past, races that opened out as 6/1 or 8/1 the field in the morning ended up with a favourite at 7/2 and a second-favourite at 6/1, as bookmakers' on-course reps moved in to shorten up the front two or three in televised events. This is particularly the case in sprint handicaps, where the public are that much more likely to latch onto the regulars. Remember Double Blue? And in '99 Mousehole, Goretski and others?

The Tote

Tote Credit account holders have the option of either taking an early price, starting price, or Tote price, and the latter is often a viable option in sprint handicaps. Telephone operators are able to tell you the latest Tote dividend over the phone right up to the off-time.

I tend to take the Tote price fairly frequently throughout a season, as long as the selection is running at a course where the pool is strong, ie, not Folkestone on a Monday. If your choice is outside the first three or four in the market, trained by an unfashionable trainer and/or ridden by an unfashionable jockey, always check out the Tote dividend if deciding to place your bet near off-time.

1999 Racecourse conclusions

The effect of the draw has changed at several courses in the past couple of years, some as a result of new watering systems, others like Goodwood as a result of the ground on one side being broken up, with the course management feeling it had become too much of an advantage to race there. My idea of the top ten courses under optimum conditions in 1997 was:-

1) Sandown (soft)
2) Ripon

3) Yarmouth (firm)
4) Newbury (soft)
5) Thirsk (firm)
6) Beverley (fast)
7) Musselburgh
8) Lingfield (firm)
9) Goodwood
10) Catterick

My idea of the top ten courses under optimum conditions now is:-

1) Beverley
2) Hamilton (soft)
3) Ripon
4) Sandown (soft)
5) Folkestone
6) Kempton (soft)
7) Thirsk (firm)
8) Windsor
9) Newcastle
10) Catterick

Of those that have disappeared from the '97 list, Musselburgh still plays a part in my punting calendar, but Yarmouth, Musselburgh, Newbury, Lingfield and Goodwood are, to use a racing cliché, best watched at present.

Ascot - The advantage favouring low numbers in straight races has become less pronounced since 1997.
Watch for (straight races only) **(before racing)** the far rail being moved to unveil a strip of fresh ground, which can favour high numbers, **(during racing)** any side being favoured in big-field races at festival meetings, **(after racing)** outliers in big-fields handicaps.

Ayr - No interest apart from at the Western meeting.
Watch for (before) low numbers in the Silver and Gold Cups if the going is soft, **(after)** outliers from those two races.

Bath - No interest.

Beverley - High numbers were completely dominant in five-furlong races when the ground was good or faster, and also held the edge over 7f 100y and 1m 100y under those conditions. However, when the ground was soft, the bias switched completely.
Watch for (before) only those runners drawn in the top six stalls in sprints run on fast ground, and only those in the bottom four or five on soft ground, **(during)** flip starts when the ground is very soft, **(after)** outliers, more so here than anywhere else.

Brighton - No real interest.
Watch for (during) runners racing towards the stands' side when the ground is soft.

Carlisle - No interest.
Watch for (before) low numbers when the ground is soft, which is rare.

Catterick - High numbers were again favoured when the ground was soft, and low numbers did best when it was fast.
Watch for (during) in round-course races, runners that race towards the outside of the field turning in and then up the stands' side in the straight, **(after)** outliers over five furlongs.

Chepstow - No interest.

Chester - Low numbers were again best off, apart from when a few races had been run on soft ground at a meeting.
Watch for (before) only the bottom half-dozen stalls on all ground, but particularly on soft in early-in-the-meeting races at distances up to 7f 122y, **(after)** any outliers.

Doncaster - Rarely of any interest.
Watch for (before) the bottom half-dozen stalls in the Spring Mile and Lincoln when the ground is genuinely soft, **(after)** outliers when one side has been favoured.

Epsom - High numbers were again best avoided in big fields over six and seven furlongs.
Watch for (during) runners switching towards the stands' side on soft ground, **(after)** outliers on the rare occasions that one side has been favoured over five furlongs.

Folkestone - High numbers held the upper hand in straight-course races where the fields split in two, apart from when the ground rode heavy.
Watch for (before) the top half-dozen stalls in straight races with 12+ runners, **(after)** outliers in races where the field split.

Goodwood - The breaking up of the ground by the far rail in the home straight seemed to balance out the draw bias, and low numbers became favoured in the Stewards' Cup. In other sprints, the draw had little effect, but over seven furlongs high numbers continued to enjoy the edge.
Watch for (after) outliers in sprints when one side has been favoured.

Hamilton - High numbers enjoyed a huge advantage on soft ground at distances of up to 1m 65y.
Watch for (after) the winner of the group up the stands' side when the field split in two.

Haydock - Unlike a few years ago, high numbers no longer seemed favoured in soft-ground sprints during '99.

Watch for (during) runners tacking over to the stands' side in round-course races on soft ground, **(after)** outliers on the rare occasions that one side was clearly favoured.

Kempton - Throughout '97 and '98, the draw seemed to have less of an effect in big-field sprints, but on soft ground the advantage was clearly back last year.
Watch for (before) only the top six or seven stalls in soft-ground, big-field sprints, **(after)** the winner up the stands' side in such events.

Leicester - Those that raced down the centre strip held a clear edge over those who raced stands' side in the first part of '99, less so in the second half.
Watch for (before) the top half in the draw in big-field straight races, **(after)** outliers when one side has been favoured.

Lingfield all-weather - The draw generally offered little advantage, apart from certain stalls not performing particularly well (see Chapter 1).

Lingfield turf - The draw rarely had any effect during '99, but high numbers should still enjoy a definite edge after recent rainfall onto fast ground.
Watch for (before) only the top three or four stalls on recently rained-on fast ground, **(after)** outliers when one side has been favoured.

Musselburgh - The draw did not play as much of a part as in previous years, but low numbers will continue to perform best in sprints on soft ground.
Watch for (before) the bottom four or five stalls in soft-ground sprints, **(after)** the winner up the far side when the field split into two groups in such races.

Newbury - The bias was not as great in favour of high numbers as in previous years, but should continue to be there on soft ground.
Watch for (during) high numbers at all distances on soft ground once the course has staged a few races, **(after)** outliers in those races.

Newcastle - The bias swung further in favour of low numbers in straight races. Whereas it used to be high on good or faster, low on good to soft or slower, it is now low unless the ground is riding genuinely fast.
Watch for (after) outliers in straight-course races.

Newmarket July - The bias remained hard to predict from meeting to meeting, but there were times when one rail was clearly favoured.
Watch for (during) one rail clearly holding the upper hand at a meeting, **(after)** outliers.

Newmarket Rowley Mile - No racing was staged at the course during 1999, so it remains to be seen if the draw biases have changed.

Nottingham - Low numbers were favoured in big-field races over 1m 54y.
Watch for (before) which side the pace seems to be in sprints, as this has more of a bearing nowadays than any draw bias.

Pontefract - The draw made little difference in '99.
Watch for (before) the top half-dozen stalls on soft ground.

Redcar - Rarely of any interest.
Watch for (after) outliers when one side has been favoured in straight races.

Ripon - High numbers clearly had the edge in big-field sprints when groups formed on both rails.
Watch for (before) the top half-dozen stalls in sprints with 12+ runners, **(after)** outliers.

Salisbury - The draw remained unpredictable and, although often comfortably favouring one side over the other in races on soft ground, it switched too often to be bullish about any advantage.
Watch for (after) outliers when one side was clearly favoured.

Sandown - High numbers generally did best over five furlongs on ground with some cut, but jockeys seem more alert now to this particular bias and are more inclined to switch across from lower stalls.
Watch for (before) the top five in the draw in soft-ground five-furlong events, **(after)** any horse that ran well down the centre in such races.

Southwell all-weather - Low numbers again did best both over six furlongs and 1m 3f.

Thirsk - High numbers continued to enjoy a definite advantage on genuinely firm ground in sprints.
Watch for whether the change in watering system brings about a shift in bias, **(after)** any outliers.

Warwick - The draw played little part in '99, but those that raced wide from high draws still seemed better off on soft ground.
Watch for (before) jockeys who realise the importance of the draw in soft-ground races.

Windsor - The draw became more important in sprints during '99, high numbers being clearly favoured on good or faster ground, low doing best when there was some cut in the turf.
Watch for (before) only those in the top half of the draw in fast-ground sprints, only those in the bottom half of the draw in softer-ground sprints, **(after)** outliers.

Wolverhampton all-weather - At the meetings where power-harrowing had taken place, low numbers did best as it noticeably shallowed the surface on the inside rail. At meetings where power-harrowing had not taken place, middle to high again fared best.
Watch for (before) whether power-harrowing has taken place.

Yarmouth - The draw became less of a factor in '99, but high numbers should continue to hold the upper hand in big-field straight races when the ground is firm.
Watch for (before) runners drawn very high if the ground is firm and the wind has been coming in from an easterly (off the sea) direction, **(after)** outliers in those races.

York - Rarely of any interest.
Watch for (before) heavy rain on watered ground, as this seems to favour horses that race hard on the inside rail, **(after)** outliers in sprints when one side has been favoured.

Changes in watering systems

Yarmouth switched from using a pop-up sprinkler watering system to a 'Briggs boom' prior to the 1999 season, and the draw bias, previously favouring runners drawn high in fast-ground straight races, all but disappeared. So, clearly changes in watering systems are something we need to keep on top of.

Like Yarmouth, Newbury dispensed with the old pop-up system in favour of the Briggs boom, and the advantage favouring high numbers in fast-ground sprints disappeared quicker than a 25% bonus on a correct tricast, although there's not a lot they can do about biases on soft ground.

As far as I know, Thirsk is the only course changing to a new system for 2000, and they will now be employing a Boom-operated Briggs Irrigator. Thirsk chairman Edward York said: "Not only will this be a more efficient way of watering the track, it should also eliminate the effect of the wind, so that all parts of the course will be watered equally."

Jockeys to follow

In my view, Jimmy Fortune and Ray Cochrane are the two top jockeys in terms of draw knowledge, with a group of seven, Kieren Fallon, Richard Quinn, Michael Roberts, Dean McKeown, Carl Lowther, Gary Hind and Dale Gibson not far behind.

I have followed Fortune closely since his apprentice days back in the late 80s, and he clearly benefited from his spell with the Ramsden stable (likewise Fallon). His riding of Bollin Ann at Beverley in July was masterful; he dropped her right in onto the rail and never left it, making a decisive challenge hard on the fence entering the final furlong.

Cochrane always seems one step ahead of the others when it comes to exploiting a new bias, his riding at the Folkestone meeting on April 20 being a perfect example. That day, Cochrane was prepared to go against the flow, racing towards the far rail (see race 765 - pages 70 and 71).

Of course, there are going to be times when racing away from the pack will not prove advantageous, and Cochrane came unstuck when unsuccessfully taking favourite Keld to race alone on the far side at Lingfield last year. I had my doubts afterwards about whether he'd be prepared to risk a similar manoeuvre again given the amount of flak he got for it but, full credit to the guy, he is still ready to pit his wits against his colleagues. It's a shame there aren't more around prepared to have a go.

There were six other jockeys who successfully went against the crowd last year; Gary Bardwell, Richard Quinn, Ollie Pears, Gary Hind, Dane O'Neill and Neil Pollard, the first two at Brighton, Pears at Catterick, Hind at Salisbury, and O'Neill and Pollard both at Windsor.

Brighton, October 29, good to soft, soft patches:-

5128 'GO RACING FREE WITH THE EVENING ARGUS' H'CAP (0-65) (3-Y.O+) (Class F)
5-10 (5-11) **5f 213y** £2,934.00 (£824.00: £402.00) Stalls: Low GOING: 0.07 sec per fur (G)

Form	Horse / details	Dist	Pos	SP	RR	SF
4276^{11}	**Swynford Welcome** ^{48} **(44)** (JPearce) **3-8-6** GBardwell(1) (lw: mde virtually all: styd far side st: rdn over 2f out: r.o wl)	—	**1**	33/1	51	30
4878^{7}	**Bataleur** ^{15} **(46)** (GWoodward) **6-8-9** RLappin(13) (b.nr hind: lw: a.p: rdn 3f out: edgd lft over 1f out: chsd wnr ins fnl f: unable qckn)	5	**2**	10/1	40	20
4986^{11}	**Skyers Flyer (IRE)** ^{9} **(47)** (RonaldThompson) **5-8-10** JLowe(5) (bhd whn rdn 3f out: hdwy over 1f out: r.o wl ins fnl f)	1	**3**	16/1	38	18
4878^{3}	**Marengo** ^{15} **(53)** (MJPolglase) **5-9-2** SSanders(14) (dwlt: bhd whn nt clr run over 3f out tl over 2f out: hdwy & hung lft over 1f out: r.o ins fnl f)	nk	**4**	6/1 ^{2}	43	23
4787^{2}	**Diamond Geezer (IRE)** ^{21} **(65)** (RHannon) **3-9-8**(5) PFitzsimons(12) (a.p: rdn over 2f out: hung lft over 1f out: one pce)	hd	**5**	6/1 ^{2}	55	34
4947^{5}	**Golden Pound (USA)** ^{10} **(51)** (MissGayKelleway) **7-9-0b** SWhitworth(17) (b.hind: no hdwy fnl 2f)	1¼	**6**	12/1	38	18
4924^{7}	**Myttons Mistake** ^{13} **(51)** (RJBaker) **6-9-0** TSprake(10) (lost pl 4f out: bhd whn hmpd 3f out: rallied over 1f out: r.o ins fnl f)	nk	**7**	9/1 ^{3}	37	17
5032^{16}	**Whatta Madam** ^{7} **(59)** (GLMoore) **3-9-4b**(3) NCallan(2) (a.p: rdn over 2f out: wknd ins fnl f)	1	**8**	14/1	42	21
4947^{4}	**Derryquin** ^{10} **(57)** (PLGilligan) **4-9-3**(3) APolli(15) (hung lft 1f out: nvr nrr)	1	**9**	12/1	37	17
4092^{9}	**Rambold** ^{57} **(40)** (NEBerry) **8-7-12**(5) RBrisland(3) (spd 4f)	nk	**10**	25/1	20	—
4431^{17}	**Oriel Girl** ^{39} **(53)** (NACallaghan) **4-9-2** AClark(6) (a.p: rdn over 2f out: carried lft over 1f out: wknd fnl f)	hd	**11**	12/1	32	12
4723^{6}	**Tong Road** ^{24} **(44)** (BRCambidge) **3-8-6** PMcCabe(16) (s.s: nvr nrr)	1	**12**	33/1	21	—
4947^{16}	**Facile Tigre** ^{10} **(51)** (SDow) **4-8-11**(3) PDoe(7) (hdwy over 2f out: wknd over 1f out)	hd	**13**	2/1 ^{1}	27	7
4824^{9}	**Level Headed** ^{18} **(41)** (EAWheeler) **4-7-13**(5)ow1 SCarson(18) (bhd fnl 3f)	2½	**14**	16/1	11	—
4656^{19}	**Key** ^{29} **(61)** (CEBrittain) **3-9-2**(7) NEsler(8) (bhd fnl 2f)	2	**15**	14/1	25	4
462^{11}	**Chi-Lin** ^{221} **(44)** (PButler) **4-8-7** RMullen(9) (prom 2f)	6	**16**	33/1	—	—
3687^{3}	**Johnny Staccato** ^{73} **(42)** (MQuinn) **5-8-5** MartinDwyer(11) (a bhd)	hd	**17**	14/1	—	—
4835^{12}	**Ok Babe** ^{17} **(44)** (GPEnright) **4-8-7v^{1}** OUrbina(4) (prom 3f)	2	**18**	33/1	—	—
				(SP 151.4%)	**18 Rn**	

1m 11.7 (4.50) CSF £355.19 CT £5,150.36 TOTE £35.40: £7.60 £3.30 £3.50 £2.20 (£270.50) Trifecta Not won; £387.06 to Newmarket 30/10/1999 OWNER Qualitair Holdings Ltd (NEWMARKET) BRED Qualitair Stud Ltd
WEIGHT FOR AGE 3yo-1lb
Swynford Welcome caused a real upset, for she has shown absolutely nothing for a very long time and full credit must go to Bardwell who enterprisingly stuck to the far side in the straight. (33/1)

In Bardwell's case, it was the first time I'd noticed him doing something out of the ordinary - he raced on the inside in the straight at Brighton when the stands' side should have been faster. I've always had him down as more of a head-down, full steam ahead jockey than one likely to try something new, so I'll be waiting to see if he repeats the dose this season before listing him as a draw jockey.

Ollie Pears wasn't backward in coming forward about showing his delight after racing away from the rest and winning up the stands' side on Cartmel Park, and he will be an interesting one to keep an eye on this year, as he's always looked a decent pilot in sprints anyway.

Catterick, October 16, good, good to firm patches:-

4911 EMERALD ISLE H'CAP (0-80) (3-Y.O+) (Class D)
3-45 (3-46) **5f** £5,312.50 (£1,600.00: £775.00: £362.50) Stalls: Low GOING: 0.02 sec per fur (G)

Form	Horse / details	Dist	Pos	SP	RR	SF
4636^{8}	**Cartmel Park** ^{17} **(73)** (JBerry) **3-9-7** OPears(15) (racd alone stands' side: overall ldr ½-wy: styd on strly fnl f)	—	**1**	14/1	79?	66
4636^{10}	**Goretski (IRE)** ^{17} **(75)** (NTinkler) **6-9-9** CLowther(6) (hld up: shkn up & hdwy 2f out: kpt on: no ch w wnr)	2½	**2**	12/1	73	60

Horse	Dist	Pos	SP	RR	SF
4555[20] **Miss Fit (IRE)** 21 **(76)** (MrsGSRees) **3-9-3**(7) AngelaHartley(10) (prom: styd on fnl f: no imp)	s.h	**3**	40/1	74	61
4755[13] **William's Well** 10 **(66)** (MWEasterby) **5-9-0b** TLucas(8) (outpcd tl styd on fnl f: nrst fin)	hd	**4**	8/1 [3]	64	51
4755[4] **Gay Breeze** 10 **(80)** (DNicholls) **6-9-9**(5) DMernagh(1) (lw: cl up centre: ev ch ½-wy: rdn & nt qckn fnl f)	1	**5**	7/2 [1]	74	61
4795[16] **Mousehole** 7 **(78)** (RGuest) **7-9-12** TSprake(11) (s.i.s: outpcd tl styd on over 1f out: nrst fin)	1¼	**6**	11/1	68	55
4713[9] **Forgotten Times (USA)** 12 **(66)** (KTIvory) **5-9-0v** SSanders(5) (b: in tch: effrt ½-wy: no imp fnl f)	nk	**7**	9/1	55	42
4795[14] **Diamond Decorum (IRE)** 7 **(76)** (PDEvans) **3-9-10** RLappin(14) (bhd tl styd on wl fnl f: nrst fin)	1¼	**8**	25/1	61	48
4427* **Blessingindisguise** 27 **(77)** (MWEasterby) **6-9-11b** GParkin(12) (led centre tl ½-wy: outpcd over 1f out)	s.h	**9**	5/1 [2]	62	49
4755[22] **Pierpoint (IRE)** 10 **(71)** (DNicholls) **4-9-5** AlexGreaves(2) (bhd: hdwy over 1f out: nvr nrr)	nk	**10**	16/1	55	42
4390[20] **Nifty Norman** 28 **(65)** (DNicholls) **5-8-13** OUrbina(4) (s.i.s: effrt ½-wy: btn fnl f)	1½	**11**	12/1	44	31
4755[11] **Pleasure Time** 10 **(75)** (CSmith) **6-9-9v** MFenton(13) (w centre ldrs tl wknd over 1f out)	1	**12**	14/1	51	38
4487[2] **Sotonian (HOL)** 24 **(66)** (PSFelgate) **6-9-0** JWeaver(9) (chsd ldrs: shkn up & outpcd 2f out: b.b.v)	1	**13**	10/1	39	26
4805[4] **Angel Hill** 7 **(73)** (RAFahey) **4-9-7b** RWinston(7) (hmpd s: a bhd)	nk	**14**	10/1	45	32
4755[18] **Westcourt Magic** 10 **(78)** (MWEasterby) **6-9-12** JCarroll(3) (chsd ldrs tl rdn & wknd 2f out: eased)	½	**15**	14/1	49	36
			(SP 134.1%)		**15 Rn**

59.8 secs (2.30) CSF £173.14 CT £6,045.83 TOTE £21.50: £4.40 £11.00 £12.50 (£233.00) Trifecta Not won; £287.39 to 18/10/1999 OWNER P G Airey & R R Whitton (COCKERHAM) BRED P. G. Airey and R. R. Whitton

Brighton, October 4, good to soft:-

4713 'SURF 107' H'CAP (0-70) (3-Y.O+) (Class E)
5-05 (5-09) **5f 59y** £2,892.00 (£876.00: £428.00: £204.00) Stalls: Low GOING: 0.08 sec per fur (G)

Horse	Dist	Pos	SP	RR	SF
4431[9] **Double-O** 14 **(64)** (WJarvis) **5-9-8b** TQuinn(10) (lw: c stands' side st: hdwy over 1f out: led ins fnl f: r.o wl)	—	**1**	14/1	68?	57
4493[11] **Facile Tigre** 12 **(51)** (SDow) **4-8-6**(3) PDoe(6) (hdwy over 2f out: hrd rdn fnl f: r.o one pce)	4	**2**	6/1 [3]	43	32
3910[14] **Whatta Madam** 40 **(60)** (GLMoore) **3-9-4** JFEgan(1) (lw: a.p: led 4f out: rdn over 1f out: hdd ins fnl f: one pce)	s.h	**3**	20/1	52	41
1232[7] **Strat's Quest** 143 **(52)** (DWPArbuthnot) **5-8-10v** SWhitworth(12) (lw: rdn over 2f out: hdwy over 1f out: r.o ins fnl f)	½	**4**	20/1	42	31
4436[2] **La Doyenne (IRE)** 14 **(54)** (CBBBooth) **5-8-12** RMullen(4) (led over 1f: rdn over 2f out: one pce)	½	**5**	4/1 [2]	43	32
4131[5] **Bramble Bear** 30 **(54)** (MBlanshard) **5-8-7**(5) SCarson(7) (rdn thrght: hdwy over 2f out: nvr nrr)	1	**6**	15/2	40	29
4493[3] **Dancing Jack** 12 **(38)** (JJBridger) **6-7-5**(5) RBrisland(2) (lw: s.s: hdwy over 2f out: nvr nrr)	¾	**7**	12/1	21	10
4493[9] **Nineacres** 12 **(49)** (JMBradley) **8-8-7b** FNorton(14) (rdn over 2f out: hdwy over 1f out: nvr nrr)	nk	**8**	20/1	31	20
4493* **Forgotten Times (USA)** 12 **(66)** (KTIvory) **5-9-5v**(5) CCarver(15) (b: b.hind: lw: a mid div)	¾	**9**	3/1 [1]	46	35
4493[5] **Half Tone** 12 **(49)** (RMFlower) **7-8-7b** DSweeney(16) (lost pl 4f out: r.o one pce fnl f)	1¾	**10**	9/1	24	13
4260[22] **Princess Mo** 24 **(44)** (TEPowell) **3-8-2** GHind(11) (lw: hung lft & hdwy over 1f out: btn whn n.m.r on ins, ins fnl f)	¾	**11**	33/1	17	6
2309[11] **Pride of Brixton** 101 **(50)** (AndrewReid) **6-8-1**(7)ow7 GArnolda(5) (b: b.hind: lw: hdwy over 3f out: wknd fnl f)	nk	**12**	50/1	22	11
4493[15] **Nickles** 12 **(62)** (LGCottrell) **4-9-3**(3) ADaly(9) (prom 2f)	nk	**13**	12/1	33	22
4493[14] **Clara Blue** 12 **(56)** (RIngram) **3-9-0** JWeaver(8) (prom 2f)	¾	**14**	25/1	25	14
3871[11] **Zola Power** 41 **(44)** (BAPearce) **3-7-13**(3)ow2 NPollard(13) (lw: c stands' side st: bhd fnl 3f)	1¼	**15**	50/1	9	—
808[16] **Don't Ask** 165 **(55)** (MrsLCJewell) **3-8-8**(5) RStudholme(3) (spd over 2f)	12	**16**	33/1	—	—
			(SP 131.0%)		**16 Rn**

63.3 secs (3.30) CSF £85.20 CT £1,637.12 TOTE £10.10: £2.00 £2.30 £3.70 £5.10 (£37.10) Trifecta Not won; £335.28 to Nottingham 5/10/1999 OWNER Canisbay Bloodstock Ltd (NEWMARKET) BRED R. K. Bids Ltd

LONG HANDICAP Dancing Jack 7-8

3571 Double-O was given a masterly ride by Quinn who brought him over to the stands' side in the straight. Running on well from below the distance, he shot into the lead inside the final furlong to win readily. This was his first success on grass. (14/1: op 8/1)

Richard Quinn's riding of Double-O at Brighton last October was perfection. He held his mount up towards the rear, waited for the rest to commit themselves to going far side in the straight, and then sneaked over to the stands' side by himself. Quinn, carelessly omitted from my list of jockeys to follow in *The Effects of the Draw*, seems to ride Brighton that much better than anyone else for some reason.

Gary Stevens was not in this country for long last season, but while he was here he seemed to grasp likely draw biases quicker than many of the jockeys that have been around for years. His riding of Torgau at Newmarket was exemplary.

Michael Roberts has shown himself a draw jockey numerous times in the past, most memorably when successfully switching Sweet Magic to the far side in a Sandown sprint when the stalls were on the stands' side, but also on many other occasions.

Of the other 'big' jockeys I would always favour Fallon, Jason Weaver and Seb Sanders over Frankie Dettori and Pat Eddery. Not that Dettori is not a jockey likely to blow a good draw, just that he's less inclined than some to go looking for the better ground. Other names to watch out for are George Duffield, Michael Fenton, Dane O'Neill, Robert Winston, Neil Pollard and Lee Newman, who tried go-it-alone tactics a couple of times during '99.

Trainers to follow

Since the inception of 48-hour declaration stages and 'draw draws' for some of the bigger Flat handicaps, often in front of the cameras, the issue of draw biases in our bigger handicaps has started to gain more media attention.

The idea to hold a ballot for starting positions in races such as the Lincoln and Goodwood Stewards' Cup means that the trainers of the first few horses picked out of the hat have a free pick. However, any biases in these events tend to be well known, so they rarely give away much about a trainer's knowledge of the subject.

The likes of David Nicholls, David Chapman, Mick Easterby, Sir Mark Prescott, Michael Bell, Neville Callaghan and less familiar names such as Ron Hodges, Tony Newcombe, Paul Howling and Karl Burke have shown draw-knowledge above and beyond the call of duty. I would be less inclined to cross out any of their representatives when they are drawn that awkward six or seven off the rail than certain other trainers. However, these days most handlers seem more up on the subject than was the case a decade ago.

David Nicholls

After the year David Nicholls had in '99 with his handicap sprinters, it would be impossible not to include a section on him in a chapter entitled 'Beating The Bookmaker'. Horses such as American Cousin and Cryhavoc (plus plenty of others) showed massive improvement after joining Nicholls' yard, and his runners could almost have been followed blind.

Nicholls has brought another dimension to training sprinters in much the same way that Martin Pipe has revolutionised training methods over jumps, and he continually works wonders with others' cast-offs.

Looking at a couple of '99 examples, Cryhavoc joined Nicholls for the start of the season. Formerly under the care of Rupert Arnold, he had won a Newmarket nursery on his final start at two and started the '97 campaign running in a rated stakes off a career-high mark of 93. By the time he joined Nicholls, his rating had plummeted to just 65, but after five wins and a string of other good efforts he finished the season running off marks in the high 80s and low 90s again. Somehow Nicholls had brought him back to his best of two years and more previously, but Cryhavoc was far from a one-off.

American Cousin made his nursery debut for Brian Meehan in 1997 on a mark of 70. After a spell with Fulke Johnson-Houghton, he went to David Nicholls and, given a few runs to find his form, turned up in a Doncaster handicap off a mark of 44, having run a blinder just a few days earlier from a poor draw at Beverley off the same rating. He won that race, plus one more after, and finished the year rated back up in the low 60s. However, it's all very well relaying what Nicholls has already accomplished, there's no money to be made from that - what does he have in store for 2000?

Legs Be Frendly ran off a mark of 88 in his first handicap at three, but only ran nine times after, with little success. The only time he made the frame was from a plum draw at Beverley, and he left Kevin McAuliffe at the end of the year rated just 65, 23lb lower than at his peak.

Flak Jacket won his first two starts in handicaps for Brian Meehan, which put him up to a mark of 85, before losing his way somewhat. He showed signs of coming back on his last two outings last year, and starts this campaign handily rated on 77.

Jacobina came to my attention when running second from a poor draw at Newcastle in July '98 and duly won next time at Haydock. That put her up to a career-high equalling mark of 67, and she is due to start this season down on 52.

Don Quixote was with Luca Cumani in '99 and it spoke volumes that the Newmarket handler was prepared to race him in maiden handicap sprints (which can't have helped his strike-rate!). Nicholls will have already seen plenty of him, as he twice finished behind American Cousin in that one's two wins, each time when made second favourite to him. His most eyecatching effort was when eighth to American Cousin down the unfavoured centre of the course at Doncaster, where his apprentice jockey did not persevere once his chance had gone. He starts the 2000 campaign on 47, having run in his two handicaps off 49 and 48, and has plenty more to come.

Grand View never actually went too much higher than his season-ending rating of 66 (reached 72 at Newbury), but he caught my eye when third, drawn away from the action, to Ambitious at Redcar. He is inclined to turn in the occasional unbelievably bad effort, but Nicholls may be the one to find the key to him and there is plenty more to come if he does.

Could any of the above be the next Rudi's Pet?

CHAPTER 5

SOME INTERESTING 1999 STATISTICS

1999 was the first year I entered the *Racing Post*'s naps table, under the *Raceform On Saturday* banner and, although having to provide a selection every day rather limited the returns, the end results were positive and interesting. Some of the bigger-priced winners included Achilles Star (14/1), Rocco Tower (14/1), Premier Baron (14/1), Central Coast (10/1), Pure Elegancia, Topton and Carlton (all 8/1) and Cold Climate and Grangeville (both 13/2).

I moved into second after Double-O won at 14/1 on October 4, before the late-season lottery stemmed the flow of winners, and would have gone closer still but for being unable to enter three selections (Bollin Ann 11/2, American Cousin 7/2 and Young Rosein 6/1) in order to ensure *SprintLine* subscribers exclusivity. This year I will be concentrating solely on *SprintLine*.

The seasonal records revealed some interesting trends. March and much of April were, as usual, very hard going, and this is a time of year I tend to leave alone unless one really catches the eye. Likewise, September, October, and the first few days in November didn't offer much in the way of success.

As in past seasons, the time for followers of the draw to strike was from the start of the Guineas meeting (late April) to the end of August. During this period, the majority of runners are fit, and the form tends to work out that much better than is often the case early and late in the season. Indeed, all the winners listed above, bar Double-O, fell within that time span.

In the spring, there are too many unexposed, well-handicapped horses knocking around, and too many others unfit, while in late summer and autumn, too many runners have plateaued, the ground becomes uneven and horses start going over the top. The table on the following page, which shows month-by-month £1 level-stakes profits on all naps entered, clearly indicates how much harder going March, April, September, October and November were compared to high summer.

March	-£6.00
April	-£3.47
May	**+£13.41**
June	**+£14.66**
July	**+£9.96**
August	**+£8.00**
September	-£14.10
October	-£12.00
November	-£4.00

Comparing spring and autumn, with the summer months, backing every nap from the former would have shown a £1 level-stakes loss of -£39.57, while backing them all from May-August inclusive would have yielded a profit of £46.03. But as I've already intimated backing one horse a day is not the way to go, which is why so many tipping services show a loss over time, forced as they are, to put up recommendations every day. I cannot stress enough the importance of maintaining discipline and of being selective.

SprintLine

The first issue of *Raceform On Saturday* was published on King George Day, July '98, not long after *The Effects of the Draw* had been released, and I started a weekly column from that date on the subject of the draw.

Throughout 1999, the column expanded to become *SprintLine*, a preview piece of each Saturday's racing, focusing on which horses had previously run well from poor draws and who were likely to show improved form on that day.

The results right from the start were very good, so much so that I received a few letters asking if there were any plans to extend the service to cover midweek racing. At the time, I hadn't given the matter any thought, but it seemed a sensible move, so the *SprintLine* e-mail and phone service kicked off on Monday, June 21st. The service ended the season well in profit on all selections (not many can boast that!), and the results of the 8-point and bigger recommendations were particularly impressive, as shown in the table below:-

Date	Rec Stake (points)	Selection	Result	+/-
June 21	**12 win**	**Misinterpretation**	**WON 11/8**	**+16.5**
June 22	5 each-way	Needwood Minstrel	Lost 8/1	+6.5
June 26	**15 win**	**American Cousin**	**WON 3/1**	**+51.5**
July 3	7 win 3 place	Wishbone Alley	Lost 4/1	+41.5
July 5	8 win	Wishful Thinker	Lost 11/4	+33.5
July 8	6 win 3 place	E B Pearl	Lost 6/1	+24.5

July 13	**8 win 4 place**	**Bollin Ann**	**WON 11/2**	**+74**
July 14	**9 win**	**American Cousin**	**WON 7/2**	**+105.5**
July 31	8 win	Pepperdine	Lost 9/2	+97.5
Aug 11	7 win 3 place	Gay Breeze	Lost 7/1	+87.5
Aug 21	8 win	Peppiatt	Lost 7/1	+79.5
Aug 26	**7 win 2 place**	**Young Rosein**	**WON 6/1**	**+124.5**
Sept 3	8 win 2 place	My Man Friday	4th 4/1	+118.5

13 sels, 5 wins (38%), 1 plcd, average SP 5/1, average wnr SP 4/1, L.S.P +£11.38

It was particularly pleasing that the three biggest win selections all went in, American Cousin (twice) and Misinterpretation, while Young Rosein (recommended at 8/1) was a fantastic result for myself and several subscribers.

The *SprintLine* e-mail and phone services will be back in action this year, and the option is there to come in either for the full season (there are always a few that crop up early and late season - Unshaken on Grand National day '99 being a perfect example), or just for the peak summer months. Again though, as for last year, the rates are being kept at an extremely competitive level.

Those coming in for the summer months will be looking at receiving somewhere in the region of 30-40 recommendations, and somewhere in the region of 10-15 banker bets, although those figures are not fixed. One of the many benefits of *SprintLine* is that the obligation to tip every day, just for the sake of it, is not there as it is for most premium rate phone services, so there will be days when no bet is recommended.

SprintLine offers genuine information, recommending horses that are invariably well handicapped, in form, and who frequently return at rewarding prices, all at a very fair subscription rate.